FEMALE SEXUAL SLAVERY

KATHLEEN BARRY

 New York University Press
New York *and* London
1984

Library of Congress Cataloging in Publication Data

Barry, Kathleen.
   Female sexual slavery.

   Includes index.
   1. Prostitution.   2. Sex crimes.   3. Violent crimes.
4. Victims of crimes.   I. Title.
HQ281.B325   1984   306.7'42   84-16505
ISBN 0-8147-1070-0 (alk. paper)
ISBN 0-8147-1069-7 (pbk.: alk. paper)

Clothbound editions of New York University Press books are
Smyth-sewn and printed on permanent and durable acid-free
paper.

To the survivors of
female sexual slavery, and to
those who attempted to survive.

ACKNOWLEDGMENTS _____

This book is a logical outcome of my own growth and activism in the Women's Movement and the result of over ten years of thinking, working, and acting with women committed to radical feminist change. The political forces of feminism which made this book possible became a source of hope and motivation for me in many of the seemingly isolated and bleak moments of writing it.

Encouragement from friends came in the form of personal support and practical assistance with news clippings, leads, pieces of evidence, suggestions, and ideas from them continually expanding the scope of my work. While many contributed important material or ideas, there are a few people to whom I am particularly indebted: Kate Bagley read each chapter in early draft form offering critical insights that often helped me deepen the analysis in my writing. In addition to her critique, the long, regular discussions that we had were a source of personal and intellectual support while the book was in progress. Throughout the research and writing I was able to count on Joanne Parrent whom I could call at a moment's notice for help in finding a way out of confusion I had woven into early drafts. As a friend and political ally, Joanne usually knew what I meant to say even when I didn't convey it clearly, and from this invaluable insight she assisted me in fuller development of ideas. I was also fortunate in being able to rely on Joan L's combined editorial skills, feminist thinking, and personal friendship.

Adrienne Rich's personal support was sustaining and encouraging as I wearily pushed through the final months and pages of writing this book. In addition she gave of valuable time and energy to work with me on substantive revisions and editorial changes. Barbara Rosenblum's critique of the completed manuscript provided me with important sociological insights, and Joan Hoff Wilson's suggestions led to several necessary changes in the final manuscript. Fatima Mernissi critiqued the chapter on Sex

Colonization while she was at UC Berkeley from Rabat University in Morocco, and in doing so she gave me a fuller understanding of women in the Arab world. Charlene Spretnak's substantive insights and careful attention to editorial details were invaluable in the final stages of book production.

In the research on this book I received considerable assistance from many individuals and agencies in the United States and Europe. Most of all I am deeply grateful to the women, the survivors of female sexual slavery, who talked with me or testified in court about their experiences, and to Marilyn Neckes who shared with me her research findings and interviews with street prostitutes in San Francisco.

In the European research I was greatly assisted by Patrick Montgomery of the British-based Anti-Slavery Society and Renée Bridel of the Federation of Women in Legal Careers. Each provided me with documentation from their own work and both put me in contact with many other individuals and organizations involved in investigating these problems. The Fawcett Library in London was extremely generous in providing me with access to the Josephine Butler papers on very short notice.

All of these people, and many more, contributed from their first-hand knowledge in various ways to my research on female sexual slavery. While I remain responsible for the interpretations and analysis in this book, it was their profound understanding of slavery practices and compassionate concern for the victims that gave me the encouragement to carry this work to its completion.

CONTENTS _____

INTRODUCTION _____

When I began to write *Female Sexual Slavery* in the mid-1970s the subject had been so effectively buried that there was hardly a trace of evidence that women were being forced into prostitution and trafficked from one country to another. "White slavery" had become an historical artifact, something that may have happened in the nineteenth century, but even that was not a certainty. The silence was reinforced by the belief that women are not *forced* into prostitution; sexual violence is simply part of their work, and further, that some women are made for that. My study broke through that silence by taking a feminist method of research which assumed that women who are in prostitution are not different in their wants, needs, desires and human rights than any other women and, therefore, that the violence against them is violation and not an acceptable part of "the life" as has been assumed.

The work on wife battery which began in the early 1970s exposed the fuller extent of violence against women in the home and created a model for understanding the victimization of women in prostitution. By understanding the experience of woman in prostitution as common to the experiences of all women, we have taken the label "prostitute" from where it had been relegated to the convenient and invisible category of "deviant" and prostitution became an essential aspect of the study of women. Now feminist theory and women's studies have broadened their scope to include prostitution in the study of women.

But there is another reason, even as critical as the violence against women in prostitution that requires attention of scholars and students to the subject of prostitution. Since the mid-1970s with the massive proliferation of pornography, the graphic depiction of what men require of whores, prostitution has been brought into the daily lives of millions of American women. Pornographic movies, magazines, video tapes and paraphernalia are no longer the province of combat zones and prostitution areas of the city. They have found their way into homes through the sexual expectations some men make of their wives, daughters, girlfriends and lovers. As a result, society is experiencing a social redefinition of woman who is reduced to her sexual utility—the functional definition of prostitute. Evidence of these changes in the meaning of "woman" can be found in the use of the popular slogan "all women are whores" which celebrates the idea that prostitutes are the new model of the sexually liberated woman, that prostitutes sell what wives give away and that prostitution should be professionalized. That idea which accepts prostitution uncritically is creating considerable confusion for many women active in women's studies and feminist groups as it denies how female sexual slavery is the underpinning of the institution of prostitution as well as marriage.

When I completed writing *Female Sexual Slavery* in 1979, I knew I had exposed only the tip of the iceberg. The evidence since then confirms this, but the change is one of magnitude; the descriptions of women's experiences of female sexual slavery now today are not essentially different than when this work was originally published. In 1980 international attention was focused on Grenoble, France when four young women who were severely tortured by pimps and customers faced their captors in the open courtroom. Their courage, a vigorous district attorney and an angry judge broke the gang of seventeen pimps, gave maximum sentences to those who had not escaped to Italy and required that extensive civil damages be paid to the women. At the same time, in the United States, Linda Lovelace revealed how she had been systematically raped, tortured and forced into making the block busting pornographic movie, "Deep Throat."

One of my major frustrations while doing the research for this work was the silence on the issue at the United Nations. But with the United Nations Decade of Women and up to 10,000 women coming together in conferences in Mexico and Denmark, female sexual slavery could no longer remain buried. Resolutions calling for more vigor-

ous investigations and intervention against the traffic in
women led to a new United Nations report by special rapporteur, Jean Fernand Laurent, which was issued in 1983
and found that indeed "prostitution is slavery" and a grave
cause for international concern.

Yet much remains to be done. Since 1979, agencies
promoting sex tourism and mail order brides have begun
operating in the United States. Now American men who
claim to be fed up with the "liberated American woman"
can *buy* women from Latin America, the Philippines, Thailand through agencies who offer them "docile" and "sub-
missive" women from the Third World. This practice, built
upon the most racist and misogynist stereotypes of Asian
and Latin American women, is a growing part of the traffic
in women which is a violation of the United Nations conventions and covenants. It is also a clear representation of
how women are set against each other for male pleasure.
Over the past decade, the singularly most effective work
against sex tourism and mail-order bride traffic has been
launched by Asian feminists, particularly the Asian Wom-
en's Association in Japan and the Third World Movement
Against the Exploitation of Women in the Philippines.
Asian and European feminists have begun to act in solidarity to confront these tours. By the early 1980s their actions caused a significant reduction of sex tours between
Japan and the Philippines, for example. It was then that
we began to see these agencies appearing in the United
States.

It was for this purpose that an International Feminist
Network Against Female Sexual Slavery was organized in
1980 and launched its first meeting in Rotterdam in 1983.
Women from twenty-four countries met to discuss the specific instances of forced prostitution, traffic in women, torture of female prisoners, sex tourism, military brothels,
sexual mutilation and other crimes against women. In doing
so they discovered the commonality of the oppression of
women globally and created the basis for international
feminist action by forming a Network. Rather than rely on
a hierarchical international organization which dictates
policy and action to the local groups, this Network is based
in each world region where women are engaged in the day

to day work of combating the traffic, forming shelters and training programs for women escaping from prostitution and demanding prosecution of pimps and procurers who traffic women. The difference now is that these local groups work with international support and can bring global attention to their causes through the Network.

Five years after completing *Female Sexual Slavery* I am excited to see that in women's studies classes, feminist research projects, grass roots political action and international feminist organizing, the work on female sexual slavery has truly begun.

PART I

Unmasking Sexual Oppression

CHAPTER 1 _____

On Studying
Sexual Slavery

There are small prostitution hotels in one part of the North African *quartier* of Paris known as *maisons d'abattage.* I was warned to stay out of this section of the 18th *arrondissement* of Paris because it is dangerous for women, at any time of day or night. But I did walk through the area. I needed to see the *maisons d'abattage.* It was early evening when another woman and I emerged from the Barbes-Rochecauart Metro station. We were jostled and pushed as we made our way through the crowded shopping section. Once we were on the quiet side streets no other women were to be seen. As we walked through the neighborhood streets of this North African section of Paris, we were suddenly struck by the sight of a crowd of about 300 men in a narrow street ahead. We stopped and gazed, assuming there must have been an automobile accident or a fight. The frantic, jostling crowd of men spanned the full width and half the length of the small street. As we approached the rue de la Charbonniere, just above the crowd of pushing and shoving men we saw a small "Hotel" sign.

We continued down the street and around the corner. We stopped again, stunned to see a small neighborhood police station with a smiling policeman standing in the doorway, while about 20 yards away from him, next door but in the same building, was another "Hotel" sign and another group of men, about 100 North Africans pushing, body-to-body, against the gates of the hotel. It was only 6:00 P.M. on Saturday of Easter weekend. The crowds of men were to grow larger as the evening progressed. Although closed prostitution houses are illegal in France, these hotels are not only tolerated but obviously supported by the police.

In each of these *maisons d'abattage* (literal translation:

houses of slaughter), six or seven girls each serve 80 to
120 customers a night. On holidays their quota might go
up to 150. After each man pays his 30 francs (approximately $6.00) at the door, he is given a towel and ushered
into a room. A buzzer sounds after six minutes, and he
must leave immediately as another man comes in. The
girl never even gets out of bed.

The girls are told that they will get a certain percentage
of the money if they meet their quota. From their earnings
is deducted the cost of room and meals; after these deduc-
tions—with the hotel doing the bookkeeping—the girls always find they are indebted to the house. Giving a false
sense of earning money, and subsequent indebtedness, are
traditional strategies for keeping enslaved prostitutes from
rebelling.

In May 1975 a French doctor submitted a confidential
report to UNESCO documenting the torture of prostitutes.
The report, which was to become the basis of testimony at
the International Women's Year Conference in Mexico
City, was based on testimony of patients she had treated
who had been held in the *maisons d'abattage*. It indicated
that the women were "detained indoors without ever having the right to move outside unaccompanied, were subjected to cruel, inhuman, and degrading treatment. Torture
was also used if it was needed to obtain their complete
submission. This form of terrorism was aimed at making
them totally subject to the wishes of those who benefited
from it, either by financial profit or sexual satisfaction."
The women were described as being of normal intelligence
and in a state of depression and considerable anxiety.
"They were passive and apathetic, unable to readjust to
freedom."

This is not the kind of work a woman looks for when she
considers becoming a prostitute. How do women get to
places like Paris's *maisons d'abattage?*

From my research, I found the women may be purchased, kidnapped, drawn in through syndicates or organized crime, or fraudulently recruited by fronting agencies which offer jobs, positions with dance companies, or
marriage contracts that don't exist. Or they may be procured through seduction by being promised friendship and

love. Conning a girl or young woman by feigning friendship or love is undoubtedly the easiest and most frequently employed tactic of slave procurers (and one that is also used for procuring young boys) and it is the most effective. Young women readily respond to male attention and affection and easily become dependent on it.

Once a procurer has drawn a young woman in by his attention to her and she commits her affection to him it is relatively easy for him to transport her to a brothel. Sometimes she can quickly be turned out on the streets by simply being asked to; he tells her that if she really loves him she will do it for him. If that fails, if she resists his request, traditional seasoning tactics are employed—beating, rape, torture. Either way she gets hooked.

When a friend first suggested that I write a book on what I was describing to her as female sexual slavery, I resisted the idea. I had gone through the shock and horror of learning about it in the late 1960's when I discovered a few paternalistically written books documenting present-day practices. During that same period I found a biography of Josephine Butler, who single-handedly raised a national and then international movement against forced prostitution in the nineteenth century but who is now virtually unknown. I realized that Josephine Butler's current obscurity was directly connected to the invisibility of sex slavery today. And so I wrote a few short pieces on the subject and incorporated my limited information into the curriculum of the women's studies classes I taught.

But to write a book on the subject—to spend two or three years researching, studying female slavery—that was out of the question. I instinctively withdrew from the suggestion; I couldn't face that. But as the idea settled over the next few weeks, I realized that my reaction was typical of women's response: even with some knowledge of the facts, I was moving from fear to paralysis to hiding. It was then that I realized, both for myself personally and for all the rest of us, that the only way we can come out of hiding, break through our paralyzing defenses, is to know the full extent of sexual violence and domination of women. It is knowledge from which we have pulled back, as well as knowledge that has been withheld from us. In *knowing*, in facing directly, we can learn how to chart our course out of this oppression, by envisioning and creating a world which will preclude female sexual slavery. In knowing the extent of our oppression we will have to discover some of the ways to begin immediately breaking the deadly cycle of fear, denial-through-hiding, and slavery.

Far from being the project I feared facing, the research, study, and writing of this book have given me knowledge that force me to think beyond the confinement of women's oppression. Understanding the scope and depth of female sexual slavery makes it intolerable to passively live with it any longer. I had to realistically visualize a world that would preclude this enslavement by projecting some ways out of it. Reading about sexual slavery makes hope and vision necessary.

To study female sexual slavery, I could start only with the slender file of material I had developed over the previous ten years. Very little information was readily available. History provided some clue to the practices that defined it. Definition and description would have to emerge from the information I would get in the field through observation, interviews, and travel.

Traditional methods employed by those who study social life were of little use. One cannot, for example, find a sample population of sexual slaves, survey them, and then generalize from the results. Nor is participant observation a possibility. And interviewing those held in slavery is impossible. I began to look for the women who have escaped. My approach was to find any evidence of sexual slavery wherever I could, and to try to fill out fragmentary facts from interviewing people associated with a particular case.

To determine the nature and extent of the slave trade *today*, I decided that except for the historical example of nineteenth century sex slavery, I would keep my research to reports of incidents that took place within the ten years prior to beginning my research (that is, since 1966). I would use earlier material as background to substantiate patterns I found. Shortly after I began, I realized that the sex slave trade is so clandestine a practice that what I would find would only be an indication of a much vaster problem. In addition, I soon realized that my assumption that traffic in women and children was different from street prostitution was invalid. From interviews and other research I learned that virtually the only distinction that can be made between traffic in women and street prostitution is that the former involves crossing international borders. The practices used to force women into prostitution are the same whether they are trafficked across international boundaries or from one part of a city to another. It is currently estimated that over 90 percent of street prostitutes are controlled by pimps. I found that street pimp strategies and goals do not differ significantly from those of international procurers. Female sexual slavery then refers to international traffic in women *and* forced street prostitution taken together.

As I received information about each case of sexual slavery, I would confirm the story by contacting people close to the case—lawyers, reporters, police, district attorneys, anti-slavery organizations, and the victims themselves whenever possible. I restricted interviews with victims to those who had either escaped or left prostitution. Interviewing these women presented a special problem as their life experiences had taught them that few if any people are willing to believe their victimization. Indeed, society has been unwilling to even name it as a form of victimization. As a result I conducted long open-ended interviews which provided an opportunity to sort out possible contradictions or exaggerations. And it provided an opportunity for confidence to be developed allowing the women to describe their experiences without need for embellishment. As a further check, I used here only portions of the interviews when I could be satisfied with their report or that I could verify against other evidence.

After days of tracking down people, getting interviews, observing trials, and filling out the details of a particular case, I would consistently find that the extreme incident that I was studying was in fact part of a pervasive practice usually existing clandestinely over many years. Not only did my investigations confirm a particular incident, but that incident in turn revealed larger practices. For example, the story of Paraguay discussed in Chapter 4 came to my attention through news reports describing how a Paraguayan woman discovered children being used for prostitution in a Paraguayan military brothel. Investigation and further interviews put me in touch with evidence of an

international traffic of women and girls for prostitution
from Paraguay. As a result of my investigations and research I came in
contact with several organizations whose titles alone suggest the seriousness of the problem. The British-based Anti-
Slavery Society, through its secretary, Colonel Patrick
Montgomery, has for years been presenting cases of female
slavery to the United Nations and any other organization
likely to take action. Then there is the French group,
Équipes d'Action, whose full title, "Action Teams Against
the Traffic of Women and Children (and against slavery by
drugs, trickery, or violence)," conveys the scope of the
problem. Their documentation amply substantiates the
traffic's pervasiveness. The French Police Department, I
found, has a Central Office for the Repression of the
Traffic in Persons. Also, as recently as 1974 INTERPOL,
the international police organization, conducted an international survey on the traffic in women for prostitution.
My discovery of these organizations and activities was further evidence of the broad scale of the practice.

Once I was convinced of the pervasiveness of the problem, the immediate question facing me was why and how
female sexual slavery has remained invisible. First, there is
direct suppression of the evidence by authorities. In addition, it is invisible as a problem to those who handle practices of female sexual slavery every day. When I would
illustrate to an authority how a particular situation fit the
most rudimentary definition of slavery, generally I found
that they saw the abuse but accepted sexual exploitation
and violence as normal for particular groups of women
under specific conditions. I noted how, *after* women are
enslaved in their homes or in prostitution, they are accepted as part of the group of women destined for that life.
When I challenged authorities, I ran up against the "don't
confuse me with the facts" attitude. Despite evidence of
force and dehumanizing violence in many cases, they were
incredulous that anyone would question prostitution or see
it as other than a necessary service for a particular group
of women to perform.

Yet other, more subtle effects have contributed to the
invisibility of the slave trade. For example, most research
on prostitution looks at female motivation rather than the

objective conditions which bring many women into prostitution, shifting the causal assumptions from those who traffic women to the psychological states of the women themselves. To those who study the victims of the practice I have called female sexual slavery, these women are the exceptions for whom exceptional behavior is normal; to sociologists they are deviants, to psychologists they are sadomasochists. Their life and experiences are construed as normal for them while they are supposedly different from the rest of us. It is in this kind of contradiction that feminists have learned to look for larger truths about female experience. It is in female sexual slavery that I have found conditions which affect all women. Because of these problems it was necessary for me to develop a perspective for analyzing both the documentation of female sexual slavery and the attitudes that define it as normal, which would reveal self-interest on the part of those who label it. That self-interest may range from the actual profit from the traffic in women to a general participation in the sexual power that accrues to men from female sexual slavery. As I studied the attitudes that accept female enslavement, I realized that a powerful ideology stems from it and permeates the social order. I have named that ideology cultural sadism. In Chapter 9 I have described the perspective or view of the world which is derived from the ideology of cultural sadism and determines what is known about sexual practices as it shapes attitudes and values toward them.

Not all thinking on prostitution accepts violence as normal for prostitutes. Prostitution is both an indication of an unjust social order and an institution that economically exploits women. But when economic power is defined as the causal variable, the sex dimensions of power usually remain unidentified and unchallenged. Consequently, economic analysis has often functioned to undermine the feminist critique of sexual domination that has gone on since the beginning of the women's movement. Feminist analysis of sexual power is often modified to make it fit into an economic analysis which defines economic exploitation as the primary instrument of female oppression. Under that system of thought, institutionalized sexual slavery, such as is found in prostitution, is understood in terms of economic exploitation which results in the lack of economic opportunities for women, the result of an unjust economic order. Undoubtedly economic exploitation is an important factor in the oppression of women, but here we must be concerned with whether or not economic analysis reveals the more fundamental sexual domination of women. As unjust as the economic order may be, this analysis spins off a set of beliefs which again contradict fact. Those beliefs assume:

1. That prostitution is an economic alternative for women who are the objects of discrimination in the larger inequitable job market—despite the fact that pimps are known to take all or almost all of the money earned by their prostitutes.

2. That only lower-class or poor women and girls turn to prostitution—despite the knowledge that most pimps recruit girls who are runaways, many of whom are from middle-class homes.

3. That only ethnic minority women are trapped in prostitution—despite the fact that many white women and girls are visible hooking on the streets, and despite the fact that pimps recruit women based on customer demand and easy availability.

4. That black men from the ghetto have no economic alternatives to pimping—despite the fact that a) most black men from the ghetto do not become pimps; b) that not all pimps are black or from the ghetto; and c) that exploitation, abuse, and enslavement cannot be justified by someone's economic conditions.

By appearing to critique the conditions which lead to prostitution these assumptions actually obscure recognition of sexual domination, which is the first cause of sexual power.

The right-wing attacks against feminism and the witch-hunts against homosexuals have further clouded recognition of female sexual slavery. Public attention has been turned to child abuse, specifically male child abuse; there has been a wave of protest over child pornography and boy prostitution. Attention to procuring young children for pornography and prostitution has singled out one aspect of sexual slavery to the exclusion of all others. Documentation of the problem of boy prostitution has led investigators to assert that sexual abuse of boys is a larger and more serious problem than female adult or child prostitution. Therefore, some people are asserting an increase in the problem. But new awareness does not indicate increased incidence. It only reveals that the homosexual witch-hunts have created an audience for those exposés. The political climate has created arbitrary and false distinctions and definitions. Child prostitution has always been a part of the sex slave trade. Separating the enslavement of children from that of women distorts the reality of the practices and conveys the impression that on some level it is tolerable to enslave women while child slavery is still reprehensible. Within that distinction lies the implication that one form of slavery is intolerable and worth attention while the other is not.

On the other hand, including male prostitution (teenage boys and adult men) with female prostitution assumes that they are the same phenomenon and thereby obscures the fundamental sex-object role of women in masculinist society. The sex-power relationship between men and women makes male prostitution quite a different practice than female prostitution. The victimization and enslavement to which women are subject in male-dominated society find no equivalent in male experience.

Finally, sensationalism has made the traffic invisible. The tendency of writers on this subject to render already horrible events in the format of a lurid novel leaves the impression that the material is less than believable, that it is fiction. Not all slave markets are lustful events where whips crack over writhing, naked bodies. Often they are subdued business transactions. Sensationalism was the method that many turn-of-the-century workers used to bring attention to the traffic in women. The net result of their paternalistic, highly dramatized concern was to characterize the victims as such poor, sweet young things as to make the stories about them unbelievable. The very effort to dramatize and create attention casts suspicion on the veracity of the stories. The issue is not whether a child, teenager, or adult woman is a poor, innocent, sweet young thing. It is, rather, that no one should have the right to force anyone into slavery.

As my research progressed, I realized that the bias that makes forced prostitution invisible as a form of slavery comes from the tendency to focus on how a girl gets into it. If she is kidnapped, purchased, fraudulently contracted through an agency or organized crime, it is easy to recognize her victimization. But if she enters slavery having been procured through love and befriending tactics, then few, including herself, are willing to recognize her victimization. Seeing this problem led me to develop a working definition which became the criterion of my research, the basis on which I decided whether or not a particular incident was one of female sexual slavery. That definition focuses on the procuring strategies as well as the objective conditions of enslavement in which a woman is held, conditions from which she cannot escape and in which she is sexually exploited and abused. Once the objective conditions of sexual slavery are recognized and analyzed, the violence that victimizes women forced into prostitution cannot go by unnoticed. Consequently, instead of accepting women's self-acceptance of their slavery, we must question whether those circumstances are tolerable for any human being.

Sexual terrorism is a way of life for women even if we are not its direct victims. It has resulted in many women living with it while trying not to see or acknowledge it. This denial of reality creates a form of hiding. One woman, overcome at hearing about some practices of sexual slavery, suggested that I put them in the Appendix of this book to allow the reader to choose whether or not to look at them. Another friend wrote, "Be patient with me about your book; it really strikes a terror in me and a paralysis and I don't know when I'll be ready to read it."

Often in hearing about sexual slavery, some people hide in disbelief denying its reality. When we do recognize the terrorism, we may simply put it out of our minds, not wanting to acknowledge it. Or we sometimes hide by sitting in judgment on the victim. When faced with examples of how women are procured for slavery, there are those who will draw themselves up and instinctively distance themselves from the situation by passing uninformed, albeit ponderous, judgments on how a girl should have behaved if she really meant to prevent herself from being procured (or raped.) "I would have . . ." "She could have . . ." "Why didn't she . . ." instantly divide protagonist from listener. Those who hide by sitting in judgment are making the assumption not that the victim did wrong, but that she just didn't do everything she could to prevent it or to get away. The judgment is that it didn't have to happen, that the victim had control she didn't exercise. Women are bullied into denying the existence of sexual violence; when we expose it, we are called crazy by those who have a quiet interest in its continuation and therefore in its secrecy. Or we are confronted by kindhearted men who would never think of committing such acts themselves and therefore are incredulous that members of their sex could be thought of as carrying out such transgressions.

Hiding has helped keep female sexual slavery from being exposed. But worse than that, it has kept us from understanding the full extent of women's victimization, thereby denying us the opportunity to find our way out of it through political confrontation as well as through vision and hope. Vision of a society that does not enslave women involves first the pain of recognizing the worst of women's oppression. But with hope there is the opportunity to create a new political structure and social order. To have this vision means demanding and finding a world that will be free of sexual terrorism. Knowing the worst frees us to hope and strive for the best.

CHAPTER 2 _____

Josephine Butler:
The First Wave
of Protest

The traffic of women into sex slavery in the nineteenth century was directly linked to state-regulated prostitution. Although the concept of state regulation of prostitution dates back to ancient Greece and Rome, there was a renewed interest in this idea in Europe at the turn of the century. Officially such regulation was seen as a mechanism for controlling venereal disease; unofficially it fostered practices that forced women into prostitution.

During the French Revolution venereal disease became a major problem in the armies; it was so widespread that it often undermined military effectiveness. This situation motivated a renewed interest in regulating prostitution. The chief concern was to find a way to prevent disease without inhibiting soldiers' access to prostitutes. The practice of regulation of brothels quickly spread from the military to the general public.

Among the first of these renewed European efforts at regulation were those in Paris just prior to the establishment of the French Empire and later codified under Napoleon. "In 1798 two private physicians were given the task of examining Parisian prostitutes; they were required to report to the police any cases of infection. In 1802 a dispensary was established, and the police began registering all public prostitutes, who were now required to submit to semi-weekly examinations."[1] By the middle of the century this system evolved into regulation of prostitution through brothels. Prostitutes were forced into the brothels as the only place they could legitimately work.

From its institution in France and Germany, regulated prostitution began to spread across Europe. In 1871 at the International Medical Congress in Vienna an international law was proposed to make regulation uniform throughout the world.[2] Regulation was accepted by many as a social reform that improved hygienic conditions. In the mid-nineteenth century it was introduced into Great Britain through the Contagious Diseases Acts, which were implemented between 1864 and 1869.

Through regulation, prostitution was officially sanctioned by the State, which did not interfere with brothels. Abuse and enslavement of women went by unnoticed, which made "white slavery" or forced prostitution a widespread practice. When the Contagious Diseases Acts became law, one woman dared to challenge them and make the connection between regulation and slavery. In doing so, she changed the direction of nineteenth-century prostitution.

Josephine Butler, a middle-class Victorian lady living in Liverpool, was already engaged, on her own, in rescue work of young girls and women from prostitution on the docks. To the outrage of her neighbors, but with the support of her husband, she brought these women to her home, nursed them back to health, and helped them construct new lives. She was deeply affected by the economic and sexual degradation to which these women were subjected and she was impressed by how quickly they responded to her kind treatment and the opportunity to get out of prostitution.

To Josephine Butler, the Contagious Diseases Acts formalized and legalized the sexual enslavement of women. The Acts were designed to protect the health of military men by subjecting any woman the special Morals Police identified as a prostitute to a "surgical examination," which involved the use of crude instruments by often cruel doctors for special vaginal examinations. The Acts were enforced in eleven garrison towns, military stations, and naval seaports. An amendment to the 1864 act required that all women identified by the Morals Police as prostitutes must submit to a medical examination. If a woman was found to be free of venereal disease, she was then officially registered and issued a certificate identifying her as a clean prostitute.

The coarse brutality of doctors, men who had only recently taken over the work of midwives, and the arbitrary police identification of women as prostitutes, combined with Victorian morality to create an outrage among women against such examinations. "The examination was demeaning because of its public character. Streetwalking at night was one thing; being forced to attend examinations during the day often taunted by young boys . . . was another."[3]

In 1869, after the final Act passed, Josephine organized the Ladies National Association to campaign for the repeal of the Acts. A statement from the Association, summarizing their position, was published in the *Daily News* on December 31. It was accompanied by the names of 130 of the 2,000 women who had signed it; among those names were Josephine Butler, writer Harriet Martineau, and Florence Nightingale. The statement said, in part:

> Unlike all other laws for the repression of contagious diseases, to which both men and women are liable, these two apply to women only, men being wholly exempt from their penalties. The law is ostensibly framed for a certain class of women, but in order to reach these, all women residing within the district where it is in force are brought under the provisions of the Acts. Any woman can be dragged into court, and required to prove that she is not a common prostitute. The magistrate can condemn her, if a policeman swears only that he "has good cause to believe" her to be one. . . . When condemned, the sentence is as follows: To have her person outraged by the periodical inspection of a surgeon, through a period of 12 months; or resisting that, to be imprisoned, with or without hard labour—first for a month, next for three months—such imprisonment to be renewed for her whole life unless she submit periodically to the brutal requirements of the law.

Along with the many responses that flowed in from this appeal came a letter from Victor Hugo encouraging the women to "Protest! resist! show your indignation!" Recognizing regulation as a form of slavery, he noted, "I am with you to the fullest extent of my power. In reading your eloquent letter, I have felt a burning sympathy rise in me for the feeble, and a corresponding indignation against the oppressor."[4]

The Percy case is an example of the way regulation was administered. Mrs. Percy supported her family by working in a musical theater on a military base. Her 16-year-old daughter accompanied her each evening and they were always escorted home by a military officer. One evening during their walk home the police approached the woman and her daughter as public prostitutes and ordered them to report for the requisite medical examination. Mrs. Percy's daughter gave the following account to George Butler, Josephine's husband, when she was taken in by the Butlers after her mother's suicide:

> They called the police and ordered my mother to go up to the Metropolitan Police Office and bring me with her. Mamma and I went. We there saw Inspector G——. He was in his room, and mamma was first called in alone. I cannot, therefore, tell what passed between mamma and the Inspector, because I was not there. I can only tell you this, that mamma was never the same person again after that hour. She told me that she assured Inspector G—— that she would rather sign her death warrant than the paper he gave her to sign. I was then called in. I shall never forget the moment when I stood before Inspector G—— and he accused me. He said, "Do you know, girl, why you are here?" I replied, "No, sir, I do not." He said, "You are here because you are no better than you should be. You know what that means, I suppose?" I said, "No, sir, I do not." He laughed in a horrible way when I said this . . . ."[5]

Mrs. Percy refused to submit herself or her daughter to the surgical examination and she made her outrage known through a letter to the *Daily Telegraph*. The Morals Police were determined more than ever to make a lesson of Mrs. Percy and her daughter. The theater which employed Mrs. Percy was forced to fire her. She and her daughter moved out of town but were induced by one of Mrs. Percy's co-workers to return to work under a false name.[6] The Morals Police unrelentingly pursued Mrs. Percy, warning lodging houses that if they took her in they would risk being cited for running a disorderly house.

In desperation, with no place to live or work, Mrs. Percy threw herself into the Basingstoke Canal. The CD Acts not only regulated and controlled prostitutes, but they showed the rest of the women that to venture out of their homes was to risk being identified as a prostitute.

In organizing the Ladies National Association and in issuing their statement, Josephine began her political campaigns against these abuses and the Acts behind them. From the beginning of this work she was acutely aware of the difficulties facing women engaged in public, political protest. The women who were organizing against the CD Acts had to fight the social attitude and the belief within themselves that men were their intellectual and moral superiors. For this reason and because she believed that the injustices of the CD Acts would always be felt more keenly by women, Josephine insisted on separate Ladies Associations throughout her political career. Men controlled the government, the CD Acts, the streets, and indeed even public thought. She exhorted the women, "We must cease to 'recognize superior wisdom' in those who oppress us, and learn to abhor the despotism of a public opinion formed by men, which has so long, and with such calamitous results, aimed at holding in bondage even the inmost thoughts of women."[7]

The Contagious Diseases Acts initiated a slavery of women. Josephine responded with a war against that tyranny, a campaign for destruction of the sexist double standard of morality, and a demand for the personal liberty of all women. She called for a return to "the mark of a common standard of purity, and an equal judgment of the sin of impurity for both sexes alike . . ."[8]

In her speeches she pointed out the results of the double standard on men's behavior:

> The language of men towards women is, and has ever been, far too much of this character. "You must make us good, and keep us good; you must continually pray for us, we having no time (nor inclination) to pray for ourselves or you; you must save our souls while you minister to our daily comfort; . . . and somehow

or other you must, you *absolutely must*, get us into heaven at last. You know how! We leave it to you; but remember you are responsible for all this." I think I should be ashamed, were I a man, to throw such awful moral and spiritual responsibility upon women, while doing little for their souls in return.[9]

Under such a double standard, state regulation of prostitution was legalized slavery. It gave governmental sanction to the chattel status of women through a Parliament that was representative of men and composed of men only. Women "not only have been debarred from attempting to deal in any large sense with this evil, but they have been systematically drilled into silence on this topic."[10] Therefore women would be the victims of men's laws as men went virtually untouched. Josephine was opposed to legislating morality. Under such inequitable conditions, she warned it would be doubly dangerous.

What distinguished Josephine Butler from many of her contemporaries was that in her recognition of sexual slavery she attacked those who profited from the practice: slaveholders, procurers, and the State (laws and corrupt governments and police). Her first goal was to purify the State, believing that if it were rid of corruption, if it were made morally responsible, and if its tyranny over women were destroyed and double standards abolished, individual morality would follow.

Hers was more than a reform campaign for equality. It was a demand for a fundamental change in values that would lead to liberty based on individual freedom and self-respect. She took that demand into the sexual arena that few others would enter in the Victorian era. On behalf of the most oppressed and exploited of women, she demanded a change in values that amounted to nothing less than a feminist revolution.

With these political principles, in 1870 Josephine began to travel throughout England, lecturing on the Acts and organizing people for action against them. From the beginning, she made her appeal to the working classes. She believed that their lack of pretense and their commitment to ethical standards were far superior to the delicacy and remoteness of society ladies of her own class. The working

classes suffered the most from the effects of the Acts and
had the greatest potential for political mobilization.

As she analyzed it:

> The position and wealth of men of the upper classes
> place the women belonging to them above any chance
> of being accused of prostitution. Ladies who ride in
> their carriages through the street at night are in no
> danger of being molested. But what about working
> women? What about the daughters, sisters, and wives
> of working men, out, it may be, on an errand of mercy,
> at night? And what, most of all, of that girl whose
> father, mother, friends are dead or far away, who is
> struggling hard, in a hard world, to live uprightly,
> and justly by the work of her own hands.[11]

Historian Judith Walkowitz points out that prostitution in
English working-class communities had been fairly casual
prior to the Acts. Prostitutes were not particularly identified as a special class and were thus allowed some opportunity for mobility out of prostitution. They were part of
the community in which they grew up. The Acts forced a
distinct separation of prostitutes from their neighborhood.
"They were designed to force prostitutes to accept their
status as public women by destroying their private identities and associations with the poor working-class community."[12] Neighborhood women rallied to prostitutes'
support in resisting the Acts. "Women seem to have been
the organizing force behind public demonstrations in the
defense of registered women. In their response to the Contagious Disease Acts, they appear motivated by personal
sympathy for the plight of a neighbor, as well as by hostility toward the metropolitan police as interlopers in their
community."[13] Further, community women assisted
women in escaping public identification by helping them
get out of the area and to rescue homes in London.[14]

Community outrage over the Acts provided a base upon
which Josephine built her campaign. But not all the reac-
tions to the Acts and to Josephine were supportive and
encouraging. As her campaigning escalated, so did reaction
against her. There was an abhorrence of her direct language. In using the words "prostitutes" and "brothels," she

defied the codes of Victorian morality for middle-class womanhood. But more important, she was challenging male self-interest where it had been most protected. Mob violence began to accompany her speeches. During one campaign against a liberal who would not support repeal of the Acts, mobs of men and young boys scuffling and throwing rocks forced her to hide in a hotel attic. The next day she was forced by the management to leave the hotel. Wearing a disguise, she sought refuge at another hotel, but the mob located her there also. Despite the threats, she insisted on addressing the women's rally as she had planned. A number of bodyguards, brought up from London by her supporters, enabled her to address the meeting, but afterwards she had to run through streets and alleys to escape the mob. She eventually made it safely to the home of a supporter where she was taken in and looked after.[15]

Josephine built her campaign from small-town organizations into a national and then international movement, with strategies similar to those employed by the suffragist Pankhursts in the Women's Social and Political Union campaigns. The strategy was to campaign against liberals who refused to introduce or support legislation to repeal the Acts. As the movement grew, it attracted different interest groups. As historian Edward Bristow points out, "There was something of interest in the new abolitionism for every possible kind of libertarian and radical, as well as for the haters of sexual sin."[16]

The movement against regulation in England began to document some of the traffic of English girls to Continental brothels. Girls were often procured through newspaper advertisements offering positions of employment, usually for domestic work, or were approached in railway stations, where young girls coming to the city from the country were easily identifiable.[17]

One of those who became actively involved in this movement was Alfred Dyer, a Quaker who published books on various religious and social questions, among them works by Josephine Butler. He became concerned about child prostitution in England and began working with Josephine and other abolitionists to raise the age of consent from 12 to 18, as a method to curtail procuring of young girls for prostitution. From this work, he learned of traffic of young English girls to the Continent where they were forced into prostitution. A friend conveyed to him an account of a young English girl who was held in slavery in a Brussels brothel and was discovered by an Englishman frequenting the brothel. Although the Englishman was taken with her plight, he did not want to risk exposing his own identity by helping her escape but he did relate the incident to a friend who conveyed it to Dyer. Dyer methodically researched the story and, confirming details of the account, he printed it: a 19-year-old girl "was courted in London by a man of gentlemanly exterior, who promised her marriage if she would accompany him for the purpose to Brussels." En route, at Calais, she was left with another man while her "lover" explained that he had to pawn a watch to get some money and would join her in Brussels. She never saw him again. Arriving in Brussels, she was taken to a closed brothel, the man with her was paid, and she was officially registered under a false name as a prostitute.[18]

When he published this story, Dyer correctly anticipated being charged with sensationalism. English newspapers published a letter from the Brussels Commissioner of Police denying the alleged practices. Dyer undertook his own investigation. He went to Brussels to investigate and visited several houses of prostitution. He went to one house where he had heard a young English girl was kept. The house was closed; customers had easy access from the outside, but they had no means of exit once inside without being let out by the person in charge. When he was alone with the young Englishwoman, she told him her story of being seduced by a man in London who promised her a job in Brussels; when she accompanied him there, she said, she was brought to this house and officially registered by its proprietor as a prostitute under a false name. Her story was similar to that of the woman who had been taken to Brussels under the promise of marriage. According to Dyer, she was eager for him to help her escape.

As Dyer reports it, he did not arrange for her escape himself but instead went to the authorities—despite the fact that Josephine Butler had exposed police corruption in regulated systems. Whether this was to test their responsiveness or came out of a sense of male bonding we don't

know, but in any event he was not successful. The commissioner of the police district performed a cursory investigation and reported that all was in order. Dyer returned to
the house on his own and was denied access.

This incident, along with many other assertions of the
traffic in women and girls for sexual slavery, have been
considered groundless by some contemporary historians.
Bristow states that the woman allegedly held in this house
was in fact a "professional prostitute." Bristow's meaning
of this term is never quite clear. The suggested role and
status of "professional prostitute," a woman who has
chosen the work of a prostitute and set herself up in
business, stand in contrast to the prevalence of casual and
temporary prostitution in neighborhoods that Walkowitz
found among the English working classes. More than that,
Bristow's dismissal of such incidents follows from his
casual disregard for the exploitation of women evidenced
in his description of how the British Embassy had been
responsible for returning home about 200 English girls in
the decade preceding Dyer's investigation. "While a few
were innocent victims, most seem to have been professionals who did not know they would be kept in more severe
circumstances than prevailed in the world of English
vice."[19] Implicit in this statement is the assumption that
prostitutes can't be forced, that they are not the objects of
kidnapping or other procuring strategies or, that if they
are, it's acceptable because they are only prostitutes. In
addition, we do not know how arbitrary the designation of
these women as "professional prostitutes" was.

When research is preoccupied with such questions as
Bristow raises, other abuses of women are obscured. Specifically, in the Dyer escapade, presuming that the woman
was sincere in her revelation to Dyer that she wanted to
escape, not only did he not accomplish it but he probably,
in fact, seriously threatened her life. When men entered the
campaign against regulated prostitution, particularly in
rescue work and investigations, one notes that consistently
their behavior was dominated by righteous heroics in
which the fate of the victim is secondary to the escapade
they are performing. Such heroics were marked by paternalism wherein the hero acted out his concern and caring
with fatherly authority. Furthermore, the men's misguided

concern for the plight of prostitutes was interpreted as sensationalism, which only discredited the reports of the traffic in women.

Josephine welcomed the support and work of men like Dyer, but she was aware that most of them were motivated by paternalistic attitudes and behavior. Meanwhile she provided guidance which for a while kept the abolitionist movement from being diverted in false directions.

When Dyer published his findings, they were vehemently repudiated by Belgian authorities. The reports created enough concern, however, that with some pushing from Josephine Butler, the British Home Secretary initiated an investigation. In 1880 he commissioned a London lawyer, T. W. Snagge, to inquire into the traffic of young English girls into prostitution in Brussels. Snagge had had no prior connection with the abolitionist movement, with Butler, or with Dyer. His official report was a complete confirmation of Dyer's allegations.[20] He found that English girls were being exported to Belgium, France, and Holland for prostitution by systematic traffic, that English girls were frequently induced by misrepresentation or false promises to leave England, that they ended up in prostitution houses, and that in those houses they were "detained by duress or subjected to cruelty and forced against their will to lead a life of prostitution."[21]

In May 1881, Snagge's findings led to an inquiry into legislation that would specifically curtail procuring and traffic of English girls to other countries. Further inquiry into juvenile prostitution led to proposed legislation to raise the age of consent to 16. Naturally, there was opposition. "Not only was the creation of a statutory offense unpopular with gentlemen who wanted to protect their dissolute sons; experts feared widespread entrapment and blackmail by sexually precocious girls."[22] (One is reminded of contemporary debates around rape legislation!)

Strong opposition to the proposed legislation raising the age of consent and repealing the CD Acts resulted in its being compromised and stalled in committees. It was Josephine's desperation over the fate of this critical legislation that caused her to become involved with the "heroic" plans of the famous English journalist W. T. Stead.

Although Stead was by reputation a somewhat sensationalistic journalist, he was a first-rate writer and editor of the *Pall Mall Gazette*. His work and newspaper were known for their respectability and were solidly entrenched in the British middle classes. He became involved in the campaigns against the Contagious Diseases Acts when he heard the reports of abuse and torture in many of London's brothels. One brothel owner, Mrs. Jeffries, who specialized in providing virgin girls, was taken to court through Butler's efforts, only to leave after payment of a minimal fine.[23]

Neither the courts nor Parliament could be moved. The abolitionists had to rely on public opinion which they would stir to outrage by exposing the exploitation and abuse in the brothels. Stead was convinced to look into allegations of abuses of children in London brothels. As he learned of the atrocities, he is said to have forgotten his middle-class securities and given way to a personal agony and anger. He interviewed little girls as young as 4 years old who had been repeatedly raped in these brothels. He spent six weeks exploring and investigating the prostitution world of London's West End. But to publish a convincing argument, he needed final unimpeachable evidence of the ease with which children could be purchased, examined for virginity, and turned over to brothels.

He proposed a plan and Josephine concurred: he would find a procuress who would actually purchase a child and go through all the steps short of turning the child over to be sexually abused. A former procuress who was under Josephine's care was asked to carry out this mission.

Rebecca Jarrett had come to Josephine at the age of 36. She entered prostitution at the age of 12 (the age of consent then), and after many years she had started her own brothels and procured young girls and women to work for her. She had tried to leave prostitution many times, but as long as she stayed in London she could not sever her connections from her former life. She was finally taken in by Florence Booth, from the London-based Salvation Army, and Florence Booth sent her to Josephine.[24] In Winchester with Josephine, Rebecca severed her connections from her past and became actively involved in rescue work. Her knowledge of the world of brothels and prostitution made her almost fearless; she was able to go into many dangerous places and induce young women and girls to leave and come back to Winchester, where she took care of them.[25]

Rebecca agreed to help Stead carry out his plan. Under his direction she made her contacts and informed an old friend that she wanted to buy a child. The friend obliged and produced various children for Rebecca's inspection. Rebecca chose Eliza Armstrong, a 13-year-old girl. Stead gave Rebecca a £5 note for the purchase and told her that she must be absolutely sure that the parents were aware the child was being purchased for immoral purposes.[26] Mrs. Armstrong reportedly drank up her share of the money and was arrested that night for drunk and disorderly conduct.[27] Without Josephine's knowledge, the child was taken by Rebecca and Stead to a midwife who specialized in certifying young girls as virgins for the brothels to which they were destined.

So caught up was Stead in his own scheme that he never questioned the ethics of subjecting the girl to the very practices he was ostensibly condemning. And needless to say, Josephine was enraged when she learned of the extent to which he had carried his scheme. But he obtained the evidence he needed. The next day Eliza was taken to France and placed with the Salvation Army there.

With this final proof, on July 6, 1885, Stead launched his attack with the first in his series of articles entitled *The Maiden Tribute of Modern Babylon*. Under the subheading "A Child of Thirteen Bought for £5," he published his first exposé, describing the story of Eliza Armstrong and the conditions of prostitution.

The public's first reaction was stunned disbelief; there were charges of sensationalism, and then outright indignation led to near rioting. "The Home Secretary begged the editor to stop publication of the articles, fearing riots on a national scale. Stead replied that he would stop them the moment he received assurance that the Bill [raising the age of consent to 16, suppressing brothels, and protecting victims] would be carried through without delay."[28] The *Pall Mall Gazette* was banned by major news agents but sold out immediately on the streets. Hundreds of London newsboys were arrested for selling the papers but the charges were dismissed. "It was on this day that George Bernard

Shaw, who was the reviewer on the *Pall Mall Gazette*, took a bundle of papers out into the Strand and sold them."[29]

"Three days after the storm broke, Richard Cross, the new Home Secretary, put the Criminal Law Amendment Bill through its second reading."[30] It moved swiftly into law. Mass meetings were held in London and elsewhere. Public indignation from the Stead exposés had finally become a national concern. These gains were not without cost, however.

The first cost to be paid was by the most immediate victims of Stead's masquerade: Eliza Armstrong and Rebecca Jarrett. When the Eliza Armstrong story hit the papers, Mrs. Armstrong's neighbors were angry at her for selling her daughter and using the money to get drunk. She defended herself by beginning a search for her daughter. First, she reported Eliza missing to the police. Eliza's father claimed that the child had been taken from him without his consent. Stead, Rebecca Jarrett, and others were arrested, charged with abducting Eliza from her parents and indecently assaulting and drugging her.[31] This turn of events gave Stead's enemies, particularly those trying to thwart repeal legislation, an opportunity to try to discredit him. Both Stead and Rebecca Jarrett were convicted and sentenced to brief terms. Just as Eliza was used by Stead, she was now being used by his opposition.

For Stead such charges and imprisonment could only heighten his personal and political sense of martyrdom in his battle for the right, the just, and the pure. But for Rebecca, a recently reformed prostitute, it meant having her past dragged up before her and hearing herself publicly condemned by the courts. So harsh and abusive was the court that Josephine wrote a tract in defense of Rebecca, blaming herself for having convinced the well-intentioned woman to work with Stead. In that tract she wrote angrily of Stead's attitude after the trial: "He speaks of having had a fair trial; compliments the prosecution; confesses himself to have been to blame; hopes that nothing will be done to reverse the sentence. . . . Perhaps Mr. Stead may think that he himself was courteously treated but what of the courtesy or even decent fairness shown in regard to Rebecca, upon whom the utmost of vituperation permissible in a Court of Law was vented?"[32]

The other costly result of the Stead exposé was political. The inherently feminist politics of liberation with which Josephine had so carefully built and guided this movement were to be swept aside by the religious moralists who began en masse to take over the movement after these exposés. Their righteous indignation was aroused over the staining of purity of innocent English girls. They were preoccupied with protecting female virtue and preserving the family. The British churches had steadfastly refused Josephine support in the beginning of her campaign; but once the issues caught public attention and created moral indignation, the church began to take an active role in the movement.

The political movement for female liberation that Josephine had built was undermined into a purity crusade, as it came to be known. Josephine had made the tactical mistake of resorting to coalition politics to build her movement. Inevitably this brought the purity crusaders in under her banner. Although she shared similar convictions with them, their political goals were decidedly different from hers.

Josephine spoke of purity, but she meant something entirely different by it than did the purity crusaders. Her demand was for a purification of the State that would protect individual liberty of women and would destroy the immoral, sexist double standards. The purity crusaders were not seeking liberation of women. Rather they wanted to return women to the confines of repressive roles and Victorian morals.

Purity crusaders appeared to be in concert with Josephine in one important respect. They, like Josephine, engaged in a secularization of religious sentiment. As David Pivar points out, "Rather than appealing exclusively to religious institutions, they directed themselves toward the 'universal' religious sentiments common to all men."[33] Josephine was a deeply religious woman whose work was inspired as much by her religious beliefs as by her commitment to individual liberty. She brought her religious beliefs into her campaigns. She called upon them in her speeches, and her rescue work with prostitutes usually involved religious appeals for their conversion. Society had little to offer prostitutes as an alternative to their life in the brothel.

The condition and status of women was so low, the availability of social opportunities or employment for women so scarce, that it is not surprising that in her rescue work Josephine appealed to the women to look to a higher authority. (The question of options for prostitutes is one that we have yet to resolve in terms of being able to provide meaningful, nonpatriarchal, well-paying alternatives.)

Looking back from historical perspective, Josephine's work, because it was in part motivated by religious beliefs, now appears to have been a part of the social purity movement. Yet the goals of the social purity movement were in direct opposition to those of Butler's feminist work no matter how much they both appealed to religious sentiment. What in fact happened was that the social purity movement by attaching itself to women's causes was able to build a mass movement and to undermine the goals of feminist leaders like Josephine Butler.

The breakdown of Josephine's abolitionist cause by male self-interest is in the same pattern as the co-optation of other nineteenth-century feminist struggles. Josephine had recognized this danger in the beginning of the movement but was not able sufficiently to protect her movement against it: "Some men who worked with us at the beginning, shocked with the cruelty and illegality of the acts, fall off when they understand the thoroughness of our crusade, and that it is directed not only against cruel result of vice, but against the tacit permission—the indisputable right as some have learned to regard it—granted to men to be impure at all."[34]

By 1886, when the CD Acts were finally repealed, the conditions of prostitution had worsened. International traffic in women was at a peak and the definition of prostitution had changed and solidified. As Walkowitz points out, the effect of the Contagious Diseases Acts was to transform the casual prostitution of working-class prostitutes "into a specially identified professional class. . . . The eventual isolation of prostitutes from general lower-class life was largely imposed from above, although it received the passive acquiescence of the poor themselves."[35] Separated from their neighborhoods into distinct red-light districts and brothels made identification of the women as prostitutes more specific and therefore their ability to leave prostitution much more difficult. In the early years of the Acts, most prostitutes were young and single; by the late nineteenth century the rigidifying of this social role resulted in women's remaining in prostitution longer. Their social mobility had been effectively curtailed.[36] Undoubtedly other social factors facilitated the formalized categorization of women as prostitutes. But clearly the impact of the CD Acts was to create among women a distinct out-group and one in which women were socially if not physically trapped. In turn, this social and geographic isolation facilitated the criminal organization of prostitution complete with pimps, procurers, and organized brothels.

Slavery was becoming more and more covert. To challenge it in all of its subtleties required the clear political vision Butler had brought to the earlier campaigns. Organized prostitution was incompatible with female emancipation and individual liberty. Women's liberties could be achieved only through forcing the State to expose and break up rings of organized procurers and brothel keepers.

But the purity crusaders, the religious moralists who campaigned against all social evils that would challenge Victorian standards of purity, now dominated the movement. The paternalism of earlier reformers like Dyer and Stead was rampant. Responsibility was placed on the victim and the need to uplift her, rather than on the oppressor and the need to eliminate him. Whereas Josephine had never interfered with or judged a woman who freely chose the life of prostitution,* morality crusaders would reassert the madonna-whore standard, condemning all prostitutes except the innocent and pure victims who could be saved and returned to their former state of innocence and purity.

One can only conjecture about the influence of Victorian male sexuality on the co-optation of the abolitionist goals and the redefinition of prostitution itself that resulted

---

* "In one statement she asserted, 'My principle has always been to let individuals alone, not to pursue them with any outward punishment, nor drive them *out of any place* so long as they behave decently, but to attack *organized prostitution*, that is when a third party, activated by the desire of making money, sets up a house in which women are sold to men.' " [Glen Petrie, *A Singular Iniquity: The Campaigns of Josephine Butler* (New York: Viking Press, 1971), p. 228.]

from these later purity crusaders. "Spending"—the Victorian euphemism for the emission of sperm—was seen as weakening, debilitating.[37] With extraordinary fervor, purity crusaders lectured that sexual containment was the ideal state. It was supposed to allow men to store up their energies. And incontinence, besides being weakening, was morally wrong, sinful. Consequently, men were advised against masturbation and urged into marriage; as husbands they would not be expected to perform frequently, as it was widely believed that women had no sexual drive. Responsibility for sexual containment rested on women. While this was the creed of Victorian male sexuality, it was never assumed that men could live by values of containment. The sexual double standard recognized the inevitability of male infidelity. That infidelity in the context of sexual repression suggests an acute need for access to prostitutes. As long as prostitutes were separate, isolated, and different from other women, Victorian men could secretly frequent them, taking care of socially suppressed sexual needs while maintaining a posture of containment in their daily lives. It obviously was not in their self-interest to see Josephine Butler disrupt the double standard on which rested the morality that assured their access to prostitutes. To see *those* women treated with the same respect and dignity as their supposedly sexless wives would defeat their need to distinguish between madonna and whore.

As the purity crusades emerged into the twentieth century, they were dominated by two themes: the immoral destruction of innocent girls' virtue and sinful incontinence in men. Therefore their call was for purity and preservation of the family. Sensationalized accounts increased, describing sweet, innocent young things being chloroformed and dragged off to foreign brothels. Girls who resisted and fought to their death were seen as martyrs. The purity crusade included other reform issues, especially temperance. Often in their exhortations, leaders would associate the evil of the traffic in women with immoral debauchery of drink. The victimization of women became the means of attacking other behaviors that flaunted religious principles —drunkenness, free love, and so on.

This sensationalism, derived from and spirited by the purity crusades, cast reasonable doubt on the actual accounts of the traffic in women and children. It created a separation between city/street prostitution and the traffic in women. Butler had been careful to focus on *all* exploitation of women from prostitution, not separating her rescue work from political campaigns, local prostitution from international traffic, white from black, brown, or yellow victims. Sensationalistic writers and speakers dramatized their cause through horrifying and likely often fictionalized incidents of sex slavery.

The victim became redefined; the less sweet, innocent, and young she was, the less likely could she be a victim. Thus the careful earlier investigations that exposed the traffic in women and created international concern were undermined by the sensationalistic appeals of reformers for the resurrection of purity through the destruction of vice.

It was in this climate that the term "white slavery" first came into common usage. While the term rarely appears in Butler's writing or speeches, when she did use "white slavery" she referred to the entire problem—regulation, prostitution, traffic in women.

The term "white slavery" was formally used at the 1902 Paris conference where representatives of several governments met to draft an international instrument for the suppression of the white slave traffic (*Les Traités des Blanches*). While the term was initially meant to distinguish the practice from nineteenth-century black slavery, it had immediate appeal to racists who could and did conclude that the efforts were against an international traffic in *white* women. So in addition to being sweet, innocent, and young, victims were also coming to be seen only as white, despite the evidence that the traffic included black, brown, and yellow women. The term eventually embodied all the sexist, classist, and racist bigotry that was ultimately incorporated within the movement dominated by religious morality. Because of the confusion and misuse resulting from the term, the International Conference of 1921 recommended that the term white slavery be dropped and replaced with "Traffic in Women and Children."[38] This was subsequently the language of the League of Nations and the United Nations studies and reports. Nevertheless, coming from the bigotry that originally brought it into common use, the term is still retained today.

The 1902 Paris meeting led to the International Agreement for the Suppression of the White Slave Traffic, which was ratified by twelve nations in 1904. It was designed to commit governments to taking action against "procuring of women and girls for immoral purposes abroad."[39] This agreement led to the 1910 Mann Act in the United States. This act (recently amended to include traffic in males as well as females) forbids transporting a person across state lines or international boundaries (exporting or importing) for prostitution or other immoral purposes. The ambiguous term "immoral purposes" suggests the extent to which the purity movement had succeeded in becoming the lawful guardians of female virtue. The question of women's will is entirely excluded from consideration and therefore the issue of individual liberty, so central to Butler, was entirely lost in the language of the act. In addition, "immoral purposes" could and would eventually be defined by the courts according to prevailing male definitions of morality.

This series of laws formalized and legalized the ideological and practical separation, engendered by the purity crusade, between international traffic in women and local prostitution, thereby distracting attention from the continuing enslavement of women in local prostitution.

Since that time there continues to be a rhetorical debate that questions the existence of white slavery. The debate first accepts the distinction between international traffic and local prostitution; second, it defines white slavery by the most *literal* criteria that can be applied. Unless it can be proven, in sensationalistic terms, that an innocent girl has been subjected to the cruelest force imaginable, the incidents have been discredited.

Teresa Billington-Grieg, who had been a member of the Pankhursts' Women's Social and Political Union but who split from that suffrage group, added fuel to this debate when she wrote "The Truth About White Slavery" in 1913. In writing the article, she gathered evidence from various police officials to prove that there is "no organized *trapping*" (emphasis mine).[40] Attributing the scandal in white slavery "in no small measure to the Pankhurst domination," she goes on to react to sensationalism. "Fed on such ridiculous scandal-mongering, these women have convinced themselves that a large number of men go regularly and deliberately to a safe and secret place of vice to engage in a pastime that is a life and death struggle to a trapped

girl."[41] As a forerunner of contemporary ideology, Billington-Grieg demands a further separation of issues—that
of sexual abuse of children from that of the white slave
traffic. In the former "an intemperate degenerate is passion-
driven into the sudden commission of an atrocity; in the
other, there is a cold-blooded, calculating deliberation
which reduces the matter from bestiality to the worst possible devilishness."[42] For the female victims, this would
seem like a hair-splitting distinction.

The debate raged in Europe and America, with contradictory evidence being presented from each new investigation. Investigating commissions accepted the formalized
distinction between white slave traffic and prostitution. The
1914 Massachusetts "Report of the Commission for the
Investigation of the White Slave Traffic, so called" concluded:

> Every story if this kind has been thoroughly investi-
> gated and either found to be a vague rumor, where
> one person has told another that some friend of the
> former (who invariably in turn referred the story
> farther back) heard that the thing happened, or, in a
> few instances, imaginary occurrences explained by hys-
> teria or actual malingering. Several of the stories were
> easily recognized versions of incidents in certain books
> or plays.

But according to Ernst Bell, the most *literal* interpretation
of white slavery was incorporated into the revised 1902
Massachusetts law, resulting in few incidents that could be
considered white slavery:

> The procuring must be fraudulent and deceitful and
> the woman must be unmarried and of a chaste life.
> If the procurer married the girl to circumvent the law
> he cannot be prosecuted; if the girl makes one mis-
> take in life, she cannot be protected from being pro-
> cured.[43]

The incidence of procuring, which is never easily measured,
is an indication of the prevalence of sexual slavery. Although its language was woefully inadequate, the Mann

Act initially facilitated prosecution of procurers in the United States. Compared to 1907, when only one alien was debarred from the United States for procuring, "in 1914, 254 procurers and five men living off the earnings of prostitutes were excluded, and 154 procurers and 155 persons living on the earnings of prostitutes were deported."[44]

Maude Miner collected significant material on white slavery from cases she handled in night court in New York and in her work in refuge shelters. She documents the procuring tactics and methods used to induce young women into prostitution. But despite these known methods, she asserted, "There has undoubtedly been exaggeration about the white slave traffic in some of the newspaper accounts and in the moving picture films which have also exploited vice. Yet the facts in authentic cases are too hideous to be told."[45]

The traffic in women and children persisted despite social redefinition. At the turn of the century in California, through the rescue work of Donaldina Cameron, an enormous traffic of young Chinese girls became known. The girls were being purchased in China, brought to the United States and sold in San Francisco in open markets or directly to individuals. Many were reported to be sold into domestic slavery for $100 to $200. Brothel slaves were sold for $1,500 to $3,000. The girls were often acquired from interior provinces and exported through Hong Kong, believing they were coming to the United States for arranged marriages. Donaldina Cameron spent many years seeking out these girls and rescuing them from back alleys of San Francisco's Chinatown.[46]

Bristow reports a considerable problem with traffic in Jewish girls in Eastern Europe at the turn of the century. Marriage was the means of procuring.

Procurers were known to go through the traditional ritual and then take their legally unmarried and largely unprotected partners off to a domestic or foreign brothel . . . . In 1892 twenty-two men were convicted in Lemberg for procuring girls from small Galician towns with promises of jobs as servants, and selling them to brothels in Constantinople, Alexandria and points east of Suez. The Austrian consul in Constantinople had rescued sixty of them from virtual imprisonment the year before.[47]

During this period, most feminists were engrossed in the battle for legal equality and the right to vote; these rights at the time were seen as fundamental to any other moral or legal changes. Some feminists addressed the issue of white slavery but it never became a major focus of the movement either in England or America. Yet a few voices continued to be heard.

Christabel Pankhurst, writing for the British suffrage movement in 1913, connected the prevalence of white slavery with the denial of votes for women. Regulation had spread to India through British colonization. Pankhurst expounded on the government's responsibility for white slavery there and showed how the absence of women in Parliament prevented legislation that would provide women fair wages and thus left them vulnerable to white slavers.[48]

Emma Goldman, writing in 1917, also associated white slavery with economic conditions. Exploitation was the cause of the trade in women, "the merciless Moloch of capitalism that fattens on underpaid labor, thus driving thousands of women and girls into prostitution."[49] And she adds, "Whether our reformers admit it or not, the economic and social inferiority of women is responsible for prostitution."[50]

Lack of economic opportunity for women was in fact the source of huge profits of procurers and madams. Christabel Pankhurst asserted:

> White Slavery exists because thousands upon thousands of ordinary men want it to exist, and are willing to pay to keep it going. These men, in order to distract the attention of the other women who are not White Slaves, are very willing to make scapegoats of a few of the Slave Traders, but all the time they rely upon there being enough traders to maintain the supply of women slaves. By force, by trickery, or by starvation enough women will, they believe, be drawn into the Slavery of vice.[51]

Feminists like Pankhurst and Goldman were reasserting the connection between morality and political conditions—

the politics with which Josephine had begun the movement. Paternalism had separated the issue of moral exploitation from the political position of women vis-à-vis men. With the political analysis of women like Pankhurst and Goldman, the focus was placed back on those who create and maintain the institution. According to Goldman,

> Fully fifty percent of married men are patrons of brothels. It is through this virtuous element that the married women—nay, even the children—are infected with venereal diseases. Yet society has not a word of condemnation for the man, while no law is too monstrous to be set in motion against the helpless victim.[52]

And Christabel's militancy is as pronounced on this issue as it is on suffrage:

> Intelligent women are revolted by men's commerce with white Slaves. It makes them regard men as inferiors. So great a want of self-respect and of fastidiousness excites their scorn and disgust. The disparity between the moral standards of men and women is more and more destroying women's respect and regard for men. Men have a simple remedy for this state of things. They can alter their way of life.[53]

And by altering their way of life she meant sexual self-control—not repression, but responsible control.

For these feminists, as for Butler, the situation called for a fundamental value change. If the moral values of patriarchy were radically altered, so would the nature of the society be. But co-optation of feminist causes successfully prevented that change. Thus it can hardly be expected that the values and conditions which originally spawned female sexual slavery would change. The only thing that has changed is our awareness of it.

Sporadic outbursts from feminists continued. Through the 1920's and 1930's studies were conducted by the League of Nations and later the United Nations affirming a continuing traffic in women and children. The issue of regulation as a form of slavery begun by Josephine Butler led to the 1949 United Nations agreement which called upon nations to punish those who procure and exploit for prostitution.

But other than these token measures, the exposure of slavery and exploitation of women in prostitution has been silenced, the enslavement of these women forgotten and ultimately denied.

CHAPTER 3 _____

Victims and Survivors

A young girl, now a prostitute, was sexually molested and raped by her stepfather regularly for four years. He threatened that if she told her mother he would leave them homeless and penniless . . .

Two runaway girls from Pennsylvania get off a bus in Sacramento. They are kidnapped, raped, and forced into prostitution . . .

A prostitute decides to leave her pimp, and when he hunts her down at her aunt's house, he takes her away with him. As a warning against future escapes, he beats her with the base of a car jack until he fractures her skull . . .

A wife gathers up her 5-year-old twin daughters and leaves home. She is hunted down by her husband, and when he finds her he beats her and fires his shotgun within an inch of her head as a warning in case she tries to run away again . . .

Several thousand teenage girls disappear from Paris every year. The police know but cannot prove that many are destined for Arab harems. An eyewitness reports that auctions have been held in Zanzibar, where European women were sold to Arab customers . . .

In one year, 2,000 girls were reported missing from a rural area of India where procurers had been posing as labor contractors . . .

These women and girls are victims of female sexual slavery. Some have escaped; others have not. When it is organized, female sexual slavery is a highly profitable business that merchandises women's bodies to brothels and harems around the world. Practiced individually, without an organizational network, it is carried out by pimps whose lifestyle and expensive habits are supported by one or two women whom they brutally force to sell their bodies for his profit. The private practice of female sexual slavery is carried out by husbands and fathers who use battery and sexual abuse as a personal measure of their power over their wives and/or daughters. *Female sexual slavery is present in ALL situations where women or girls cannot change the immediate conditions of their existence; where regardless of how they got into those conditions they cannot get out; and where they are subject to sexual violence and exploitation.* Sexual slavery, whether it is carried out by international gangs, or individual pimps, is a highly criminal and clandestine activity, and the slavery carried out by fathers and husbands is kept secret and is socially tolerated as well. Its setting may be an Arab harem, a German eros center, an American pimp pad, or a suburban home. Wherever it is located, it brings both monetary gain and personal satisfaction to its perpetrators.

Female sexual slavery is not an illusive condition; the word "slavery" is not merely rhetorical. This is not some condition in which a woman's or child's need for love allows her to fall into psychological patterns that make it possible for her to accept abuse with love or to feel joy in pain. Slavery is an objective social condition of sexual exploitation and violence. The experiences of sexual slavery documented in this book reveal that it is not a practice that is limited to international traffic but it is pervasive throughout patriarchal societies.

THE RAPE PARADIGM

As long as a woman or girl is held in sexual slavery, sexual intercourse is, by definition, rape. If one is not free to consent or reject, one is forced; and forced sexual intercourse, whether physically brutal or seductively subtle, is rape. The fact of rape is determined by its objective conditions. If those are conditions which a woman or girl cannot leave or alter, then they are conditions of slavery.

Rape is the primordial core of female sexual slavery, extending from the most public international traffic in women for prostitution to the most private slavery in a suburban home, city tenement, or rural cottage.

It is a political crime of violence against women, an act of power and domination. Kate Millet coined the term "sexual politics." Sexual slavery is the very essence of sexual politics in its most extreme and ugly form. From Susan

Griffin's ground-breaking article, "Rape, the All-American Crime" to Susan Brownmiller's exhaustive study, *Against Our Will*, we have come to understand rape as a political act rather than the isolated, private experience of individual women.

One of the most important findings in this survey of female sexual slavery is that the rape paradigm, the sexual politics of rape, forms the social and political context in which victims are sexually enslaved. The rape victim's experience is, in essence, the experience of all female victims of sexual violence in terms of how the entire social order reacts to and treats her experience. Recognition of the commonality of women's experience in female sexual slavery breaks the time-honored separation of women into competitive and incompatible categories of madonna and whore and makes it possible to understand that "victim" can mean also prostitute, battered wife, incestuously assaulted child, veiled woman, purchased bride.

The rape paradigm is best illustrated in the way rape is routinely handled by the police, in the courts, and by public attitudes. The response of these institutions to rape victims reveals the structure in which sexual violence and slavery thrive. When raped, a victim is expected to have escaped unharmed against overwhelming odds that include fraud, deception, physical force and violence, manipulation, and sheer terror. If she cannot extricate herself from the situation in which the rape takes place, then it is assumed that she was to some degree complicit in the assault; consequently it is no longer considered an assault and she is not truly a victim. Her victimization is proven or disproven on the worth of her word, the test of her character, the chasteness of her past sexual life, the mode of her dress, the glint in her eye, and the smile on her face. Each rape victim is treated as a self-contained sociology of why men do what they do to women. No other explanation of social forces or male behavior needs to be considered. Nothing outside of herself, not even her assailant, explains the rape. This is the rape paradigm.

The theories that explain why prostitutes stay with pimps, or why battered wives don't leave their husbands, or how incest victims "participate" in their experience, or how veiled women in arranged marriages "choose" living in seclusion are derived from the rape paradigm. Each uniformly sees women as driven by their own needs into abusive situations and enslavement.

Making the victim responsible for her victimization declares her the cause of her own anguish. The woman who is declared in court by judge and jury as the cause of her own anguish when she tries to prosecute a rapist or get protection from her violent husband is subject to the same judgments as the woman who is hidden behind a veil and kept behind the walls of her home, or who is subjected to genital mutilation in order to protect her from bringing down on herself the dishonor of being raped.

Penalties for rape differ from one culture to the next, but the sanction for it in the rape paradigm is constant across cultures and classes. The raped woman in America is likely not to see her attacker prosecuted, nor will beaten wives or prostitutes be likely to get protection from violent husbands or pimps. If they leave, they will both live in fear of being hunted down. In practice, punishment for rape and beatings falls more heavily on the victims and consequently acts as a social control of all women.

TERRORISM

Sexual violence, by definition, constitutes acts of excess that are unlimited in potential, scope, and depth and that are therefore terrifying to both victims and nonvictims alike. Terrorism goes beyond one woman's experience of sexual violence. It creates a state of existence that captures the hearts and minds of all those who may be potentially touched by it. In the face of terrorism people reorganize their lives. In several California cities different rapists have been carrying out reigns of terror that have continued for many years. In Sacramento many husbands and wives now sleep with loaded guns next to their beds. In Berkeley single women are making alternative arrangements rather than living alone. Windows are nailed shut; doors are equipped with two and three dead-bolt locks. Conscious plans for self-protection stem directly from prevailing sexual terrorism. People are forced to live in ways they would not normally choose; they have fears they hope can be overcome.

Terror—sometimes openly expressed, more often tacitly understood—permeates lives, often through something "known" but never stated. Such is the way a legacy of terror passes from mother to daughter. Many inner-city mothers wait and worry, knowing their daughters must return home from school through streets with cruising pimps. Suburban parents wait at the school or bus stop to ensure their children's safe return home. And mothers explain to teenage daughters why it is unwise for them to go out at night even though their brothers do. Sexual terrorism has become a way of life for women.

For its direct victim, sexual terrorism usually begins with initial disbelief that gives way to fear and ultimately a terror that overrides all other emotions. When a victim is subjected to sexual violence, the questions whirl dizzyingly: Could this be happening to me? When will it end? What will he do next? Can I escape; should I even try? Will he turn to my child next? And always the ultimate question in terror: Why? Why? Why?

After the assault a woman is likely to keep asking these questions for the days and weeks and months ahead as she integrates herself back into her normal life's activities with lingering terror. But if she is held in slavery, terrorism becomes her "normal" life and those questions have to be answered in some way that will enable her to cope with the immediate situation. She cannot look at her situation as something that will be over soon, or as a past event from which she tries to predict her future. As she must live with it day in and day out, so we must find a means of understanding how and what she goes through.

VICTIMISM

The feminist confrontation of rape has demonstrated that, by means of mutual support and knowledge, terrorism can be dealt with through political action and personal confidence. In confronting sexual violence, the first task of feminists has been to challenge the rape paradigm and prove women's victimization in order to have rape taken seriously. Public opinion did not favor the exposure of this hidden abuse. Nor were courts or police ready to accept that women were truly victimized by rape. The legitimacy of rape as an issue of sexual politics had to be proven also to those of the left whose class bias denied rape as real oppression, and to members of the right who said that we had doors opened for us and electric kitchens and what more did we want?

Through testimony of women, through campaigns to change rape laws, and through rape crisis centers, sexual violence has come to be understood as a social force, a political act, and not a collection of isolated, unrelated incidents. First in consciousness raising groups, then in speakouts and hearings, women began to describe their experiences of sexual violence. The horror of rape came out. The victims of rape found compassion and understanding from other women. Making rape no longer the personal, private problem of the victim shifts the focus of attention and the responsibility for the violence back to the assailant. With that change of emphasis, rape began to be taken more seriously in general and became known as more extensive and severe a problem than anyone was initially willing to believe. But this new consciousness has been a mixed blessing.

In the redefinition of rape, causal assumptions have been shifted away from the life history and state of purity of the victim and directed toward the assailant and his act of violence. In the process, attention has been drawn to the victimization of the woman, the brutality she endured, the traumatic psychological effects, and the havoc it has created in her life. Furthermore, with subsequent changes in law and police procedures it may become possible to prosecute more rapists, although police and courts' reaction to new laws reveal their resistance to punish rapists.

In creating new definitions we always risk incorporating the rigidity in the new that exemplified the old. Redefining rape, demanding recognition of women's victimization, has led to creating a new status—the victim. The status of this role is awarded according to the nature and extent of the abuse a woman suffered. Creating the role and status of the victim is the practice I call *victimism*. A women who has been sexually assaulted often finds she can only be understood if she takes on the role of victim; she is assigned a victim status and then seen only in terms of what has happened to her. What was done to her, the bruises, broken bones, and psychological pain she suffered makes her known only as the object of abuse. The status of "victim" creates a mind set eliciting pity and sorrow. Victimism denies the woman the integrity of her humanity through the whole experience, and it creates a framework for others to know her not as a person but as a victim, someone to whom violence was done. Assigning this role extends the terrorism of the act of sexual violence by continuing to rob her of her humanness, an act begun by the rapist. Yet because women receive so little support from this society when raped, many have only the status of victim to hold on to in trying to find justice and understanding. The assigned label of "victim," which initially was meant to call awareness to the experience of sexual violence, becomes a term that expresses that person's identity. Once one has been raped, one is not ever again a nonvictim. Victimism is an objectification which establishes new standards for defining experience; those standards dismiss any question of will, and deny that the woman even while enduring sexual violence is a living, changing, growing, interactive person.

The practice of victimism is not limited to sexual politics. It has its heritage in the political and academic left-liberalism of the late 1960's when the cult of the victim was the liberal's answer to urban racial violence. In an attempt to respond sympathetically to the plight of oppressed racial minorities, academic and political liberals delineated and stressed black victimization at the hands of a white racist society. William Ryan describes how the practice of *Blaming the Victim* shifted from the old-fashioned, conservative approach, which saw "victims as inferior, genetically defective, or morally unfit," and came to attribute "defect and inadequacy to the malignant nature of poverty, injustice, slum life, and racial difficulties."[1] Ryan notes that while the latter view attributes the causes of victimization to environmental forces, it still focuses the causes on the victim. Consequently, remedial programs and reform projects don't treat the objective social conditions which produce a racist society and trigger racial violence but try instead to improve the environment of the victim. Those left-liberals, whether academic or political, who respond from this perspective to social injustice, are as unable to see the victims of racial injustice as full human beings as they are unable to see the victims of sexual violence as real persons. To them minorities and women are only passive receptors of injustice. Because of them the true aggressors remain unchallenged.

Victimism is not a role necessarily sought by the victim but instead a status assigned to her by those who are judging her experience. I refer here not only to those who would judge her from sexist bias but also to many of those who seemingly bring support and caring to the plight of victimized women. Even those who are supportive will often shackle a woman with the judgments of victimism. For example, they usually identify passivity as a criteria for victimism—not passivity in the experience of violence, but passivity in accepting the noninteractive role of victim —the simple object of abuse without response whatever that response may be. While women are encouraged to fight back, we still recoil from recognizing the interaction a woman is necessarily engaged in when she is raped or enslaved; she is responding moment by moment. In slavery women are active and doing; often they are or appear to be complicit with their enslavement as a means of survival, a way of staying alive and coping. As a psychological device for dealing with their situation they may, for example, fall in love with their captors or their work. For these women, the practice of victimism imposed on them denies the reality of their circumstances and the very human efforts they make to cope with those circumstances. That is why women, whose experience of sexual violence is carried over into their enslavement, usually are not seen as victims— even by the very people who are demanding recognition for women as victims of sexual violence. How often we find some feminists chafing against the actions of a victim of sexual violence, as those actions could undermine the woman's status as a victim in the eyes of the public. Yet her actions were part of a complicated process of survival.

SURVIVING

More than victims, women who have been raped or sexually enslaved are *survivors*. Surviving is the other side of being a victim. It involves will, action, initiative on the victim's part. Any woman caught in sexual violence must make moment-by-moment decisions about her survival. She must be able to bring whatever resources she has to bear on the situation. If her husband suddenly starts beating her after several years of marriage, or the pimp she has just met and dined with tells her what will happen if she doesn't turn out on the streets, she has to decide if this is a crisis, if she is truly being threatened, or if this too will pass.

She is likely to have had little experience with facing this kind of trauma and may assume, as many rape victims have, that passive acceptance is the best way to get through the moment. She is likely to be unaware of the extent to which her crisis decision for survival will affect her later, particularly when she is in a situation where she cannot change the conditions due to the violence surrounding her.

On the other hand, she is also likely to be aware, even if subtly, that the society around her—friends, family, police, courts—will be judging her actions harshly. Passing up an attempt to escape because one is either frozen in terror or not yet able to see that one is in danger can be the pivotal point around which the court will try to destroy a woman's character. While it isn't likely in the moment of crisis that she will analyze specifically how judge, jury, or family will perceive her actions, the madonna-whore criteria, under which all women always live, is ever-present in her mind.

To be defined as victim in the context of victimism is to deny that identity is ongoing and changing; it is to deny whole parts of our active self in the experience of surviving the assault or slavery; it is to deny that women construct ways of coping and dealing with that violence in its aftermath, ways that are necessarily defined, though, by the limited options for women in the society.

Women are accustomed to seeing their acts of survival become grossly distorted or go by unnoticed. Some years ago a woman I knew was accosted as she was getting out of her car in front of her home. Knowing that her ex-husband was inside baby-sitting with her daughter, she convinced her assailant to go into her house. When the case came to court, the would-be rapist was acquitted because the victim had indicated motivation to have sex with him

by inviting him into her house. The fact that in the moment of crisis she had not become paralyzed in fear but
figured out a way to try to get herself to safety was never
acknowledged. If she was not an empty victim, a victim
who does not interact, who cannot be seen as engaging in
survival, could she even be a victim at all? On the other
hand, when Patricia Hearst was first kidnapped and locked
in the trunk of the car outside her Berkeley apartment, she
did think of trying to pull her blindfold down enough to
pull the plugs on the taillights, hoping to draw the attention of the police. She didn't carry out her idea, however,
perhaps because she was afraid Cinque would kill her, as
he threatened when she was put in the trunk, or perhaps
because being bound hand and foot prevented her from
getting her blindfold off enough to move. One juror saw
her lack of follow-through as an indication of guilt without
ever recognizing how resourceful and daring it would be
for a person in her situation even to come up with an idea
like that.

Surviving is a muddy business made all the more difficult
by a socialization that in no way prepares women for dealing with it. Women handle survival in a variety of ways,
usually haphazardly, making questionable decisions or
problematic nondecisions. Sometimes they are effective;
often they are not. Surviving is not written into the code of
socialized female behavior. Girls do not go to boot camp
or battle it out on the football field and in the locker room,
where survival tests of one form or another are played out.
Girls do not learn the survival skills that are automatic in
male socialization; instead, their socialization assumes a
life where they will not need to rely on survival skills.
Husband replaces father as protector. Life is seen in terms
of being, not doing. One is to *be* pretty, *be* smart, *be*
sociable. Being does not bring with it the problems of
survival that *doing* requires. To go out and do is to be
active and interactive, and action necessitates considerations of survival. Of course, women don't just "be," even
though they are trained to think that their existence is a
passive one. Even the most passive woman is acting in her
daily life, making decisions, interpreting her environment.
Yet she is not encouraged or trained to see herself as active.
Thus when she is unexpectedly faced with the question of

her own survival, her decisions, her analysis of the situation, her attempts at handling it may likely reflect her lack of awareness of herself as a survivor. But however she handles it, she is attempting to survive.

The only way to understand a woman's survival is to put oneself in her place. In order to do that, we must know the situation she faces, understand what the objective conditions are that she must handle when confronted by a rapist, pimp, or violent husband. The limitations of victimism confuse active survival with complicity, making it difficult to understand why a woman thinks and acts the way she does. She is in fact not fulfilling the assigned role and status of "victim." Infliction of victimism by the well-intentioned becomes as oppressive and destructive to the victim as the sexist act of completely denying women's victimization. Understanding the situation and putting oneself in the place of the victim makes it possible to comprehend the interpretations she will make and the actions she will take when facing violence, particularly in light of her background of female socialization. When the victim is an active, striving agent in her own behalf, whether her actions are effective or not, there is something to try to understand and some reason to hope.

To recognize women as survivors is not enough. There is a difference between survival and *effective* survival. Effective survival necessitates women's coming together over the serious threat of sexual violence and organizing against it. That massive numbers of women are organizing against rape and other forms of sexual violence is a statement of hope, a move toward effective survival. Until public consciousness is mobilized and the terrorism of women is taken seriously, we will not have a world where basic human freedoms belong to women as well as to men.

Third World women in the United States today have gained an edge on survival that many white women have yet to understand. For example, black consciousness, the awareness of racism in society, the political and civil rights movements that continually address the issue of racism, all make it very difficult for blacks to grow up today unaware of the danger they are in—physically, socially, and economically—from a white racist society. Racism is a serious problem to black people; they know it as a constant threat.

Survival is not taken for granted. Growing up black in a racist society means learning and incorporating survival skills into one's life. Learned survival becomes automatic over time when threats are recognized as constant and serious.

Despite their awareness from surviving in a racist society, black women are no less often its victims. They face the double jeopardy of living in a society that is both racist and sexist. Yet in having learned survival skills and in taking seriously the threats of this society to their well-being, they are a model for all women.

The women discussed in this book are enslaved. Whether in suburban homes, prostitution hotels, or Arab harems, they are not free to change the conditions of their existence. They have been denied basic human rights that should be theirs because they are living beings. The first step toward freedom is to lift the curtain of secrecy that surrounds their enslavement.

PART II

Female
Sexual Slavery

CHAPTER 4 —————————————————————

The Traffic in Sexual Slaves

Zanzibar, the fragrant island of spices, lies off the coast of Tanzania. Cloves are its main export. There is evidence that not long ago slaves were also being exported from the island. "If you were to visit the island, you would be shown where the slave auctions used to take place and told that that doesn't happen here anymore," said a European businessman who told me his story of attending slave auctions in Zanzibar in 1970.

Zanzibar became an independent Arab state in the early nineteenth century, at the height of the slave trade there. In 1890 Zanzibar was made a British protectorate, and from then until independence from Britain in 1964 the majority black African population was ruled by the British and Arabs.[1] Although slavery was officially abolished in 1897, it continued openly until the 1964 Zanzibar revolution which ended Arab rule of the island. The auctions witnessed by this European businessman in 1970 took place six years *after* independence from British colonialism, the revolution, and the loose unification of Zanzibar with the moderately socialist regime of Julius Nyerere's Tanganyika which created Tanzania.

As a European resident of East Africa for many years, the businessman who witnessed the auctions was constantly in touch with trade and politics there. He was living in Africa and doing business in Zanzibar at the time of the Sultan's deposition in 1964. When I interviewed him, he explained his involvement in Zanzibar: "I went to Zanzibar many times," he told me. "I was building a factory and was anxious to get an in with the ruling party." In 1970, while living on the African mainland, a friend approached him suggesting the European might be interested in seeing a slave auction on his next trip to Zanzibar.

"The first time I was taken to one of these events it was an auction of people for slave labor. The auction was held indoors near the housing projects in the center of the city. There were about 30 or 40 men and women milling around the way cattle do. They didn't look well fed. There was no obvious bidding. I learned later that the actual selections had taken place at another time. The purchasers were of Middle Eastern extraction, most of them Arabs."

By remaining silent about what he had seen, he had apparently "passed a test." About eight months later he was approached by a member of a family with whom he was doing business. "I was on the island and I was asked if I wanted to see a *real* auction. What they meant by *real* was the fact that they were selling girls."

Sexual slavery has been part of the traffic in and out of Zanzibar for many years. According to Sean O'Callaghan, author of *The White Slave Trade*, in the 1960's the traffic through Zanzibar was controlled by one man who had brothels in nearby Mombasa, Kenya, as well as on Zanzibar. "He posed as a spice dealer, invited women who took his fancy to Zanzibar for a holiday."[2] After being wined and dined and taken off guard by his suave manners and gracious behavior, he was able to get them to his estate, where he is reported to have drugged them. They then became part of the traffic into Saudi Arabia.

Traditionally the slave trade in Zanzibar had been controlled by the Arab minority. Since independence, more and more Africans were reported to be getting into the slave trade and they now had some concern about how long they could continue it since Nyerere was officially opposed to slavery. The young man who made the arrangements for visiting the second auction was peripherally involved in the slave trade. My informant supposed that this man was informally seeking some kind of outside support in the event that efforts should be made from the continent to limit the practice.

The second auction was held in Pemba, the more remote of the two islands of Zanzibar. It took place in the evening, behind locked doors. "Most of the girls being auctioned, and there were about fifty of them at this auction, were of European extraction. I assume they were part of the statistics of the girls who go on holiday to the Mediterranean area and disappear. They appeared to range in age from eighteen to thirty. A few of the girls were Indian, a couple were from South Africa. They were in a variety of dress—some in evening gowns, others in plain dresses, and others still in shorts, leaving the impression that they still had on the clothes they were wearing when they were acquired.

"The girls were in a central area, free to move about. They all looked slightly drugged. It was like a cattle market but there were no beatings nor was anyone screaming or shouting. The girls just moved around and suddenly you would see some girls escorted from the ring by one or two men. They were treated as important pieces of merchandise. Again there were no auction signals that I could see. But I was told by my contact that they had all been inspected by buyers before this event, which was where the official buying took place.

"It was required that all the men attending the auction wear long flowing Arab tunics that hung from shoulder to the ground and that they cover their heads with turbans; they completely masked their identity by covering their faces with the loose material from the turban. It was pretty hard to identify anyone there; nevertheless, I recognized two Africans who were city fathers. Except for the few Africans most of the purchasers were Arab. I was told by the person who took me there that eighty-five percent of the girls were destined for harems in the Middle East. The prices varied enormously. In conversations, I heard prices mentioned which were as high as $10,000.

"I was told that these auctions took place about every two months, when there were enough girls brought in to warrant one. I did hear of individual deals taking place with procurers who supplied certain harems and who didn't come to market at all."

During our interview he reported to me details that were given to him at the auction, but there were large gaps in information: where the women came from, for instance, and how they were taken out of the country remain unknown; discretion and safety suggested that he not ask these questions.

In 1978 a French policeman who had worked in the Central Office for the Repression of the Traffic in Persons told me that it is well known by authorities that many of the several thousand French teenage girls who disappear every year end up in Arab harems. The gang that operates the traffic is well known to the police but highly organized and very elusive. It is not known whether they find their way to harems through Zanzibar anymore, but as the businessman who saw the auctions said, "I can't imagine that it has stopped. There were a lot of people getting very rich on it."

Nor is there any indication that Nyerere intervened in the slave trade as some islanders feared he might. In the same year that these slave auctions were witnessed, the Revolutionary Council which governs Zanzibar was carrying on its own slavery. In September 1970 a truckload of soldiers under governmental orders went to the homes of four Persian girls in Zanzibar and held their families at gunpoint as the girls were dragged off screaming. They were taken before the Revolutionary Council, where they were forced into Muslim marriages with high-ranking government officials, most of whom had other wives. The abduction, forced marriage, and enslavement of these girls were carried out under the direction of Vice-President Karume, then dictator of the island, in accordance with the post-revolutionary policy of compulsory racial integration through intermarriage.

When this incident became known, shock waves were felt through the international press. Appeals were made to Nyerere to intervene. He remained silent. In July 1972, an All-Africa Women's Conference was held in Dar es Salaam, Tanzania. According to the Anti-Slavery Society in Britain, "A petition for the release of the four girls was handed to the Secretary General of the Tanzania Women's Organization, Mrs. Sophia Kawawa, wife of the Second Vice-President of Tanzania, and copies were handed to almost all the other delegates to the Conference. The appeal was not heard, however, lest the host government be embarrassed."

In 1973 three of the Persian girls managed to escape and were taken by guides through the night on a secret route out of Zanzibar. Their stories of the forced marriages, beatings, and torture created a larger wave of concern for the one girl who remained behind, Nasreen Hussein. She had been heavily guarded and could not escape. According to Stephen Barlay in his study of sexual slavery:

> An African politician of great integrity, international reputation and influence made a personal appeal to Julius K. Nyerere for the life and freedom of just one Persian slave girl. The President of Tanzania chose to ignore the appeal. His reason is thought to be political—the good of the country, the unity of Tanzania and a dream of some larger East African federation under his leadership.[3]

In 1973, after the escape of the three girls, the case of enslaved Nasreen Hussein was taken up by the United Nations Human Rights Commission as a human rights violation. A fully documented appeal was sent to the Tanzanian government, but again there was no response. The appeal died from inaction.

But the Anti-Slavery Society continued to mount pressure for the release of Nasreen. In 1975 Colonel Patrick Montgomery, the Secretary of the Society, received a visit from the Attorney General of Zanzibar telling him that Nasreen was now reconciled to her marriage and demanding that he cease his campaign for her freedom. Montgomery indicated that he would stop when Nasreen could tell him that on free soil.

The following year, in August 1976, the Anti-Slavery Society made another appeal to the United Nations Commission on Human Rights on behalf of Nasreen. In his appeal Montgomery presented a letter which had been smuggled from Nasreen to her parents the previous month.

> To my dear parents,
>
> I, your dear daughter, have heard that you want to leave me behind to be without parents or relations. If anything happens to me, who will be there with me? My parents, don't be deceived by anyone to believe that I don't want to accompany you. That is completely false. If today I am left free, I am ready to come to you . . . .
>
> As you know the marriage was performed without my consent and without my parents' consent. It was

> performed by force . . . . I have nothing more to say, except to beg those merciful guardians of human rights to see that I am given the right to decide myself where I want to go . . . .

Nasreen's father has remained on the island and continues to seek his daughter's freedom. Amnesty International has tried to make arrangements for Nasreen to visit her family in Teheran but she has been denied a visa. She remains a slave in a marriage to a man who has since taken another wife in addition to her.

The United Nations' token action and Nyerere's silence reinforced the virtual sanction of sexual slavery Zanzibar has enjoyed for many years. Diplomacy at this level is reduced to a conspiratorial brotherhood. The silence that surrounds slavery is awesome and makes it one of the best-kept secrets of the twentieth century.

SUPPRESSING THE EVIDENCE

INTERPOL has been aware of and has been reporting on the traffic in women for years. Since 1965 they have prepared two comprehensive reports based on their own international surveys which they have suppressed. The reports have had only a limited circulation to delegates to IN-TERPOL conferences and some United Nations officials and delegates. The first report, in 1965, documented several patterns of traffic in women which still underpin slavery today. On the basis of responses from seventeen countries to their survey, it was later reported that INTERPOL concluded:

> The main immigration route at the time was reported to be from Europe to the Near East and to Sub-Saharan Africa. It was stated that traffic had its main source in European countries which acceded to the 1949 Convention and closed their licenses to brothels.

> When women were hired, the forms of contracts were generally vague nor did they conform to national regulations of work conditions. In the result, the women who leave their countries on the strength of a contract were really without any protection.

Constraint of various degrees stemmed from the clauses and also from the relationship between the employers and the employees. Threats, indebtedness, and fear of destitution were constantly present which contributed to prostitution among such members.[4]

When this 1965 report reached Colonel Patrick Montgomery at the Anti-Slavery Office in London, he immediately contacted INTERPOL for permission to release it to the press, indicating the urgency of informing the public as a way of exposing the traffic and slavery. INTERPOL refused permission. It is typical of police organizations to refuse to divulge information even when it could help prevent these practices. INTERPOL had an additional motivation in this case. According to their response to Montgomery they refused his request "in order to avoid compromising countries which had shown their confidence in INTERPOL by giving certain information."

The patterns and practices that had been reported in 1965 but never released to the public were still apparent in a report made ten years later. In 1974 the General Secretariat of the International Police Organization prepared and submitted to the United Nations a report on the "Traffic in Women." It contained the following conclusions:

South American women—mostly Argentine women or women who have visited that country—are "exported" to Puerto Rico, to the European Mediterranean countries, or to the Middle East.

There is a European regional "market," mainly in French women who "work" in neighboring countries, mostly in Luxembourg and Federal Germany (in eros centers), but women from South American and other countries are sometimes involved. There are links between this "market" and other regions, notably the Middle East.

Some traffic networks apparently recruit women in Europe and send them to certain African countries which have reached a point in their development which allows the international exploitation of prostitution (Ivory Coast, Senegal).

There is an East Asian market which recruits women
—mostly from Thailand, but also from the Philippines
—and sends them to other countries.

The statistics received from Lebanon give reason to
believe that there is a concentration of prostitution in
this country. The women involved come mainly from
other Arab countries. The situation would appear to
be the same in Kuwait.[5]

This report, like previous ones, has been suppressed not
only by INTERPOL but by all those individuals working
in the field of slavery who have abided by INTERPOL's
sanction against making public such information. After
failing to obtain the report from INTERPOL officials, I
made repeated attempts to acquire a copy of the report
from those who had attended the 1974 INTERPOL conference in Buenos Aires, where the report had been disseminated to delegates. I was given a multitude of excuses;
one man insisted that the report had been stolen from his
car and that he couldn't get me a copy of it. Nevertheless I
did obtain a copy of the report. It is no longer limited only
to those who share INTERPOL's silence; it appears un-
expurgated in Appendix A of this book.

There is no way to estimate the incidence of sex slavery.
Full and accurate statistics are impossible to calculate on
this practice. While statistics are frequently used to verify
facts, any attempt at this time to quantify sexual slavery
based on known incidence would undoubtedly underesti-
mate the actual incidence. INTERPOL found from its
1974 survey the same thing the FBI has found about rape
statistics. Reported incidents do not reflect the true picture;
"the number of cases of traffic in women which have never
come to the attention of the authorities is quite high."[6]

Estimating the prevalence of sexual slavery is further
complicated by the inability of authorities to distinguish
between victims and volunteers. As with rape, with the
traffic in women there is an automatic assumption of complicity on the part of the victim in any sexual attack
against her. More often than not, officials receiving reports
of international traffic will make the determination that the
woman is not a victim and the case will be treated as a

typical prostitution offense, contributing to the low *re-ported* incidence of sexual slavery.

International law derived from the 1949 United Nations Convention for the "Suppression of the Traffic in Persons and of the Exploitation of the Prostitution of Others" and from other international conventions, makes it "an indictable offense to hire, induce, or lead astray a woman or girl . . . even if she consents—with a view to making her engage in prostitution" outside her own country.[7] Only 49 nations of the world have ratified the 1949 convention agreeing to take direct action against the exploitation of persons in prostitution. The United States is not one of those nations. (See Appendix B for list of nations.) Similarly the Mann Act, passed in the United States in 1910 and recently amended, forbids the transportation of anyone across state or national boundaries for prostitution or other immoral purposes. These laws reflect the contradictions in social attitudes which, at one extreme, in the early twentieth century held that any time a woman traveled to another country in the company of a man and engaged in prostitution she was forced. The sexually liberated 1960's and 1970's presented the opposite extreme, which assumed that women are *never* forced into prostitution. Neither view reflects the reality of female experience, nor does it consider the objective conditions of enslavement.

In an effort to highlight the reality of forced prostitution, INTERPOL defined "disguised traffic" as

> the act of hiring women in one country with a view *to making them engage in* certain types of employment in another country . . . and in conditions in which they are subjected, incited or exposed to prostitution.[8] (emphasis mine)

Force was implicit in their definition which like international law is focused on procurers and pimps. From their survey they found that "disguised traffic in women still exists all over the world." But even with this definition and these findings, victims still were synonymous with volunteers:

> Here again, a certain number of *victims are more or less consenting*, and when they accept various kinds of employment abroad, *they probably know* what is expected of them and occasionally engage in prostitution to supplement their income. However, in this field, there are a certain number of naive women who are attracted by the promises made to them by some employment agencies or by organizers of artistic tours, etc., and who eventually find themselves in a situation where they are forced into prostitution and may finally think that this is the only way they can earn their living.[9] (emphasis mine)

When distinctions are blurred and confused, facts lose their poignancy. By confusing victimization with consent, language is used to mediate the horror of slavery and ultimately to still any outrage against it. In the 1975 INTERPOL report of the following cases, the very language used reveals women taken against their will and their knowledge:

> *Belgium.* In 1973, a procurer engaged three young Thai girls in Thailand and took them to work as prostitutes in Belgium.
> *Federal Germany.* In 1973 and 1974, German nationals persuaded young women from Hong Kong and Ethiopia, by making them false promises, to go to Germany to work as "masseuses" in "massage parlours," or as barmaids in nightclubs.
> *France.* A network of procurers was broken up. The network, composed of 6 Guadeloupe nationals and 2 Germans, had recruited about twenty young women from Pointe-a-Pitre to make them work as prostitutes in Paris and in the "Eros Centers" of Dusseldorf and Essen (Federal Germany).[10]

These incidents reflect only the surface of the problem. In his international survey presented to the United Nations in 1966, Dr. Mohamed Awad, U.N. Special Rapporteur, found slavery still to be a major world problem. Subsequent updatings of that report by the United Nations Human Rights Commission have come to the same conclusion. While 70 nations responded to the survey, 40 did not. (Again Tanzania and Zanzibar's silence is noted here.)

The action of the United Nations in response to this report was as revealing as the lack of cooperation from 40 countries. On the basis of his survey and the expressed needs of individual countries, Dr. Awad proposed "that the United Nations should establish a committee to deal with the problem of slavery in all its aspects, and to act as an advisory body to the Economic and Social Council."[11]

> The American delegate gave the proposals a very lukewarm reception, declaring that the problem of slavery did not warrant the cost of a new committee. The Soviet delegate condemned slavery but insisted that apartheid, racialism and colonialism were even more pressing problems and only these should be regarded as manifestations of modern slavery.[12]

An alternative resolution was proposed which emphasized apartheid and colonialism, eliminated the proposal for a new committee, and referred the whole problem to the less powerful, heavily overworked Commission on Human Rights. The delegate from Tanzania moved the alternate resolution and "hit out at everybody who appeared to support Dr. Awad's very meagre findings. . . . He asked the Indian and Iranian delegates if they wished to have a committee of experts inspecting their countries and reporting on imaginary slavery."[13] The alternate resolution was carried and the subject of slavery and traffic in women was effectively buried.

In August 1974 a Working Group on Slavery was established within the Commission on Human Rights under the Sub-Commission on Prevention of Discrimination and Protection of Minorities. This Working Group consists of five members who "meet for not more than three working days, prior to each session of the Sub-Commission, to review developments in the field of slavery and the slave trade in all their practices and manifestations."[14] According to the Chief of Research for the Commission, they are just now trying to renew reporting procedures for member countries to document "the traffic in persons and the exploitation of the prostitution of others." But informally it is generally recognized that there is not much official interest in seeing the issue of sexual slavery reopened.

Such attitudes as those of a Pakistani delegate, when approached by Colonel Montgomery of the Anti-Slavery Society, reflect the underlying mood and motivation for silencing the subject of slavery. In response to a request for support on a resolution on slavery, the delegate said, "I shall not waste your time by reading your resolution. We have no slavery in my country, but we have neighbors who have slavery in theirs and I'm not going to embarrass them."[15]

International pressure has been felt by organizations like the International Abolitionist Federation. That group, originally founded by Josephine Butler, planned a major conference to be held in Egypt in the summer of 1978. They had to cancel the conference due to refusal on the part of the Egyptian government to assist in supporting the conference and reported threats by others on the lives of organizers and potential participants.

Within the United Nations, atrocities are being covered up or sanctioned by inaction and neglect. Attrition from the amount of knowledge to the extent of action is overwhelming. There were 23,000 complaints of violations of human rights filed with the United Nations in 1973 under a new procedure that had been adopted for dealing with slavery practices. Only eight cases survived the bureaucratic procedures and evaluations. One was that of Nasreen Hussein.

Thus the slow, disinterested machinery of the Human Rights Commission has carefully avoided addressing issues of international sexual slavery and forced prostitution. However, a new hope in the 1970's was the newly appointed United Nations Commission on the Status of Women under the leadership of Helvi Sipila, as well as the 1975 International Women's Year Conference in Mexico City.

At that conference Marie Pierre DeBrissac (then Herzog), at the time Director of UNESCO's Human Rights Commission, speaking for the Director General of UNESCO, asked for an international investigation of the imprisonment of girls and women in closed houses of prostitution; she indicated that she had evidence of "sexual torture for sexual ends." The World Plan of Action proposed at the conference stated in part:

> Specific legislative and other measures should be taken to combat prostitution and the illicit traffic in women, especially young girls. Special programmes, including pilot projects, should be developed in cooperation with international bodies and non-governmental organizations to prevent such practices and rehabilitate the victims.
>
> Governments which have not already done so should ratify or accede to the United Nations Conventions for the Suppression of the Traffic in Persons and of the Exploitation of Prostitution of Others (1949).[16]

The year following the International Women's Year Conference, Renée Bridel, representing International Federation of Women in Legal Careers, a nongovernmental organization in consultative status to the United Nations, proposed to the Status of Women Commission that they support a legal study "to expose an important area of oppression and injustices to which women are subjected through the power of highly organized and financially powerful criminals." The areas to be studied were slavery from the traffic in women and children, torture of prostitutes, the exploitation of migrant women, refugees, and children.[17]

While Helvi Sipila encouraged Renée Bridel to make the proposal, she cautioned her that she knew the United Nations did not want to get involved in those issues. The proposal was made, the Commission members listened to it, and without a motion or any discussion they immediately went on to other business.

The United Nations has many reasons for keeping the sex slave trade off their agenda. Some member nations still practice it with impunity; also, closer to home, some U.N. officials and diplomats engage in the related practice of domestic slavery. Domestic slavery is a widespread international practice. Young girls are procured from poor Third World countries and taken to the United States or Europe to work in households as domestics or household servants. There they are usually confined to the house, forced to work long hours, doing menial chores for little or no pay; sometimes they are subjected to sexual abuse by their employer and they are threatened with deportation to keep them in line.

From 1971 to 1974, 165 federal cases of involuntary servitude and slavery were investigated in the United States. It was reported that "Many of these cases involved holding of domestic servants in a state of servitude by their employers . . ."[18] No statistics were available on cases investigated on the state level. The flood of cases up to 1978 concerning domestic slavery in the United States suggests that several thousand slaves are now serving diplomats in the United States.[19] In 1977, I. G. Patel, United Nations Deputy Administrator for Development, a post that is equivalent to United Nations Undersecretary General, was sued for holding a Philippine girl named Natividad Diza in slavery. The lawsuit was filed in United States District Court against Ruben Mendez and I. G. Patel and their wives for involuntary servitude and peonage. When legal action was initiated against him, Patel, under advice from the United States attorney, pled diplomatic immunity. He resigned his United Nations post and became governor of the Reserve Bank of India.

According to the brief filed in court, Natividad was procured for employment from the Philippines in 1973 by Ruben Mendez, a United Nations official. She was brought to the United States, where she worked as a servant in the Patel household until January 1976. Natividad's duties included cooking, serving, entertaining many guests, caring for Patel's child, cleaning house, and laundry. She worked for a minimum of 14 and often as many as 19 hours per day, seven days a week, without any holidays.

Several years before, in 1969, Mendez had procured her sister Perlita and brought her to the United States. According to Perlita, whose hours and working conditions matched those of her sister, she was not permitted to leave the Mendez residence except to walk the dog or do required shopping. She was constantly threatened with deportation to keep her in line. When she finally was able to leave the Mendezes, she demanded the $50 per month that was to be kept in trust for her during the six years she was there. They gave her a check in the amount of $2,431.78, claiming that from her earnings were deducted food, clothing, and transportation.

The court found that force had not been proven in the case of Perlita and her sister. On appeal the women were awarded a monetary settlement by the court, but the finding of the lower court was upheld. In denying the claim of Perlita and Natividad, the court indicated that diplomatic immunity given to such officials makes them exempt from the United States laws such as those governing minimum wages. The judge referred to a recent decision which stated that "Congress has accorded the foreign diplomatic or semidiplomatic officials . . . the privilege of bringing into and employing in this country nonimmigrant aliens who are attendants, servants, or personal employees, free of any minimum wage requirements," and he found its "reasoning eminently sound."[20]

In light of the practice of domestic slavery that exploits Third World women, and the protective United States laws that support these practices, it is not surprising to find the United Nations acting as an international brotherhood to protect its own. It will not interfere with its member nations' abusive practices toward women when its officials are themselves privately carrying out these practices. One would have hoped for more awareness and less complicity from the Status of Women Commission.

Usually many factors coalesce to create conditions of female sexual slavery. Often but not always, the conditions of poverty combine with female role socialization to create vulnerability that makes young girls and women susceptible to procurers. Social attitudes that tolerate the abuse and enslavement of women are reinforced by governmental neglect, toleration or even sanction. At levels of governmental and international authority where action could be taken against the slave trade, one finds at best suppression of evidence and at worst complicity in it.

Recent information from Paraguay reveals how interdependent various forms of slavery are on each other and how they in turn depend on other social and political factors.

In Paraguay where, according to a United Nations report an Ache Indian can still be purchased for $2.00, there is evidence that the sex slave trade begins with young peasant girls who are either purchased from their poverty-stricken parents or promised work in the cities. These *campesinas*, unlike the Indians who are sold for slave labor, are usually destined for one of the 200 brothels in Asunción (a city of 300,000) or a house of prostitution in the United States or Europe. According to a commission studying prostitution in Paraguay, at least 90 percent of the prostitutes in Paraguay's cities are naive, uneducated girls from the countryside, between the ages of 15 and 18.

Female slavery and the traffic in women in and from Paraguay are attributed to the corrupt military dictatorship of Alfredo Stroessner. Epifanio Mendez Fleitas, political refugee and exiled leader of the opposition to Stroessner, attributes the proliferation of prostitution to the corrupt dictatorship. According to Fleitas there was only one bordello in Asunción before Stroessner's rise to power in 1955.

The large demand for prostitutes in the cities, combined with the easy availability of girls from the countryside, has stimulated the traffic in women to other countries. There is evidence that young peasant girls from Paraguay are taken to the United States and Europe for prostitution. In the past several years over 700 girls from the rural area of Caraguatay are reported to have come into the United States in groups of ten to twenty, passed through Miami and Chicago, and then by bus to New York City. Many have never been in a city before. None could have afforded the air fare to come themselves. In one incident a local bishop was known to have assisted a procurer by bringing twenty Paraguayan *campesinas* to a house of prostitution in Flushing, New York. It was reported that a lawyer from Caraguatay was paid $250 for preparing documents, including passports and visas, that were easily certified through the American Consul there.[21]

There are conflicting reports about the fate of these girls. Many of them insist they work only as domestics. According to one girl who escaped, the girls also work as sexual slaves. Fifteen girls are reportedly kept in one small house run by a madam. The others work during the week as domestics in nearby houses and on the weekends they are expected to work there as prostitutes. If the girls refuse to work, they are threatened with deportation. They are young, usually uneducated, and alone in a foreign country, and their procurers are aware that they have no other option than to comply with what is expected of them.

Stories of the use of young girls within Paraguay by some Paraguayan military leaders reveal the abuse and torture to which these girls are subjected. In Asunción a house of prostitution is reported to be run by Colonel Perrier of the Paraguayan Army and visited by General Stroessner. An eyewitness account from a Paraguayan, Ada Rodriquez, reveals that young girls 8 to 14 years old were purchased from poverty-stricken parents for this bordello and sexually abused by the military government's VIP's.

Ada Rodriquez was from a Paraguayan family of considerable wealth and influence. She told columnists Jack Anderson and Les Whitten in an affidavit that in November 1975, while she was having lunch in Asunción with her husband, a naval officer, "they were summoned by neighbors to a house next door," where Ada "saw the unconscious bodies of three little girls, two of them age 8, the other age 9, lying naked on a pile of sand in the rear of the home." They were bleeding from the genital area, had "marks on their bodies evidencing sexual abuse." Ada called the police, but when they found that the children were from Colonel Perrier's house they left immediately without any action.

Ada began investigating and asked her friends to help but was told to remain silent. Finally, "in absolute desperation she turned to a man named Miguel Soler, who published an underground Communist paper called *Adelante*. She is opposed to his politics, but he promised to publish the story. He was unable to keep his promise. In December of 1975, Soler was arrested and Ada's story was found among his documents. Shortly after midnight on January 9, 1976, three men broke down the door of her home and dragged her off to the offices of the Paraguayan secret police."

She was beaten and tortured continuously for three days. At one point, after a particularly hideous torture session, during which she tried to commit suicide, she lost consciousness and awoke hours later in a hospital. "It took the political connections of her influential family to gain her release on February 13, 1977."[22]

THE MARKET FOR SEXUAL SLAVES

The traffic in women, like the traffic in drugs or black market babies, depends upon a market. Although police occasionally break up a gang of procurers, or the United Nations notes a new route of traffic from one part of the world to another, the actual demand that gives impetus to the traffic in women has been ignored.

The demand for sexual service is most significant where men congregate in large groups separated from home and family. The sexual demands of military men, traveling businessmen or sailors, and immigrant laborers create a major market for women's bodies. That market is kept supplied through procurers and gangs that run the traffic in women and children.

Procurers work the poverty-stricken countryside of Third World nations as well as bus and train stations of major cities, acquiring girls and young women. They maintain a constant supply to serve the market.

1. The Military Market

Around the world prostitution is considered a necessary and even patriotic service to "our boys in uniform." The time has long since passed when anyone bothers to wonder how women get into military prostitution. Procurers work freely and almost unrestrained in acquiring females to stock military bordellos.

In February 1977, authorities broke up a ring of procurers who were part of a well-known gang operating out of Lyon, France. The gang, who were convicted in Marseille in March 1978, had been procuring women and girls from the Continent for a military bordello called Pouf in the barracks of the French Foreign Legion in Corsica. The bordello, which was called a cultural center, was uncovered when a Frenchwoman reported to authorities that she was forcibly sent to the Legionnaires camp at Calvi in the southern part of Corsica. The women there reported that they were forced to receive 60 to 80 Legionnaires a day.

Corsican women were not involved, as Corsican gangs would likely keep their women away from that form of prostitution; therefore the women had to be brought in from other countries.

The French Foreign Legion has been considered an elite army known for its bravado and brutality; Legionnaires are known to be the toughest fighting soldiers in the world. About 60 percent of the Legionnaires are from other countries while some 40 percent are from France. Among them are criminals who assume new identities upon joining the Legion. Three thousand of the 8,000 Legionnaires are based in Corsica.

When the gang of procurers was convicted, a former Legionnaire gave an interview to the French paper, *Le Matin*. Ten of his fifteen years in the Legion had been spent in Corsica. He stated that he was astonished that military officials were not also accused in this case. He reported that the bordellos, known as BMC's (*Bordel Mobile de Campagne* or mobile field brothels), were set up by military leaders who worked with rings to supply the girls.[23]

The BMC's found in Corsica were the French cultural contribution to the Vietnam War. Susan Brownmiller in *Against Our Will* pointed out that "by the time the Americans had fully replaced the French in Indochina, the war had sufficiently disrupted South Vietnamese society to a point where it was no longer necessary to import foreign women for the purpose of prostitution." She described how prostitution was introduced for the American military in Vietnam by degrees. First bar girls, then massage parlors for the Marines at Da Nang, then "a shanty town of brothels, massage parlors and dope dealers, known as Dogpatch, soon ringed the bases."

> By 1966 the 1st Cavalry Division at An Khe, in the Central Highlands, the 1st Infantry Division at Lai Khe, twenty-five miles north of Saigon, and the 4th Infantry Division of Pleiku had established official military brothels within the perimeter of their base camp . . . .
>
> Refugees who had lost their homes and families during the war and veterans of the earlier Saigon bar

trade formed the stock of the brothel . . . . The American military, which kept its hands partially clean by leaving the procurement and price arrangements to Vietnamese civilians, controlled and regulated the health and security features of the trade.[24]

By 1972 prostitutes were officially welcomed to U.S. bases in Vietnam as "local national guests." At Longbinh, near Saigon, it was reported that soldiers could take onto the base as a local national guest any of the 50 to 60 girls who waited outside the base. In addition to military brothels and those that ringed the bases, closed prostitution zones developed. These areas, like the streets of Hamburg's eros centers, which were forbidden to anyone under 18, were found in many South Vietnamese cities. It was reported that the government was taking 30 percent of the receipts from prostitution in these zones.[25]

Procuring for military prostitution in South Vietnam had by 1965 become a major problem in Southeast Asia. Laos, in its response to the 1965 U.N. slavery survey by Dr. Awad, noted a sizable increase in the traffic in women and stated that "procuring is spreading from South Vietnam and Thailand to Laos."[26]

At the close of the war and the time of military withdrawal from South Vietnam many American soldiers made valiant efforts to "save" prostitutes in South Vietnam from the North Vietnamese forces and government that would be taking over:

Within a week, there were few beautiful prostitutes in Saigon. Young Americans made the rounds of virtually every bar and whorehouse in the capital to round up the women and sponsor them out of the country. One man claimed he made four trips in and out of Saigon, each time leaving with another "wife" and several "sisters-in-law." One prostitute who turned down the offer to leave said her would-be "husband" told her he planned to start an all-Vietnamese whorehouse in Honolulu. She said he worked for the CIA.[27]

One can assume that only a small percentage of the estimated 300,000 to 500,000 prostitutes in South Vietnam were "rescued" by American GI's. According to official government pronouncements from the new regime, prostitutes were considered victims of the political, social, and economic order of the old regime in South Vietnam. As such, they were able to receive emergency aid which included medical examinations and treatment. Venereal disease was a major problem and it has been estimated that 54 percent of the prostitutes suffered from it. Those women who came into prostitution from rural villages were said to be returned to those villages for work and, where possible, reunited with their families. Women and girls who were originally from urban areas were sent to boarding schools, "Schools to Rehabilitate Woman's Dignity," where they were trained in a trade or profession, attended political lectures, and participated in cultural activities. The cost was to be borne by the revolutionary administration of each city.*[28]

Procurers have found other ways to deal with the excessive number of prostitutes left from the booming sex industry created for and by American GI's in Thailand. They became victims of a drastic crash in that industry and therefore pawns in traffic in women to other more lucrative or profitable areas. The sex industry was one of the largest businesses in Thailand until the withdrawal of troops from Southeast Asia. After the troops left, journalist Tom Weber, writing for the Chronicle Foreign Service, visited Thailand and found some of the prostitutes left in the Village of Night Girls—a prostitution area he described as full of pimps who would offer "a young virgin from a farm for $300 American dollars." Black market operators were doing a big business in orphaned children, many fathered by GI's and left behind; they were being sold through adoption agencies. Weber asked to be taken to a typical massage parlor in Bangkok.

> There is an expensive look about the whole operation. Inside the entrance is a large department store display window. The walls are draped in red velvet. The glare

* Representatives of Humanitas indicate that so far as is known, prostitutes in these centers were not part of the population of political prisoners being detained and tortured as charged in an open letter to the Socialist Republic of Vietnam from Joan Baez, May 30, 1979.

> of 30 spot-lights shows off the merchandise; nearly 200 girls, all pretty and painted and wearing bright colored dresses and platform shoes. They sit on tiers of benches, looking like an all-girl choir. I asked if any of them spoke English. A few were pointed out.

After making his selection and paying the equivalent of ten dollars, he was taken by the young woman to a small room.

> After the routine of the bath she started to take off her dress. I told her to keep it on and we spent the rest of the time talking.
> She grew up on a farm northeast of Ching Mai. When she was 16, an American came to the farm and told her parents he wanted her for his wife. He paid his gift of money and took her to an army base.
> She thought the marriage was forever. But after her daughter was born, the "husband" was transferred back to the States, and just before he left, he "gave" her to his buddy. Then there was another and another. Now there are no more Americans to "marry" and she lives in the Village of Night Girls.[29]

While large numbers of women are sitting in places like the Bangkok massage parlors, procurers have been busy locating still other markets and other strategies for capitalizing on women. New agencies have opened to develop a disguised traffic in women to places like Hong Kong and the eros centers of Germany, which will be discussed in the next section of this chapter.

Some myths die hard. But the evidence of sexual slavery in military prostitution argues against the traditional assumptions that easy availability of prostitutes to the military, in a situation controlled by the military, would lower the rate of venereal disease and reduce wanton abuse and rape of peasant girls. Arguing in support of the French BMC's, author Bernard Fall found that "The BMC has the advantage of providing soldiers with a controlled sexual release, thus cutting down on desertions, on rapes of hapless girls of surrounding civilian population and also on venereal disease."[30]

Susan Brownmiller's articulate analysis of the prevalence and sanction of rape in war has put to rest this myth. Rape, as a military strategy and as personal outlet, is inseparable from prostitution, especially when one considers countless naive, poor girls from the countryside of Paraguay, Vietnam, Thailand, Laos . . . for whom prostitution would have remained unknown had the demands of the military not brought them into the cities and onto the bases. And of these countless numbers of girls, a large proportion would never have known of venereal disease. It is one of the most serious problems the new regime of Vietnam had to face at the end of the war. Health officials have estimated that even with an intensive campaign, it would take six to eight years to conquer it.[31]

The colonization of women's bodies in war begins with massive raping. It culminates in sexual slavery, as the description of postwar Japan reveals:

After its defeat in World War II, the Japanese government presented Japanese women as "comfort girls" to the United States Occupation Forces. It is reported that at the cabinet meeting held on August 21, 1945, only six days after the V-J surrender, Konoe Fumimaro, then State Minister without Portfolio, made the following proposal: "We must take emergency measures to protect our women and children from sex-starved American soldiers." Three days later, the Metropolitan Police Headquarters began to gather members of the red-light trade and request, "As a stopgap measure to protect the flower-like purity of 40,000,000 respectable Japanese women, we would like you to open facilities to 'comfort' the American troops." The government proposed to contribute indirectly 50 million yen (roughly equivalent to $5 million at the present exchange rate) to help meet their expenses . . . .

A ceremony to proclaim the establishment of the "Association for the Creation of Special Recreational Facilities" (later the "Recreation and Amusement Association," nicknamed R.A.A.) was held in the square in front of the Imperial Palace on August 28 to coincide with the landing of the first contingent of

American occupation troops. Soon the first R.A.A.-sponsored army brothel, Komachi Garden, was opened in the Omori district of Tokyo. On August 30, about 100 women, some of them former prostitutes and others deceived by advertisements reading "Recruiting the new Japanese woman: lodging, clothing and food provided," had to surrender their bodies to American soldiers. R.A.A. army brothels literally sprouted up before the smoke could clear from the bombed-out rubble of Tokyo, and within three months there were twenty-five such brothels . . . . At its height, R.A.A. is said to have employed 70,000 "comfort girls."[32]

2. The Businessmen's and Sailors' Market

The women that men no longer need after a war are often recycled from the military market to major cities where businessmen congregate and sailors dock.

Kisaeng tourism from Japan to South Korea is the practice that resulted from military markets at the close of World War II. According to Japanese journalist Matsui Yayori, until women were forced to serve the military, *kisaeng* originally referred to independent women who took on lovers. Now *kisaeng* means "prostitute" and refers to brothel tours that take Japanese businessmen and tourists to South Korea, often supported by their companies. "Chartered tours of two nights and three days cost no more than $200—including the price of sex."

> Many Japanese men are attracted to the stories of *kisaeng* girls in their colorful native dress waiting on men at parties and even putting food into the customer's mouth for him. It is advertised that the *kisaeng* spirit is so self-sacrificing and dedicated that when a man brings a *kisaeng* girl back to his hotel, she will even do his laundry if he will leave her a big tip.[33]

Yayori notes that there are over 8,000 *kisaeng* in South Korea in conditions of sexual slavery.

Because sexual slavery is not only a crime against women but is also a shameful activity for them, extortion can be as lucrative for racketeers as prostitution.

Many women are being trafficked from the military prostitution industry in Thailand to Germany's legalized brothels serving tourists, businessmen, and sailors. They join with local women and women brought in from other parts of the world to respond to the demand.

In Hamburg, prostitution is legal and confined to the Reeperbahn. This area is immediately accessible to sailors coming into port and its thriving sex industry is promoted in travel brochures. Within several blocks one can pass through almost all levels of prostitution, from streets lined with hookers, through noisy pinball machine arcades and pornographic quick flics, to closed streets that forbid passage to children and discourage women from entering except those who are housed behind the iron gates in eros centers.

Abuses surrounding prostitution in Germany are difficult to document because legalization has created an atmosphere that sanctions prostitution and assumes that the problems associated with it have been solved. Nevertheless, due to the demands for women in Hamburg, pimps have flocked to that city, and recently authorities have broken some gangs and rings of procurers surrounding other eros centers in Germany. (See Chapter 5.)

Many eros centers are kept out of the view of all but pimps, clients, and prostitutes. Prostitutes within these centers need not venture out into the city, since the compound provides canteens for meals, boutiques and beauticians. In a city like Hamburg which boasts of its liberalism and its sexual openness, it is incongruous to find prostitution conditions that are not open to public view. At the very least it raises the question of what needs to be hidden.

Many other international port cities have been implicated in the traffic in women over the years. In its response to the 1975 Interpol Survey on Traffic in Women, France reported a continuing traffic to port cities in the Ivory Coast and Senegal.

It was estimated that in 1973 there were about 40,000 prostitutes in Dakar, the port city of Senegal. Most were Portuguese, some were Senegalese, and a few were other Europeans.[34] Much of the influx of the young Senegalese girls into prostitution results from a flight from rural poverty. While their plight is usually attributed to their inability to cope with urbanization, inquiry needs to be made into the manner in which they find their way from rural villages to street or hotel prostitution in Dakar. Several international organizations, including *Terre des Hommes*, are investigating reports of the kidnapping and sale of children from rural villages into sexual slavery.

Veronique had been a prostitute for several years when her pimp kidnapped her four children, held them hostage, and threatened to kill them if she did not obey him and follow the arrangements he made for her to go to Dakar. Fearing for her children's safety, she was forced to go to Dakar in 1973. There she was enslaved in a brothel for two years, during which time there was no opportunity to escape or leave the premises. When the ships came in, she was forced to take on 100 men a day. After two years, as a result of beatings and the demands made on her body, she became seriously ill and was taken to a hospital. There she confided her story to a doctor, who took pity on her, contacted the police, and helped arrange for her escape. Upon returning to France she sought refuge with Le Nid, a French refuge for prostitutes. She contacted authorities and testified against her pimp. As a result of her testimony, he was found guilty and imprisoned, and her children were returned to her.

The Ivory Coast has long been associated with the slave trade in women and children. Abidjan is the port center of this West African country, as Dakar is in Senegal. It is estimated that about 80 percent of the prostitutes in Abidjan come from the neighboring countries of Nigeria, Ghana, and Liberia; 5 percent are European, and 15 percent are from the Ivory Coast.[35]

Rabatteur, which is the French word for procurer, means "one who beats down, reduces, lowers, and humbles." *Rabatteurs* working the trade into the Ivory Coast are professionals: they can easily spot young, attractive, and naive women who are seeking adventure. The men, well-dressed and with slick manners, can procure such young women to come to Abidjan to work as barmaids or entertainers in cabarets.

The procurement of one Ghanian woman follows the classic pattern of this form of sexual slavery. She was a typist working in Accra, Ghana. While at the airport, waiting to meet a friend, she got into a conversation with a handsome, charming, and well-dressed man who later took her and her friend by taxi into the city. He told her that he owned a large cabaret in Abidjan and that he was in Accra for a few days only to build a house there. She could not tell if he was lying as she found him so persuasive. They dated, going out to many of the cabarets in Accra. After several days, he asked her to marry him. She accepted immediately. Later she reflected on how difficult it would be for a young girl to resist the influence of such a seducer.

Arriving in Abidjan, she realized that instead of the man of her dreams she had married a *rabatteur* who put her to work in a closed house of prostitution with other young women in the same situation. She was there for a month when by chance she met a fellow Ghanian who was well known in Abidjan and was able to arrange for her release. When he got her out of there, he took her to his house, contacted her parents, and arranged for her trip back to Ghana.[36]

In 1969 the swift action of *Équipe d'Action*, the French group that combats traffic in women and children, prevented the enslavement of two French women from Toulon in a brothel in the Treichville quarter of Abidjan. One of the young Toulonese women, who was worried about how she was going to support herself and her child, was approached by a smooth-talking man who offered her a job as a hostess in an Abidjan bar and also offered to take care of her child while she was gone. She and her girlfriend were told that they would need to work for only a short time and that from the money they made they would be able to save enough to return to France without financial worries. A friend who didn't trust the arrangement tried to talk them out of it, and when she failed she went to the *Équipe d'Action* for help. Jean Scelles, President of the *Équipe d'Action* and a former French Parliamentarian and resistance fighter, contacted the French Ambassador in the Ivory Coast. He in turn made inquiries and arranged for police to be at the airport when the women arrived. The men who accompanied the women from France were identified by the police as part of the gang that operated a well-known bordello in Abidjan. After checking the women's papers, the police determined that the women were destined for a bordello. They were both sent home; the pimps were taken into custody and returned to France, where they were tried and sentenced.

3. The Immigrant Laborers' Market

When men from underdeveloped countries leave home and immigrate to countries of higher technological development seeking work, wives and families are often left behind. The men plan that, when they earn enough money, they will have their families join them or will return to their families. Such men form some of the poorest classes in the areas to which they immigrate, but they are exploited by procurers and bordellos as a likely source of revenue. In turn they form a market for female sexual slaves whom they use and abuse.

In Paris, *les maisons d'abattage* are the prostitution hotels that immigrant workers flock to at night and on their days off. *Maisons d'abattage* are found in a small section of the 18th *arrondissement* of Paris, the immigrant *quartier* which teems with poverty and has the highest crime rate in the city and the most oppressed population. Of that oppressed population, the most tortured and exploited are totally invisible, except to the men who buy time with them.

The small hotels in the North African *quartier* are frequented by Algerian and Arab immigrant workers, men who are usually not accepted as clients by the rest of Paris's prostitutes. Some charge the Parisian prostitutes with racism. That may be likely, but it is also likely that it is the conditions of work that make the prostitutes stay away from the houses serving these men. Women who have a choice of clientele, location and conditions would surely not seek work in a *maison d'abattage*, where they would be forced to take up to 120 men a day.

One evening in 1976 an 18-year-old Frenchwoman named Marie went out dancing at a club. There she met a young woman and her boyfriend, who invited her to join them at the same club the following night. The next evening the young couple brought another man with them. The four enjoyed an evening of dancing and left to go to the other woman's house for a last drink. That was where Marie was forced onto a bed, stripped, and sexually forced by the woman and then raped and beaten by the two men.

The three then took her to a *maison d'abattage*, and she was sold to the house. She never saw them again. In the house she was locked in a room and customers were brought to her. She told every one of them that she had been kidnapped and forced there and that she was not a prostitute. She begged each to help her get out. Over three days only one client responded at all: he gave her his phone number in case she did get out.

On the third day the police received an anonymous tip, raided the house, and found Marie there. All the girls, along with the three men and one woman who ran the house, were taken to the police station. Marie reports that in the police wagon on the way to the station the other girls, frightened for their lives, begged her not to tell anything to the police. At the station the police separated her from the others and took her into another room. She told one of the staff at *Équipe d'Action*, where she went for help in prosecuting the pimps, "When I passed through that door I changed my universe completely; I came back to the real world!"

The *Équipe d'Action* made sure the case was successfully taken through the courts. When the court finds in favor of a victim in France, it may award a monetary settlement. In 1977 the court awarded Marie 20,000 francs, or $4,000.

But slavery begets slavery. The court could not locate Marie. They forwarded the money to *Équipe*, who called her parents. After some hesitation Marie's father agreed to have his daughter contact them. An hour later Marie called. She had changed her name and married. "I am especially afraid my husband will find out what happened to me," she said. "He is very jealous and if he discovered that I got all that money he would find out what happened to me and demand a divorce. So please, you keep the money."

Procurement practices similar to that imposed on Marie are beginning to come to light in the United States. Periodic reports reveal how young girls from Mexico and poor areas in the United States are provided for migrant workers. Loretta Schwartz, writing for *Ms.* magazine, discussed the system of indenture in migrant camps on the east coast. She found that "To keep such men further in debt and sexually appeased, crew leaders often forced women into prostitution. Sometimes the prostitutes are retarded or emotionally disturbed women. They are taken across state lines, held prisoner, and forced to serve as labor camp prostitutes in return for food."[37] Sociologist Richard Morrison, Coordinator of the Interagency Council on Migrant Services on the Eastern Shore of Virginia told her about finding Patricia, a young black woman:

> "She had been shanghaied in Florida. After being discharged from a mental institution, she was told by a crew leader that she would be brought to work in Virginia. Actually, she was forced to service a work crew of a hundred and fifty men, mostly alcoholics. When our staff encountered her, she had been beaten and her body was badly bruised.
>
> "The crew leader allowed us to take her out of the camp. We arranged with the Migrant Association to provide funds for her trip back home. We brought her some clothes and arranged to pick her up the next day. But when we returned, we were told that she had wandered off. Shortly afterward, we found her in a ditch. She had been badly beaten . . .
>
> "We could not prosecute because these people are so frightened of retaliation that they won't come forth with plaintiff-type information, and the truth is that they are in real danger. The body of a woman who tried to talk to one of our workers was found on a highway three days later.[38]

An Illinois Legislative Investigative Commission took up the problem of illegal aliens in 1971. Their report stated that "illegal Mexican alien prostitutes are purposely smuggled into Chicago Heights for the adult males who comprise almost all of the illegal alien population in that area. These prostitutes operate from local taverns frequented almost exclusively by Mexican aliens."

According to the Chief of Investigators for the San Francisco Office of Immigration there is no problem with the traffic of women for prostitution into California. He said he knew nothing of Mexican girls and women being procured into prostitution by force or fraud. Conveying the same confusion found in the INTERPOL report on disguised traffic, he added "There is quite an immigration problem with girls being smuggled into the United States to work in migrant bars as hostesses and prostitutes. But I never heard of any of them being forced." He went on to explain that some bar owners do their own procuring while others hire professional smugglers to bring girls into the country. Immigration is aware of several of these bars in California. I asked him, "Do the girls know they will be expected to work as prostitutes when they are procured to work as hostesses in migrant bars?" "Probably not," he answered. "They start out as barmaids and progress from there."

SUPPRESSION THROUGH SELECTIVE PERCEPTION

Amassing one hundred, one thousand, or many thousands of sex slavery cases will not prove the existence of the practice to those who have a vested interest in keeping it invisible. It is a practice that is controlled and dominated by highly skilled, heavily armed, and very menacing gangs and individuals who have been able to buy police protection in most countries. Any case that does make it to court or even to the United Nations appears to be an isolated incident but, in fact, is most often the tip of an iceberg.

There is no way to estimate what proportion of prostitution results from cases like the ones presented in this chapter. Physical force and fraudulent seduction are important agents causing many females to be prostitutes. For them prostitution is slavery in the most standard, traditional meaning of that term—not as a euphemism for a slightly less than totally free experience. Prostitutes have long been socially regarded as women who are constitutionally predisposed to engage in their work. No one is predisposed to be a slave. A person may be unwittingly trapped into a slavery condition; no one goes out looking for it.

While psychologists, sociologists, and criminologists have studied prostitution laws, prostitutes' motivations, the effects on society, sexual practices and behaviors, few researchers have asked the obvious question that known cases of slavery demand: "Are these women able to change the conditions of their existence?" Inaccurate assumptions of freedom at the most basic level of existence have produced research that is fragmentary at best and usually distorted as a result of the selective perception with which the subject is approached.

Selective perception has made it possible for many to see situations of forced prostitution as voluntary. For example, the director of Le Nid, the prostitute shelter in Paris where Veronique went after escaping Dakar, told me emphatically that forced prostitution doesn't exist anymore and that prostitutes end up in brutal situations with pimps out of sadomasochistic needs for such relationships. Similarly, on numerous occasions when I've inquired of police authorities about forced prostitution, I have been told that they never get cases like that anymore; then, as they give me examples of women or young girls who are fraudulently procured they never recognize that they are revealing cases of sexual slavery. And when Elizabeth and James Vorenberg, in their study of prostitution, found in France the *maisons d'abattage*, they ignored the enslaving conditions and noted: "At the bottom of the ladder is Barbes . . . where prostitutes work in small hotels and rooming houses, each serving as many as eighty men a day at 50 francs each. It is hard work. . . ."[39]

Undoubtedly not all women are physically forced or fraudulently seduced into prostitution. Many resort to it out of economic necessity. Some, seeking fun and adventure, find the illusions of glamour associated with it appealing. Others will try it as a rebellious act of defiance against traditional moral standards. Many of those who enter prostitution voluntarily will learn once they are in that they can't get out and some fewer women may not want to get out.

Selective perception that assumes all prostitution is voluntary ignores the self-interest of procurers, their broad range of techniques for procuring the women, and the diverse number of prostitution situations in which women exist. Instead, it focuses on the prostitute's internal motivation. One way out of such patriarchal bias is to redefine the questions we ask about prostitution.

In addition to asking, "Are women forced into prostitution?" we should also want to know, "What is in it for them?" What improvement in lifestyle, economic conditions, or personal freedom does their situation afford them? For example, in an exposé of CIA practices during the Vietnam war, Victor Marchetti and John Marks reveal how the CIA recruited mercenaries from the national minority of Chinese hill people in Vietnam. "Their function was to observe North Vietnamese and Vietcong supply movements and on occasion to make attacks against convoys . . ."[40] The Nungs, as these mercenaries were called, demanded that for these remote and dangerous missions they regularly be supplied with beer and prostitutes. "The agency had no choice but to provide flying bar and brothel services . . ." Yet the CIA was concerned about security and the problem of prostitutes learning about the Nungs' mission. To solve the problem, they used the CIA's own airline, Air America, and "brought in only prostitutes from distant parts of Southeast Asia who had no language in common with the Nungs."[41]

This incident raises important questions not addressed by the authors and probably unasked by most of their readers like "How and where were these women acquired?" Most significantly it must be asked "Would women actively seek to sexually serve mercenary soldiers in a remote and dangerous area of Vietnam when they do not even have a common language with them?" The evidence presented in this chapter suggests some other questions:

> Is it likely that French girls and women wanted to go to Corsica to work for the sexual well-being of the ruthless men of the French Foreign Legion?
> Is it reasonable to assume that young Algerian and French girls seek jobs in Paris's *maisons d'abattage*?
> Do Mexican girls ask smugglers to bring them into the United States so they can be confined to the back rooms of shabby migrant bars?

By shifting the weight of explanation off the victims and onto their captors, we find that the "oldest profession" is not prostitution but *pimping*.

CHAPTER 5

Pimping:
The Oldest Profession

The arbitrary and false distinctions made in the nineteenth-century purity crusades between the international traffic in women and local prostitution still dominate thought today. Those distinctions, with the accompanying assumption that women are driven to prostitution (by economics, sado-masochism, or mental deficiency), screen the procurers, hiding their strategies and making pimping appear to be other than what it is.

Together, pimping and procuring are perhaps the most ruthless displays of male power and sexual dominance. As practices they go far beyond the merchandising of women's bodies for the market that demands them. Pimping and procuring are the crystallization of misogyny; they rank about the most complete expressions of male hatred for femaleness. Procuring is a strategy, a tactic for acquiring women and turning them into prostitution; pimping keeps them there. Procuring today involves "convincing" a woman to be a prostitute through cunning, fraud, and/or physical force, taking her against her will or knowledge and putting her into prostitution.

THE PATTERNS OF PROCURING

I have been able to document five different patterns for procuring women. Some were patterns noted in Stephen Barlay's work on sexual slavery.[1] But he, along with most workers in the field, continues to hold to the arbitrary distinction between foreign traffic and local prostitution. I have found that distinction misleading and unnecessary. Strategies for procuring therefore include any and all situations to which they apply whether they involve taking a woman across town, to the next state or across international boundaries. They are (1) befriending or love, (2) actions of gangs, syndicates, and organized crime, (3) use of recruiting agencies (for employment, dance companies, or marriage), (4) purchase, and (5) kidnapping.

Procuring cannot always be categorized as one particular strategy or pattern. There seem to be an endless number of combinations of these strategies that procurers may use to get a woman into prostitution. The various strategies and the flexibility in their execution reveal the extent to which any woman, regardless of class, race, or educational level, is vulnerable to the craft of slave procurers.

1. Befriending or Love

Procurers who employ the strategies of befriending or love and romance use both tactics together. They may begin by befriending a forlorn runaway and then calculate a romantic connection. The strategy of befriending and love is designed to fit the vulnerabilities of its potential victim. A procurer's goal is to find naive, needy teenage girls or young women, con them into dependency, season them to fear and submission, and turn them out into prostitution.

The world of pimps and procurers is a well-defined hierarchy leading from the lowest—the street pimp with one or two girls—to gangs or rings of pimps who control specific circuits encompassing large areas. As in any hierarchy, the largest numbers of pimps and prostitutes are at the lowest level, living fast and trying to climb.

A pimp, whether he procures his own whore or has her provided by procurers, is legally defined as one who lives off the earnings of a prostitute. He is seen as one who acts as her protector. He puts her on the street or in a house, sets daily earning quotas, takes most or all of her money, sometimes hustles customers, and is supposed to get her out of jail if she is arrested. In the United States the stereotyped pimp is the flashy black street hustler with smooth-talking jive and apparently extravagant spending habits, one whose life is imbedded in crime and violence. Abuse of his prostitute is almost synonymous with his title. His cunning and violence often exceed human understanding, ironically making him a legendary folk hero to many.

In American cities almost all street pimps are black; white pimps operate less visibly because they run prostitution houses and massage parlors. Both black and white pimps see the trick (customer) as a con, an easy ripoff, a pitiable man for whom they have no respect. They teach their prostitutes how to steal from tricks and take the maximum money for minimum performance. Both black and white pimps abandon their woman when she faces the trick's wrath for being conned.

Contrary to the stereotype, not all street pimps drive Lincolns or Cadillacs. Those luxuries come only to the few who work their way up, building their stables and moving into larger rackets. Most street pimps are decked out in fake fur with an old Ford around the corner. They are not a pretty lot. Their flash is only an exterior appearance.

Whether black or white, whether operating on the street, from a house, or in higher levels of organized gangs, all pimps have a clear rundown on the pimping rules. They see themselves as players running a game. Iceberg Slim, a notorious pimp in his day, now retired from the life, called this knowledge "whorology." It is learned on the streets and in the prisons. The first rule is that "The best pimps keep a steel lid on their emotions and I was one of the iciest . . . any good pimp is his own best company. His innerlife is so rich with cunning and scheming to out-think his whores."[2]

A favorite philosophy of pimps is to liken their game to movies: they are producer and director and they run everything according to their own will. Iceberg Slim recalled the best philosophy he ever heard while in prison: "I picture the human mind as a movie screen. . . . Son, there is no reason except a stupid one for anybody to project on that screen anything that will worry him or dull that vital edge. After all, we were the absolute bosses of the whole theatre and show in our minds. We even write the script."[3]

Likening pimping to a movie set was the basis of a contract confiscated from a pimp in a Washington, D.C., raid in 1977. The terms of the contract read:

> You are reading this because you have passed one of the requirements to become a member of the illustrious family of ⎯⎯⎯⎯⎯⎯. This life is just like a large scale movie production with me as the producer and you as the star. The world is your audience for the

entire universe is your stage. It is also like a large
scale business; you are the stockholders. In this business there is a president, director, and a teacher and a
treasurer. All of these offices are held by me. In this
business, there is no room for confusion. Anyone or
anything opposing my will must be and will be destroyed.

As they set up and run their game to con a woman into
prostitution, pimps also exploit the boredom in female socialization which makes many young girls seek excitement
in their lives. One pimp who wrote of this described the
state of many teenage girls from the pimp's perspective:

> . . . here we have a group of "have-nots" plain women
> who have, as a result of their plainness, lived plain
> unexciting lives, perpetuating their drab, plain exis-
> tence, their drab morality on a potentially beautiful
> girl child . . . . Mothers, teachers, school nurses, aunts,
> grandmothers, etc. in collusion to put a beautiful girl
> child in her place. . . .
>   Most potentially beautiful women arrive at the age
> of seventeen or eighteen for all intents and purposes
> a shell . . . like an unfinished house which is potentially
> a mansion; while the structure may be there, it needs
> to be finished on the outside . . . a woman who is po-
> tentially beautiful must also be finished, inside and
> out.[4]

One of the most effective covers for forced prostitution is
the refusal of police, courts, and the public to acknowledge
disparity between the reality of the pimp and his game and
the perception of the girls he seduces. Pimps know all the
cards and how to play them. The young girl or woman he
sets as a target is likely to be naive, lonely, and bitter at the
family she has just run away from or the marriage she has
just left. She is also likely to be broke and without job
skills.

Suddenly a man appears who is friendly, who offers to
buy her a meal and, later, a place to spend the night. She
hears compliments for the first time in ages, as well as
promises to buy her new clothes and have her hair done.

The romantic movie scenario is being played out and it may be days, weeks, or even months before she figures out what has happened to her.

The pimp's approach fulfills all the star-studded romantic images that popular magazines, TV, and movies have promoted. When Officer Mary Christenson went undercover for the San Francisco Police Department to arrest pimps for pandering, some of their opening lines were, "You are going to be my star lady," or "I'm going to make you my foxy lady" or "my sportin' lady," or, as one pimp put it, "you are going to be MY hope-to-die woman . . . cause that's how long we going to be together."[5]

After his initial come-on, a pimp will follow with what he discerns to be the most likely way to win her over. If the girl he is procuring appears to be rebellious and daring, he can come right out with his proposal, offer her a challenge. Mary was making herself apparently easily available in one particular case:

Pimp: *I'm a businessman. We could be partners. You've got nice cord pants on, but you look like you should be wearing satin. I can take you to the hairdresser and buy you some nice clothes.*
Mary: *What is my role in this?*
Pimp: *Well, you'll be my woman. I'll turn you out on the street. Give you some schooling. If you are my partner you'll have your pockets filled with money and you'll fill my pockets too.*

Lots of money, new cars, travel, the best clothes, flash, and glamour are the promises. Another pimp who first explained that he would take care of business, be her protection, stay with her forever, later made it clear that tricking would only be necessary until he got a big settlement from an insurance company on an accident. This, according to vice officers, is a frequent procuring line used by street pimps, who often represent themselves as about to come into some big money. Ultimately the appeal is to glamour:

Pimp: *I'm going to be sure that you have your clothes, everything else you're suppose to have.*
Mary: *Like what?*

Pimp: *Anything that you want, anything. No limit to what you'll have, things of that nature . . . . Do you understand me? Seeing my lady getting it together and saying you understand me . . . . You're suppose to have the best. I like to see my lady with the best on. I like every mother-fucking body around to look at my lady . . . .*

For many girls it is attention and apparent affection that wins them over. In testimony to the New York Select Crime Committee, a young woman reported being picked up at a bus stop in Minneapolis and eventually put in prostitution in New York City. She stated:

At the time I did it because I really liked him and it was more or less having someone, you know, and he said, you know, to prove to him that I really love him I had to do this because we needed the money. It was things he said, but I did it because I liked him. He made you feel like you were somebody important.[6]

When a pimp hits on a female who is resistant, "prudish," or scared, he will not introduce prostitution immediately. He'll just be a nice guy who buys her a meal and offers her a place to stay. Finally he professes his love to her. When a sexual relationship between them is established and he is sure she loves him, he employs the "if you love me, you'll do anything for me" line. To prove her love she must have sex for money with someone else she does not know. If she resists or refuses, he will likely pout, create a scene, and insist that she does not truly love him. To restore his affection, she finally agrees to do what he asks, believing that one time won't hurt. He has her hooked. After she turns one trick, he starts pimping her, giving her nightly quotas, taking the money she earns, and making her believe that she is truly a slut and that only he out of the goodness of his heart will have anything to do with such a despicable creature. The attitudes of the rest of society and of the police, johns, and others in the world of prostitution confirm to her that he is right.

Instead of the psychological destruction and character breakdown of the love-con, the pimp may use direct physical violence. Late in 1976, Blood Stewart picked up 14-

year-old Jennifer in the vicinity of Penn Station in New York City. She had run away from her parents' Long Island home and was confused, bewildered, and alone in the big city. Blood befriended her until he got her to his room. There he beat, raped, and tortured her for three days.

Journalist Mark Schorr unraveled the details of this case: Blood Stewart presented himself as Ralph Moss and listened to her sad story.

> She decided to trust him, so she told him her real name and age. Then she showed him the letter she was sending her father. "I know you tried stuff with her (Jennifer's girlfriend) . . . and she told me where you touched her." Still, the note was apologetic: "Daddy I'm really sorry. I feel like dying for what I've done to you."
>
> Ralph Moss offered to help. He would act as a go-between, speak to Jennifer's father man to man, and straighten out the problem. Jennifer could sleep over in his hotel room that night, and the next day they'd return to Long Island to work things out.[7]

When she entered the Cort Hotel with Stewart, the young girl had no idea what was ahead of her.

> To demonstrate his absolute power and reduce Jennifer's defenses, Blood stripped her naked, then raped her, police say. They maintain that he terrorized her with his big "007" gravity-blade knife and told her, "If you don't do what I tell you, I'll use this on you."[8]

He then informed her that she was going to work the streets for him. After three days of such abuse he sent her out to work in front of the New York Hilton. She hurried inside and hid in the women's rest room in the lobby. When she finally got the courage to come out, she spotted a security guard and ran to him asking for help. In a back office she poured out her story; the police were called and ultimately Stewart was arrested.

What Jennifer experienced after being procured was a seasoning that was meant to break her will and distort her perceptions. It is designed to facilitate turning a procured girl out as a prostitute, but unlike many, Jennifer escaped before she was broken.

Seasoning is meant to break its victim's will, reduce her ego, and separate her from her previous life. All procuring strategies include some form of seasoning. Often the extent or form of it is determined by the resistance of the woman or girl, sometimes it is a measure of the sadism of her procurer. Seasoning inculcates dependency and indebtedness in the victim. The meals, new clothes, and a place to stay all must be paid for. What appears at first to be freely given is later tallied up to be paid back, whether it is an act of affection, a meal, or some seemingly mutual sex. Affection and love-making are meant to hook a woman, make her dependent emotionally and psychologically. Meanwhile she is thinking in terms of a mutually developing relationship.

In breaking down their victims, some procurers rely only on the dependency that results from taking their acquisition so far away from home that they can't get back without money for transportation. The language barrier that a victim of international traffic faces will make it difficult for her to fend for herself in a new country. Harsher methods may involve beating, rape, sodomy, drugging, and starvation before turning a female out on the streets or over to a brothel.

Seasoning does not always precede prostitution. It is as effective in forcing some women to remain in prostitution as it is in putting others into it. Some women who willingly try out prostitution do not realize until later that they cannot get out. When they try to leave their pimp, the physical brutality and torture have the same effect as it would have had if they were used earlier. One sixteen-year-old who was procured in Minneapolis described the "going-away present" her pimp gave her when she tried to leave:

> Well, first he put his foot in my face which broke my nose and knocked me out and I got out the door— we lived on the third floor of this building and I couldn't get out the door in time before he caught me and there was just punches in the face and he had long fingernails which scarred up my body pretty much and kicking because I kept falling on the floor

> from being hit in the head. . . . I finally got out the
> door and was running out the middle of the street and
> he was trying to drag me into the place again when
> the police came.[9]

A critical early step in seasoning a girl is changing her
identity. She is given a new name and any necessary papers
such as a false driver's license, social security card, and
birth certificate, so that the police will not be able to trace
her real identity or determine her true age. New identification serves a more important function than cover from the
police. It separates the woman from her past and focuses
her totally on the moment in time when she belongs to this
man. According to anthropologists Christina and Richard
Milner, "a pimp wants his woman's mind more than her
body. It is love, loyalty, and obedience he requires as well
as a capacity for self-discipline."[10]

The Milners in their field research on pimps found
"Turning out a square broad means that you must literally
change her mind."[11] (And Richard Milner appears not to
question the ethical limits of research behavior. When he
was posing as a pimp for purposes of his research, he
reports how he was required to recommend a particular
pimp to a new girl the pimp was trying to procure. Even
though Milner from his research likely knew what the fate
would be for the girl, he provided the recommendation
anyway.) Steve, a pimp, discussed with the Milners why a
new prostitute's mind must be changed:

> She must cut all family ties, because, you see, she can't
> be with her family and ho [whore] too. You can't cope
> with bringing disgrace upon your mother or father,
> your sister, or whoever it is. You have to get away
> from them. There's nothing I could do with you over
> there because they're telling you one thing and I'm
> telling you something else.[12]

Brock, another pimp, put it to the Milners this way:

> You create a different environment. Its a brainwashing
> process; the whole thing is creativity. When you turn
> a chick out, you take away every set of values and

morality she had previously and create a different environment. You give her different friends.[13]

Seasoning, among other things, creates perfect obedience in the newly procured woman. The pimp must have complete authority. One pimp who tried to procure undercover Officer Mary Christenson told her that when she went to work for him "I am not going to beat on you . . . I don't want no tricks to beat you up." She responded, "You won't beat me?" "I ain't that stupid," he replied, "long as you obey, understand me, and act like a lady, then I don't think we should ever have any misunderstanding, okay? Just do like I say, 'cause I'm not going to tell you to do nothing wrong. . . ."

Another pimp described how he would protect her out on the street: "The only thing is, you can't make me mad at you. I don't want you hiding out any of the money you make. You give it all to me and I take care of you."

The idealized role of protector stands in sharp contrast to the actual methods and behavior of procurers. Convincing his women and society at large that he is the prostitute's protector is just another one of the pimp's con games. By and large pimps do not protect prostitutes from violent customers. Often they are hanging out down the street in the local pimp bar when their woman faces a sadistic trick in a room by herself. Sometimes pimps, particularly those who run houses or massage parlors, will set their women up with a violent trick to teach her a lesson if she isn't working hard enough.

Nor do pimps automatically respond when their prostitutes get arrested. Depending on his mood and circumstances, a pimp may choose to leave his woman in jail, ignoring her call to be bailed out, or he may get her out immediately if he wants her back on the street working. All the promises made in the first meeting—glamour, travel, money, affection, protection, even child care if she is on her own with a small child—turn out to be means of enslavement. A certain glamour is necessary for the pimp's display of his new acquisition to other pimps and for her work in hooking customers. As to travel, she soon finds out that *she* finances it with her work, and when they go to another city, state, or country she will continue to work her long hours to meet her daily quotas.

Prostitution is not the economic alternative for women that many have believed it to be. The money a woman makes is usually not her own. The pimp takes most or all of it. He tells her where to work, how many hours a day, and what quota she must make before coming home. If he is angry at her or just wants to instill some obedience, he will threaten to "pimp her hard," that is, raise her hours and quota. Often a pimp will make arrangements for his woman to leave the money she makes in a convenient place when she comes in at night; he will pick it up the next day. This technicality is meant to protect him from prosecution: since he doesn't take money directly from her, he can't be charged, he hopes, with living off the earnings of a prostitute.

Even the child care he proposes to provide for the young woman with a small child is part of the strategy. Almost always when a prostitute with a child is taken in by a pimp, she will ultimately find her child used as a weapon against her. By offering to take care of the child, to take the child to the baby-sitter or to school, to provide for his or her well-being while the mother works, a pimp acquires physical control of the child. If a woman wants to leave her pimp, she may find her child held as hostage, forcing her back to work.

When the pimp controls his woman body and soul, then she is set up to bring other women to him. One pimp told Mary Christenson, "You get them for like, you know, sisters, you know, understand what I'm saying. Just get 'em to come and help you and the more, you understand, more that you get, the more sisters that you can get, honey, the better it is for you. They'll help you and by you being my main lady, you see, you don't have that to worry about, see, 'cause they ain't going to never be able to take your place, you understand me? You bring 'em home, I'll do the rest." And the cycle of loving her, seasoning her, and pimping her starts all over again.

2. Actions of Gangs, Syndicates, and Organized Crime

While local prostitution in the United States is usually an individual "free-lance" operation set up by one pimp, there is evidence of involvement in some areas of prostitution by gangs and organized crime. Organized crime appears to operate behind the scenes in the United States, controlling much of the distribution of pornography and leasing many prostitution hotels and massage parlors in New York's Times Square area.

Organized crime may be defined as anything from an informal group of people organized to commit crimes to highly sophisticated national and international syndicates. According to Hank Messick, author of *The Mobs and the Mafia*, the Mafia no longer exists as a centrally controlled family organization. Rather, organized crime at this level consists of a number of loosely related groups that work independently or may cooperate with each other on joint ventures.

Pimping and procuring that appears to be only free-lance could not take place without a social network of male bonding that supports and facilitates it and is itself "organized" crime. At this level, organized crime exists in informal working relationships and loose organization. It is a brotherhood of pimps, procurers, hotel and motel managers, police, bailbondsmen, doctors, lawyers—all of whom form a protective network that facilitates the traffic in women to customers.

The combined action of the loosely affiliated brotherhood and organized crime can be discerned behind the "Minneapolis pipeline," for example. In 1977 the testimony of several young girls to the New York State Select Crime Committee and the investigation conducted by Minneapolis policemen revealed a steady flow of teenage girls from Minneapolis to New York City Times Square prostitution. What became known as the "Minneapolis pipeline" was not organized traffic but a large accumulation of street pimps who were acquiring girls, mostly teenage runaways, from the Midwest who had flocked to Minneapolis. In many cases the girls, mostly blonde and blue-eyed, were turned out in Minneapolis and then taken to New York. They reported having to work seven days a week, some averaging sixteen hours a day. The nightly quota set by the pimps was usually about $150 and the girls charged about $20 a trick. When they used a hotel, the trick had to pay an additional $10 or $15 at the door. One hotel charged $5 for twenty minutes.

According to Jeremiah McKenna, Chief Counsel to the

Crime Committee, the Committee was able to determine from testimony of some former prostitutes that the Senton Hotel was being used by pimps as a place to keep their girls. The girls worked out of other hotels but lived at the Senton with their pimps. It was observed in stakeouts that several young girls likely to be from the Midwest were staying at the Senton.

In November 1977 Sidney Baumgarten, Director of the Midtown Enforcement Project, obtained a search warrant and set up a raid on the Senton Hotel. The raid was kept secret beforehand, even from the local precinct. On the day it was to take place, those in charge asked the local precinct for cooperation. However, the precinct refused to participate and called the Police Department's Legal Bureau, which decided that the warrant was illegal. The Enforcement Project people had to call off the raid, but their surveillance of the Senton continued.

In another case of aborted action, Jason Huntsberry, a pimp, was arrested for putting a 15-year-old runaway into prostitution at two midtown Manhattan massage parlors. The young girl, who earned $3,000 in the month she worked for him, contracted a severe gonorrheal infection. According to Ralph Marino, Chairman of the Select Commitee on Crime, the pimp's sentence of $300 or 90 days in jail "amounts to no more than a tax of 10% on the pimp's earnings off this child's body."[14] Baumgarten again received a court order to close the massage parlors. In subsequent court action the owners were sentenced to 30 days to be served intermittently over four weekends.

In 1973, Gail Sheehy, in her important book on New York prostitution, *Hustling*, reported that after inspecting every midtown massage parlor one police sergeant found that all but four had the same overlord and connections to organized crime. "The other apparent gimmick is the use of attorneys as a front. The incorporation papers carry not the names of the actual owners but the names of their lawyers."[15]

In 1975 there were 117 massage parlors in New York City. Forty-three were closed by police action in that year, 28 were closed in 1976, and 22 in 1977.[16]

Besides making money off the lease of the buildings, some lawyers who have been connected with organized crime are also taking fees from the women. In January 1978, at a Public Hearing on Operations of Massage Parlors in New York City, testimony revealed that many massage parlors required the girls who worked in them to pay a $5.00 per day lawyers fee.[17] A sizeable income is suggested when it is realized that some parlors have as many as sixteen girls working for them seven days a week.

Pornography is a form of prostitution. Its producers and distributors can be defined as pimps, as they are living off the earnings of prostitutes. Pornography is estimated to be a $4 billion-a-year industry. The Adult Filmmakers Association claims that an average weekly audience of 2.5 million people paid an approximate total of $455 million to see hard-core films in 1978, and in 1978 an estimated 400,000 X-rated video-tape cassettes were sold for private consumption. Organized crime is said to hold a virtual free hand in the distribution of pornography. In 1975 it was estimated that it controlled at least 80 percent of hard-core magazines, books, and newspaper publishing.[18] It is said to have moved into pornography distribution after the 1967 Supreme Court decisions that lifted restrictions on pornography, making it a lucrative racket.

Pornography is probably the largest procurer of children for sexual slavery. If knowledge is a requirement for consent and maturity is necessary for sexual knowledge, then the use of children in pornography is by definition forced, and therefore a form of sexual slavery. Here is where the connection to organized crime and international traffic is found. Methods for acquiring children for the multimillion dollar profits of organized crime reflect the scope of present-day child sexual slavery. In August 1978 an international child pornography ring was broken up. Nine men were indicted for allegedly selling children for immoral purposes at prices ranging up to $1,000 and using them for lewd acts. The victims of the ring were seven girls and one boy, aged 4 to 12, from Southern California.[19]

Inspector Lloyd Martin of the Los Angeles Police Department's Sexually Exploited Children's Unit confirmed to me that the international market in 1978 was for blond-hair blue-eyed American boys and girls. In this case it is usually pornography that is trafficked, not the children, although Martin did cite one case of a man from Europe who flew to California and paid $500 for sex with an 8-year-old girl.

In California the Attorney General's Advisory Committee on Obscenity and Pornography determined that some producers of child pornography are child molesters "who take photographs of their victims and either sell the photographs to more sophisticated pornographers, both in and outside California, and/or distribute them through small mail-operations. Others photograph the children and use the photographs to produce sophisticated books, magazines, and films which sell for high prices in bookstores and are distributed by large-scale mail-order operations."[20]

There are pedophile organizations which encourage sexual activity between adults and children, promoting such activity through their meetings and in newsletters. Some make pornographic films and pictures available to their members. According to investigators, they are involved in the exchange of children for sexual services. Some magazines and privately circulated pedophile newsletters have become the market for selling children's services.

Through these magazines and privately circulated newsletters, out-of-state clientele and foreign contacts are made. According to one informant, "Individuals travel great distances to avail themselves of these services. Often, other children are brought along to these assignations for use as exchange chattels to avoid paying the fees, which range from $250 to $500, the asking price for use of a child from noon until the following noon."

The informant found that "The children who are used in this manner are rarely the legal daughters of the procurers, although often described as such in advertisement to create an illusion of family togetherness and safety from exposure. More often than not they are children from fatherless families, where the mother is befriended by the procurer, kept happy with material possessions that she would not otherwise be able to afford. The children accept the man in the father-figure role, usually responding without hesitation to bribes such as outings, toys, etc."

The New York State Select Crime Committee has gathered evidence to indicate that when child pornography is too hot to peddle in the United States it is sold from

Denmark or Amsterdam. The pictures or movies depicting children in a variety of poses and sexual acts are shot in the United States but shipped abroad for sale back to customers in the United States as well as other countries. The same children who appear in simple nude poses that can be found in bookstores in this country are seen in hard-core pornography produced in Denmark or Amsterdam.

For example, Robin Lloyd, while writing his book on boy prostitution, *For Money or Love*, ordered some child pornography from Amsterdam from an ad which promised delivery in plain wrappers and several small packages. The packages he received were postmarked from Van Nuys, California, and pictured several youths he could identify as boys he knew from his research on the street prostitution scene in Los Angeles.

While there appears to be an increase of free-lance prostitution in Europe, organized crime has always been more prevalent in pimping and procuring there than in the United States. In the 1960's, Beirut, where prostitution is legal and regulated, was the center of one of the most powerful and well-known syndicates providing women to Mideastern brothels and harems. In the 1950's that traffic had been conducted through Algeria and Morocco but it was disrupted by the Algerian war of independence. Most procurers and pimps moved on to Beirut, where regulated prostitution made it easy to set up business in nightclubs and brothels. Beirut was also where oil sheiks from Arab countries visited and vacationed. O'Callaghan, in his book, *The White Slave Trade*, distinguished three types of slavery operated by the syndicate in Beirut. "The slaves who cater to the Arab oil sheiks and who might be called the white slaves of the harems; the white slaves of cabarets or nightclubs; and the white slaves of brothels. . . ."[21] The syndicate kept a ready supply of girls who were procured in other countries and sent to Beirut. Women were procured from Europe as well as places like Ghana. In March 1973, nine Ghanians and a Lebanese faced charges in Accra "when the police discovered that twenty fourteen-year-old Ghanian girls had been sold to buyers in Lebanon."[22] Traditional strategies of seasoning and indebtedness were employed to keep women from running away.

In recent years, throughout the war in the Mideast,

Beirut has been continually under siege. The syndicate appears no longer to have direct control over traffic in women and children. The prostitution traffic is now operated by more loosely affiliated gangs of procurers and pimps.

Despite the German claim that they have solved the problems of prostitution and eliminated any need for pimps, gangs of pimps continue to move in and out of Germany. Traffic of the syndicate appears to have been taken over in part by some procurers connected with the thriving sex industry in Germany. According to a report in *Der Speigel* in December 1977, the largest ring of procurers ever found in Germany was broken up when eleven men and one woman from Argentina and Uruguay were arrested for procuring women from those countries and bringing them to Frankfurt, where they were put into prostitution on the street as well as in eros centers. Authorities became suspicious when they observed that a large number of prostitutes in the Frankfurt area were not from Germany but from southern countries. After the arrest of 50 prostitutes in a large raid, information on the gang came to light. According to the report, so many women were procured that if a woman escaped or ran away from the gang they never bothered to go after her but were able to replace her immediately. The prostitutes who were brought in from Argentina and Uruguay worked for three months on tourist visas and then were taken to Italy, where they were married to unemployed or retired Italian men who were paid $1,000 for the marriage. Italian marriage made the women members of the European Common Market and therefore able to return to Germany and continue their work.

It was with the boom of the German eros centers in the mid-1960's that Austrian pimps started to move into the German scene, according to Wolfgang Hollreigal, a Viennese reporter who has spent considerable time studying prostitution in Austria. These large state-sanctioned prostitution hotels where women (through their pimps) lease rooms or apartments created a new boom in business. The competition that Austrian pimps offered to the German pimps created rivalry between gangs. Gang rivalry and, later, a decline in profits, caused Austrian pimps to return to Vienna, where prostitution is governed by laws similar to those of Germany. According to Hollreigal, there is one well-organized gang that dominates prostitution in Vienna. It has about 75 members and controls 600 prostitutes, in addition to being involved in other criminal activities. Certain "assistants" in the gang travel the Prater (the Reeperbahn of Vienna) every night to collect their money from the women working for them there. The women are paying the gang for protection from the gang.

In 1976 two Austrians who were part of a ring of procurers were arrested and six others from West Germany were the object of a nationwide manhunt. The case broke out after one girl escaped from an eros center in Essen and reported to authorities that she had been taken there from Villach, Austria, by procurers and forced into prostitution. Further investigation revealed that many young girls were missing from the Villach area, and several Villach girls were located in Essen.

When I inquired into the case two years later, authorities explained that the other Austrian women found in Essen were prostitutes with expired passports who claimed that they too had been forced when they were picked up by the police. Assuming they were lying, authorities dismissed the issue of force completely, even though police know that many women when picked up are terrified of giving evidence against pimps and procurers. Prostitutes' unwillingness to testify is often an easy excuse for not investigating cases police would rather not handle anyway.

I pursued the question in the INTERPOL office. There even the victimization of the one girl who did testify was denied. "No, there were no girls forced into prostitution," said Dr. Kohl of the Austrian office of INTERPOL in Vienna. "By the time it came to court, it was only one girl; the whole thing was blown out of proportion." I asserted that I had heard that she had escaped from the eros center and I thought that suggested that she had been forced. He said, "At first it seemed that she might have been, but during her testimony it seemed that she had some opportunities to escape that she didn't take." Then Dr. Kohl's underlying interests became apparent: "We don't have any problems with prostitution here in Austria. That incident involved only one girl and she may not have even been forced."

Staff from the *Équipe d'Action* in Paris told me that

because so much of French prostitution is dominated by gangs, many women find it difficult to escape from their pimps. When a woman tries to escape, her pimp will usually hunt her down. If she successfully eludes him and testifies against him to the authorities, when he is a part of a gang, the gang will try to locate her, put her back out on the street, collect her money, take their cut, and save the rest for her pimp, who will be out of jail after his usually short jail sentence. Several times members of *Équipe d'Action* have had to hire bodyguards in order to accompany a woman to court to act as her advocate.

Within this mutually interdependent brotherhood, violence and abuse of women are considered a natural, basic right. Physical and verbal abuse of prostitutes is understood as part of "the life." There is little danger that anyone who sees or hears a prostitute being beaten will intervene directly or call the police. The security of a supportive brotherhood protects the pimps.

In 1976 Cynthia testified before a San Francisco Grand Jury about the times she tried to leave her pimp. The first time she left him, she went looking for an apartment when he began following her down the street. "I ran into a restaurant. I was running around the tables screaming. I told the man to call the police. The man told me to get out of the restaurant." The pimp forced her to return to him and beat her so badly she couldn't work.

Some time later she was beaten again by her pimp. She got away from him and was recuperating from the beating in a motel. He tracked her down, got the key to her room from the motel manager, entered her room and began beating her again, claiming she was avoiding him and not working. She managed to escape from him and ran to the motel office for help. The motel manager was subpoenaed by the Grand Jury investigating this case. His testimony under cross-examination is illustrative of the bonding within the brotherhood.

District Attorney: *She ran around your motel screaming for someone to call the police, right?*
Manager: *Yes.*
District Attorney: *You grabbed her, pinned her arms back, and told the guests in the motel not to bother calling the police.*

Manager: *I tried to get her out of the office.*
District Attorney: *She was saying that A. was trying to kill her? Did it ever occur to you that he was trying to kill her?*
Manager: *No, it didn't occur to me.*

While the manager was holding her, the pimp came in, grabbed her, and carried her out. She finally got away from him and went to the police. He was arrested and pleaded guilty to one count of pimping. When he was sentenced to one to ten years, he complained to the judge that the court was picking on him: he charged that it is known that pimps who plead guilty never have to go to prison.

A prostitute is known to be "out of pocket" with her pimp when he punishes her for talking back to him, disobeying him, or contradicting him. When the word goes out that she is "out of pocket," she is fair game for any other pimps around who have a free hand with her without triggering a pimp war. When I rode on patrol with San Francisco Police Officers Rich Oaks and Vince Repetto of the Prostitution Detail in the summer of 1978, we stopped to talk to one prostitute who had been kidnapped by two pimps from Oakland three nights earlier. She was picked up off the street, taken to Oakland, beaten, raped, and robbed. As she was telling us about this, she lifted her wig slightly to show us that they had shaved her head before dumping her back on the streets of San Francisco. It is a common occurrence in the Tenderloin, the high crime prostitution section of the city. While we were talking to her, another prostitute joined us and reported that a similar thing happened to her a few months earlier. The kidnapping had somewhat dimmed in her memory. She was presently concerned with the slashes on her arm and back. She took off her jacket to show us her slashed arm and lifted the back of her shirt to display her back, which had been criss-crossed with razor blade slashes by a trick a few nights earlier. She didn't consider reporting it to the police. She appeared to accept the violence as inevitable.

3. Employment Agencies
The use of phony employment agencies or dance companies offering exciting jobs abroad has long been a common method of procurers. It is easy and effective. An ad

placed in the newspaper offering exciting work in a foreign country with "no experience necessary" immediately attracts young women who are bored and frustrated with their lives and have to face the job market in times of high unemployment and discrimination. Or procurers posing as labor contractors need only spread the word in rural poverty areas of jobs available.

Employment agencies, whether they are recruiting secretaries, dancers, actresses, or domestic workers, are very effective covers for transporting women to foreign countries. They are what INTERPOL referred to as disguised traffic and they remain one of the major procuring strategies. The phony agency provides a job contract with which passports, visas, work permits, and other necessary documents are obtained or falsified. There is no difficulty passing through immigration, and the young women offer no resistance because they assume they are off to an exciting adventure in another country. Through this strategy women and girls are trafficked into domestic slavery as well as forced prostitution.

Once women procured for prostitution arrive at their destination, any number of tactics may be employed to put them to work. Sometimes they are told that the original job is no longer available and that they will have to repay the air fare and other expenses the "agency" has incurred. The procurer will then suggest that he can get them jobs in a particular bar. When they arrive they find their duties extend far beyond being a hostess and serving drinks. They are trapped into prostitution, believing initially that they must do the work in order to earn the money to buy their freedom. Other times the seasoning is more direct: physical violence is used to persuade women to accept prostitution.

In 1970 two women dancers in a club in Madison, Wisconsin, were approached by two men who offered them jobs as dancers in Saigon for three months. They signed contracts for the agreed-upon work but when they arrived in Vietnam they were taken to a walled posh villa, where they were told they would be beaten unless they worked as prostitutes. They managed to get away and later reported what happened to them; ultimately five men were charged in the case. One pled guilty at the beginning of the trial and the other four were convicted.[23] But on appeal these men were acquitted; they argued that the women had volunteered to go to Vietnam to do research for a book they were writing!

In June 1975 *Le Monde* reported that a prostitution ring was broken up and Marseilles authorities arrested five people who for two years had been operating between Marseilles and Antwerp, Belgium. The alleged cover for the ring was the temporary-work agency Diano-Interim, which was reported to recruit women between the ages of 18 and 30 and sent them to Antwerp, where they were forced into prostitution. According to one woman who escaped, if a woman refused to submit to prostitution, her captors didn't hesitate to use torture, including beating and genital mutilation with cigarettes.

Not all promises of jobs take women abroad. In April 1978 indictments were handed down in New Jersey against a ring of five men who procured twelve women, some of whom were working as Playboy Bunnies. The women were promised an opportunity to be taped for a television promotion and given an address to report to for an audition. When they arrived, they were drugged, tortured, forced into pornographic poses and scenes, and photographed. They then were blackmailed. The ring was broken when one woman risked her life and reported the operation to the police. In the police raid, videotapes and Polaroid pictures of the women were found. The bedrooms in the house were equipped with video cameras and recording equipment.

4. Purchase

Selling women for cash still takes place all over the world in a variety of settings. In the poverty-stricken rural areas of South American countries like Paraguay, teenage girls are purchased from their parents. In metropolitan areas like Paris or New York City, pimps sell their prostitutes to other pimps. One Minneapolis policeman found the going price of a blonde, blue-eyed, Midwestern girl in New York City in 1977 was $1,000.

When the American military withdrew from South Vietnam and Thailand, the overwhelming sex industry created in Thailand for their rest and relaxation had to find new markets. Pimps and procurers had to do something with the estimated 100,000 prostitutes who had been recruited to meet military needs. The German economy and liberal prostitution laws made that country a likely focus for traffic from Thailand. One report indicated that Thai girls were purchased for $1,000 each by a ring in Frankfurt, who then were reported to rent them out for $2,200 a month.[24] Some were taken directly from Thailand to German brothels with no ruse or pretense. In 1977 a Thai welfare worker, who went to Germany to bring home one young woman abandoned on the streets there, estimated that there were over 1,000 Thai girls working as prostitutes there at that time.[25]

One means of disposing of the excess prostitutes was through agencies who ran ads in European newspapers offering a "Super Sexy Tour" which included a vacation in Thailand and the opportunity to buy a wife. According to one British journalist who found that these tours were legitimate, the first week of such a trip is spent picking out the girl one wants (after trying out several, if you like). The second week a final selection is made with "Sightseeing and sweet nothings on a romantic palm-fringed beach. See a Thai style boxing match, eat a traditional Thai dinner, see traditional Thai dancing . . . by week three the tour operators will have made all the wedding arrangements . . . and be ready to hand over all the documents needed to export your new acquisition." The prices ranged from $1,500 to $3,000.[26]

Other reports indicate that some agencies were taking the men's money but not delivering the merchandise. One ad in a German paper offering three weeks in Thailand and the bride of your choice for $3,000 simply took the man's money, arranged a ceremony, and promised that the "wife" would be sent to him later. She never arrived. Similarly, in Hong Kong over 100 men complained to authorities in 1975 that they bought brides from Thailand (some paying as much as $1,000) but found the girls disappeared soon after the marriage.[27]

The Thai sex-marriage tours are advertised in men's magazines in Europe. According to one report, "Norway's foreign minister Knyt Frydenlund now says if diplomatic pressure on the Thai government doesn't halt the tours, Norway will take legal action to stop them." The Norwegian parliament investigated the tours. The foreign minister reported that the prostitution, pandering, and slave trading is in violation of human rights and the resolutions of the 1975 International Women's Year Conference.[28]

In terms of sheer numbers the heaviest traffic in women and girls purchased for prostitution is from rural poverty. In a 1972 report from India an investigator for the state criminal division of the state of Orissa documented the sale of seven girls to individuals and brothels and said that he knew of many more sales. Two thousand girls were missing from that state in 1972 and it was assumed by authorities that they had left through persons posing as labor contractors visiting the villages and offering the girls jobs in other cities.[29]

Purchase does not affect only those in rural poverty. Judie was from a middle-class, religious fundamentalist home in Arizona. A 16-year-old runaway, she had taken a bus to the mining town of Totz, Kentucky. There she bought her first pack of cigarettes and had her first drink with Orie. Undoubtedly Orie was not an organized procurer; more likely he was a local opportunist who could make a fast buck off of a young naive girl.

He invited her to his cabin. It was a crude place with a dirt floor, but she stayed and fell in love with him. One night three months later, when she thought they were going to a dance in Hazard, Judie was drugged by Orie. She passed out, and when she regained consciousness she was in the back seat of the car, which was parked in front of a bar-dancehall. A huge man was holding a gun to her head. She saw him give Orie $300. Orie took the money, turned to her, and said, "You belong to him now."

The next thing she remembered was that a woman who called herself Goldie was walking her around through some graves that were behind the dancehall. Pointing to the graves, Goldie explained that this is where girls end up who try to get away. "Naked terror gripped me, like nothing I had ever known. I could not run and I was afraid to stay," Judie recalled. Still not knowing the full extent of what was expected of her, she tried to numb the reality with a drink. "Goldie offered me a slug of whisky . . . I gulped the liquid down rapidly. Maybe this would stop the raw fear and blot out the recurring memories of the past few months."

Writing about her experience years later, Judie recapped Goldie's instructions to her: "First, ya gotta serve the cocks drinks. We kin only serve beer in the hall, case the 'noses' are 'round. They don' bother much no more, some are 'in' now. . . . The regulars don't pay 'cepting their monthly chits. They git anything they ask for. Ya supposta dance with all the cocks—anyway they want. Strippin's not agin the law here, this bein' Dead Man's Territory. So's ya better learn, ifin ya don' know how to do it good. The he-goats like ta look and feel ya. That's what Earl boughtcha for."

Judie's clothes were taken away from her and she was given a costume and makeup. She was confined to the dancehall and her room behind it. Earl always carried a gun as a reminder to her and the other girls of what would happen if they tried to leave. She worked from about noon to 4:00 A.M. and then slept until the next noon. There was no time to think or do anything else but "work" and sleep. She awakened many mornings with her body writhing with pain from bruises, gashes, or wounds inflicted by customers the night before. Earl provided them with a variety of chains, whips, and clubs to use on the women. Awakening, Judie would think, "Oh my God, why?" But thinking only made the pain worse; there was nothing she could do to stop it. Drink deadened both her pain and thoughts.

Most of the customers were truckers and state highway patrolmen from both Tennessee and Kentucky; the brothel was near the border of those two states. While Judie was there, she saw the new grave of a girl who had tried to escape by running to the highway, where she was picked up by a customer and brought back for Earl's vengeance.

Earl had never made sexual demands of Judie in the three years she was confined in his brothel. But when he came to her room drunk one night with his gun in one hand and a spiked club she knew was meant for her vagina in the other, she knew she had to defend herself against him—it was now a matter of life and death.

Somehow, all those other men did not have a personal connection for Judie. But Earl's wife was right next door in their house; she brought Judie two meals a day and new makeup when she needed it. That small personal connection made the thought of Earl's approach additionally impossible.

She fought back when he approached her, and some minutes later she left covered with blood. Her mind is still blank regarding what happened—25 years later the horror of it is still inaccessible to her. She remembers grabbing $30 from the cash drawer, an act which caused her guilt for a long time.

To avoid the highway she ran through the hills most of the night and finally reached a highway just when she was ready to collapse. A friendly trucker picked her up. After her initial fear that he might take her back, her next fear prevailed for many years—that her mother would find out what she had been doing. She blacked out in the truck and was taken to a hospital in Memphis, where she spent a long time recuperating from hepatitis, malnutrition, anemia, and damage to her internal organs from the severe sexual abuse of the customers.

In the 25 years since her escape, through 19 years of marriage and three sons, Judie has had to fight the long battles of alcoholism and severe overweight. These were the prices of hiding her story, suppressing her pain for the comfort and acceptance of her family. In recent years her story has come out and she is conquering the last vestiges of control sexual slavery has held on her.[30]

5. Kidnapping

In the 1975 revision of his earlier work on sexual slavery, Stephen Barlay stated that "outright abduction has become an antiquated, unnecessarily troublesome rarity."[31] This view has also been expressed by some anti-slavery workers who believe that girls are now much more easily procured through ads for jobs abroad. However, when sexual slavery is considered in its total context, which includes both foreign traffic and local prostitution, the incidence of kidnapping is still very significant. I have found the following accounts to be illustrative:

In May 1978, two black men and one white woman were arrested for kidnapping, raping, and forcing two 14-year-old girls into prostitution. The girls, who were runaways from Pennsylvania, reported to the police that they had been kidnapped from a Sacramento, California, bus station and held for three days until they escaped.

Describing another kidnapping as "bizarre and reminiscent of white slavery traffic," an FBI official revealed the bare facts of the kidnapping and forced prostitution of a 27-year-old woman from Hartford, Connecticut. She was beaten and taken to a motel in Schenectady, New York, where she was forced into prostitution under the constant guard of a woman who worked with two men in the kidnapping. Three days later she escaped.[32]

In 1976, according to the London *Times*, as many as eight teenage girls, including the daughter of a Dutch count, were abducted in Brussels and forced to work as prostitutes in Zaire. Belgian police were holding a riding instructor and two sons of Zaire's consul general in connection with the girls' disappearance.[33]

In 1973, a husband and wife kidnapped a 29-year-old advertising executive who was traveling through Chicago on business. After slipping a knockout drop into her drink in a bar, they took her to their home, where she was stripped and told she would be trained for prostitution. The victim escaped and contacted police. The couple was arrested.[34]

In August 1972, a 15-year-old runaway girl from New Jersey escaped a New York City Times Square massage parlor, where she had been forced into prostitution after being kidnapped. As a result of her escape, police raided the parlor. They found tape recording facilities and television monitors which may have been used for extortion.[35]

In January 1972, Grand Jury indictments were handed down in Dane County, Wisconsin, against four men and two women for kidnapping and torturing more than twenty women to force them into prostitution. According to a newspaper report, "Some of the victims were kidnapped from go-go bars in Minneapolis, tied up and thrown into autos, and driven to Madison . . . the victims were kept in a house on Lake Kegonsa and were taken by force to a sauna parlor in Monona, a suburb of Madison, where the prostitution took place, according to the indictment."[36]

Runaways, girls who have a background of delinquency, and women who dance in bars are easy prey of sex slave procurers and are not easily recognized as victims. When they are kidnapped, many of these girls and women fear that the police will not believe them. So they alter their stories, which usually makes it impossible to prosecute their captors. Kidnapping, like other sex slave practices, continues to appear nonexistent. The background oi many of its victims overshadows the actions of their captors.

ESCAPING THE BROTHERHOOD

Forced prostitution is the result of procuring strategies and seasoning practices. How do women escape this slavery and the brotherhood conducting it?

According to Melinda, a former San Francisco prostitute:

> Once a woman starts hoing [whoring] for a man, there's no way out—unless she runs. Once I started, my man wasn't going to let it stop. He wasn't a flashy pimp. He was a lazy good-for-nothing who leeched off of women!
>
> The first time I came home without enough money and he put his foot in my ass—that's when I realized I was his ho and he was my pimp and that's the way it was going to be. Then the beatings were regular. He'd hit me up side my head with a 2 by 4 or a dog chain. When I was pregnant he'd kick me in the stomach. He put me in a tub and tried to drown me once . . . .
>
> Pimps have two ways of holding on to women. One is verbal abuse, psychological beatings where they make you feel like you are worthless, like you're trash. The other is fear. Beatings are the other way he'll keep her because by having so much fear in her heart she is afraid to leave him. Yet by that time I was so much in love with him it really didn't matter as long as he was there. When he put his arms around me nothing could hurt me. When he told me he loved me I believed everything would work out all right. I'd been alone for so long and he'd told me I'd be with him for the rest of my life.

Melinda recounted some temporary escapes she devised as her pimp grew more and more vicious and she was too dependent on him to leave. She would spend long evenings over dinner and drinks with her girl friend before they would start working the streets together. Prison was also a temporary escape. "I got busted left and right. I knew if I'd get convicted that would be one way I could get away from my man for maybe four months. I could get away to regroup my mind to deal with another year."

Many prostitutes feel that they can divert their pimp's attention away from themselves if they bring another woman to him. If she can convince a sister of the streets to "choose" her pimp and he accepts her, she may get some peace from his attention and she may even get an opportunity to leave.

But when a woman tries to escape from the life, whether or not there are other women around, she will invariably be hunted down. If she goes to relatives or friends, her pimp knows to look for her there. Once he locates her, he will "sweet talk" her until he gets her alone, by telling her how much he missed her, how he had lost his mind the last time he beat her and could never do that again, and how miserable and lonely life is without her. This line, or sweet talk, just like procuring strategies, is the same across cultures. Jeanne Cordelier's graphic description of her attempt to escape her pimp in France in her book *The Life* is the same as I've heard from prostitutes in San Francisco and New York. Once he gets her away from her friends, the sweet talk turns into hard punches and probably the worst beating yet.

In San Francisco in 1977 Joey was convicted and sentenced for pimping and pandering. Jessica began dating Joey in January 1975 when she was 19. Soon after she fell in love with him, he began to talk to her about the easy money to be made in prostitution, telling her that "within a month or two I could get him a car and I could get myself a car and we would travel around the world." He was persistent and convinced her to try prostitution if she really loved him. He instructed her on how to approach customers, set prices. He got her phony identification with a new name "so that you can have a life under your real name that won't be soiled."

She wasn't a very good prostitute and when she came home three nights in a row without any money he began to slap her around. She was with him for a year and a half, during which time the beatings increased. She eventually realized that despite her love for him her dreams were not going to come true. She decided to leave him and that was when she realized the extent of her enslavement.

He hunted her down, burst into her aunt's house and broke down the door. After terrorizing her he left, but returned three days later. "He told me to bring my baby. So I got the baby and stuff. And we got on the freeway going towards Oakland. . . . I went with him because there was no other way out. The back yard was all fenced up and I knew—the door was already pushed open, it couldn't close—I knew if I didn't walk out, he would come and get me. We got on the freeway. He asked me about an incident that happened when I first left him and he accused me of lying to him and he hit me in my nose. It started really bleeding bad. Then he said 'I'm going to pull off, take the next exit off and beat your ass until you can't move.' And I kept asking him, 'What about Michael?' Because Michael [her baby] was right in the back. He was looking at me with the blood on me. He just said, 'You're going to get it now.' We got off the freeway and he started beating me real bad . . . hitting me with his fists and trying to turn my neck. I lost track of how many times he hit me. I just know he hit me so many times that after a while I was so weak, and then he said 'I'm not going to hurt myself hitting you.' And so he went to the trunk and got the base of a jack and he hit me on the head." He took her home with him. His other prostitute, her stable sister, seeing the severity of her condition helped her get out and call the police a few days later. When she got away the police took her to the hospital where she found that her skull was fractured.[37]

Some pimps will allow a woman to buy back her freedom for an arbitrary amount of money which she must raise and pay him. In some cases women have been able to walk out of the life after paying the required fine. But most often the fine is just like the sweet talk, part of the game he has been running, another fraudulent means of holding on with no intention of letting go.

Some women manage to elude their pimps and escape into another town or state, taking on a new identity and the enormous task of putting their lives back together. Others, overwhelmed emotionally as well as physically, escape through suicide.

In some countries, particularly France, there are refuge

centers for women to go to. But in the United States, where the victim is herself a condemned and hunted criminal, it has been nearly impossible to get public support and funding for such centers. Covenant House, a refuge for teenage runaways in New York City's Times Square, is one of the few that does exist. It provides a teenage prostitute with a place to sleep and meals for a night or two. But it runs only on an emergency basis and doesn't have the capacity to keep the teenagers any longer. This is not enough time for a young woman to sever her ties; when she is back out on the street she is likely soon to be back to her pimp, but with some rest and good food behind her.

The last resort for escape is to the police. It is hardly an option to women who know they are legally and morally condemned by those from whom they would seek help. Police brutality of prostitutes is periodically reported by women working the streets.

One night in March 1977 Mary, who was working the streets to get enough money to pay her rent, solicited an undercover police officer. When he told her she was under arrest, she didn't believe him. She later said that she thought he was a trick who was going to take her someplace and beat her. A rapist had been working the area and the prostitutes were quite anxious about who his next victim would be. Mary tried to get out of the car, at which point she alleges she was severely beaten. A nearby taxi driver noticed a man beating a woman and rushed to intervene; then another man (who turned out to be the backup for the first police officer) appeared and beat the taxi driver. Mary was arrested and taken to a police department's holding tank, a room in a downtown hotel where police hold prostitutes each night as they are arrested until there are enough to get a paddy wagon to come and pick them up and take them to the police station. (The holding tanks in prestigious downtown San Francisco's hotels are usually arranged through informal agreements between police who work part time as guards there and hotel management.)

Another prostitute was already in the holding tank when the officers arrived with Mary. She saw and testified to the beating that Mary received in the hotel's lower chambers. According to Mary and the witness, Mary was beaten to unconsciousness. I saw her when she got out of the hospital a few days later. Her face was swollen and puffy, both eyes blackened; a bone behind her eye had been fractured and part of her cheekbone was crushed.

Still dazed and bruised from the beating and surgery she had to have while in jail, she kept saying "Why did they beat me so badly? Why did they have to mess up my face?" As a victim of incest from her stepfather and later battery from her boyfriend, Mary had come to accept beatings as inevitable, but she just couldn't understand why it was so bad this time. The officers claimed that in the room at the hotel holding tank Mary had tried to kick them and her injuries resulted when they tried to restrain her and they all fell to the floor.

The only thing unusual about this case is that it ever went to court. That was the result of agitation raised by prostitute organizations and some feminist groups. Their support led to the officers being suspended and formally charged with assault.

In court the defense's winning strategy was a prostitute conspiracy theory which alleged that Mary and the other prostitute, along with the prostitute organization, were out to dishonor and discredit the police department. In addition, like so many victims who try to help their case by making the story more believable, Mary testified that she had been hit by a police officer at the hotel holding tank when it was already established in court that she was unconscious when the officer hit her. An acquittal for the officer followed.

I talked to Mary after the trial and tried to encourage her to continue with her plans to get her high school equivalency diploma and enter a vocational training program. But she was bitter—not at the police, but because, as she saw it, she had been suckered into trying to get justice through the courts. She was ridiculed by her friends on the street and felt, as they did, that she would have been better off if she had just accepted the beating and let it go at that.

Escaping the brotherhood that controls prostitution involves escaping the wrath of society, especially in its social and legal institutions that condemn prostitutes.

ESCAPING INVISIBLE ENSLAVEMENT

The question that has never been objectively asked about the victim of female sexual slavery is why, if there is a possibility of escape (which often there is not), will some women fight their captors and get away while others give in and passively accept their fate?

Part of the answer must lie in the fact that these victims are faced with an experience that is an invisible reality—this is a victimization that has no name. Until we name the practice, give conceptual definition and form to it, illustrate its life over time and in space, those who are its most obvious victims will also not be able to name it or define their experience. We are faced with the question: if a tree falls in the forest and no one is there to hear it, did it make a noise?

Of course it did! Things simply do not exist only as perceptions. There is an objective reality which precedes perception and is presumed by perceived reality. Objective reality *is*, whether or not it is perceived. It is not merely a matter of perception or opinion that women are sexually enslaved. It is a fact. But social perception is presently inconsistent with objective reality. The decision to suppress evidence of sex slavery is but one means of maintaining the disparity between social perception and objective reality. As a form of selective perception, it allows the patriarchal brotherhood in high diplomatic circles, in science and research and on city streets, to keep the practice unknown and nameless.

When victims have no way of naming what has happened to them, they cannot understand themselves as victims. They suffer the same madness that raped women experience when their victimization is denied and equated with sexual intercourse. It is the same madness undergone by battered wives who are told the police don't interfere in "marital disputes."

Because sexual slavery is not perceived as a reality, young women are easily vulnerable to it, particularly if their history or background has been one of abuse. For many of its victims, the present reality of sex slavery is in accordance with past experiences. It is in this context that the background of victims urgently needs to be known.

From a recent study of San Francisco prostitutes, it is possible to conjecture on the effect of background for one group of sexual slaves, street prostitutes who are controlled by pimps. This survey of thirty San Francisco street prostitutes by Marilyn Neckes and Theresa Lynch found the average age of the women was 22. They began prostitution at an average age of 17 after completing tenth grade in school. Most of the women were white (67 percent), single (60 percent), and childless (63 percent), and most had been runaways (63 percent). Prior to entering prostitution, 80 percent had been victims of physical or sexual abuse (37 percent incest/sexual abuse in the home, 33 percent physical abuse, and 60 percent rape). Eighty percent of the women had pimps, a fact that partially explains why 83 percent of them reported no savings even though they earned an average of $140 per day.[38]

For one who comes from a background of physical and sexual abuse, or even just verbal or psychological abuse from those who are the most significant in her life, anonymous and violent sex is possible. The young woman who has been sexually abused by her father, brother, or uncle, or beaten by her husband, will begin to see herself as those who have abused her do, as someone worth nothing more than the treatment she has received. If her mother berates her, calls her a whore when she tries to explain that her father has been molesting her, or if her husband accuses her of infidelity when she tells him she was raped, she will eventually take on the definition that has been attributed to her, particularly if there is no one in her environment to contradict it. Her self-image is at least partially derived from interaction with those with whom she is the closest— parents, lover, spouse, or friend. If the people she is closest to deny her affection and instead shower her with abuse, then she will eventually begin to think of herself as someone who deserves that kind of treatment.

Necessarily, then, if such a girl is procured into prostitution, or if she tries it out on her own and then finds herself enslaved, she may not resist the slavery. It is inconsistent with the way she was defined when growing up.

Furthermore, a young woman who has grown up physically, sexually, or verbally abused may place her need for affection above the abuse she is subjected to from a pimp. Physical contact with another person breaks the agonizing loneliness; it is at least a form of recognition by the other. This does not mean that she likes it, needs it, or wants it. It is the attention and affection that she craves and she becomes willing to take almost anything to get it. Turning tricks seems little to ask of her in exchange for the attention she receives. She is not sexually liberated, not beyond puritanical moral standards and repressive sexual habits. Rather, she has taken on the same perception of herself and her body held by the people who have abused her over the years—the self-image of a throwaway.

Accepting the perception of others is taking the path of least resistance; that is survival for some women. It is the other side of madness. Those who are not broken either by seasoning or earlier childhood abuse, will be able to resist the definition imposed on them by others and even recognize their own unnamed victimization. But those who comply with their captors' definition will take on their work in earnest. It becomes their only source of self-respect. Such a woman will try to prove that she is the best goddamn whore on the block and the toughest. She learns to roll tricks and shoplift for her pimp. In interviews with exprostitutes I have often noticed a lingering pride in their work. When they tell the rest of us that we are straight, judgmental, and prudish, they are surviving by defending the definition they have accepted of themselves and making the most of it.

CHAPTER 6

Throwaway Women

All kinds of women are vulnerable to slave procurers. The assumption that only women of a particular class, race, or age group are potential victims of female sexual slavery has followed from the inability to recognize sexual domination as it underpins all other forms of oppression. It is true that some procuring methods are adapted to particular groups of women and the strategy that works in rural poverty may not work in an urban bus station. But it is primarily procurers and their interests and only secondarily women's age, race or economic class that determine who will end up forced into prostitution.

The other major cause of sex slavery is the social-sexual objectification of women that permeates every patriarchal society in the world. Identifying women first as sexual beings who are responsible for the sexual services of men is the social base for gender-specific sexual slavery. As most women know, being sexually harassed while walking alone down a street, or sitting in a bar or restaurant without a man, is a poignant reminder of our definition as sexual objects. Spurning those advances and reacting against them are likely to draw indignant wrath from the perpetrator, suggesting the extent to which many men assume the sexual objectification of *any* woman as their right. Under such conditions, sexual slavery lurks at the corners of every woman's life.

Increasingly, stereotyped female-gender characteristics are becoming the means of identifying prostitutes. In 1975 a Danish court ruled on a prostitution case that had ramifications for all women when it agreed that a policeman could identify a woman as a prostitute *from the way she walked*. The court fined the woman for soliciting based only on the testimony of a policeman who said, "I took action only when she was obviously soliciting, and that was easily determined from the way she walked."[1]

British prostitutes have been organizing against a twenty-year-old law which permits conviction of a woman as a "common prostitute" on the basis of police observation of her standing on the street. The law requires no indication that she was disturbing anyone.[2]

In 1976 the New York State legislature enacted a law against loitering for the purposes of prostitution which in effect makes any woman walking or standing on the street vulnerable to being identified as a prostitute. In challenges to that law the New York Civil Liberties Union has raised the issue that loitering "for the purposes of prostitution" is determined almost solely on the observations of the police officers. In reviewing over 200 loitering arrests, NYCLU attorneys found that in not one arrest was any other evidence gathered to support the arresting officer's observations. According to NYCLU attorneys, in depositions with arresting officers it was found that officers defined loitering for the purposes of prostitution based on their observations of the women on the street, what they were wearing, with whom they were associating, and repeated beckoning to men. Susan Heeger is one woman whom the police apparently saw as fitting their definition of a prostitute.

In July 1978 Susan Heeger emerged from the subway at Park Avenue and 28th Street in New York City. She was returning home from the movies and, being new to New York, was a little scared to be out on the street late at night. As she reported:

> As I turned the corner to go east on 28th toward Lexington Avenue, I saw an old battered car with some people around it who were making noise and talking loudly. The street was quite dark. I was apprehensive and started to run toward the light at the corner. When I reached the corner of Lexington and 28th I noticed the battered car behind me as I stepped into the intersection.
>
> Before I got across the street, the car had pulled over near the northeast corner and a man in casual clothes jumped out.
>
> The man started coming at me so I went around the front of the car. He ran around his door to the front of the car and in the middle of the intersection grabbed me by the hair and dragged me to the ground.

I started screaming as he dragged me by my hair across the intersection toward the car. My body was scraped and my neck was wrenched. I kept screaming and crying for help. He told me to "shut up" and "be quiet." Then he handcuffed himself to me. My screaming brought some witnesses. . . .

The man finally took off the handcuffs and tried to get me into his car. I kept screaming: "Don't let them take me away. Don't let them put me in the car." Another man got out of the car and one of the plain-clothes officers said to the crowd, "She's a psycho." The man who had gotten out of the car said, "Come on, I'm a police officer, we've chased her twice to-night."

Despite the protests of the crowd, she was put in the car, where six other women were cramped into the back seat. At some point between the scene of this incident and their arrival at the precinct station, Heeger was apparently able to convince the plainclothes officer that she was a writer and a Harvard graduate and that she worked at St. Martin's Press. At the station the other women were taken in but according to Heeger, the officer started pleading with her to not do anything about his "mistake."

As she recovered from her harrowing experience, Heeger realized that "in addition to being battered and falsely accused, people would think I was a prostitute just because the police picked me up." It was then that she decided to take action through the NYCLU as "it was too important to me and other women to let it go."[3]

In my interview with Melinda (who described her life with her pimp in the preceding chapter), she told me how she was "turned out" when she was 15. One day, after going to the movies with her girl friend, she was waiting for a bus when a man approached her and told her he'd pay her $50 for a date. She talked with him for a few minutes and she naively believed he just wanted to take her out so she accepted. She did not know he had actually solicited her as a prostitute until she got to the hotel room with him and he told her his expectations. At that point she had no alternative.

Women like Melinda who don't escape the arbitrary definition of prostitute are recycled into the world, where they are sexually used and abused and disposed of when no longer of use. Like the no-deposit, no-return beverage bottles—they are throwaways. Jeanne Cordelier recalls warning her friend, "They're going to chuck us into those trucks with a few other foolhardy girls, and then off we'll go to Zanzibar, Bahia Blanca, Conakry, and Dar es Salaam! The expendables."[4]

A picture of a prostitution homicide I saw in the police investigation file graphically illustrated this point. As I was looking through a series of pictures evidencing torture in the murders of prostitutes, one picture puzzled me. It was of a huge trash barrel in the basement of an old building. I peered at the picture for a few moments before I realized that a dead girl's body had been stuffed into the barrel. Only her arm, curled above her head, was showing. In New York City alone in 1975, official police statistics document 71 prostitution homicides. At least 54 of them were committed by pimps or tricks.[5] This figure is undoubtedly conservative. Frequently street prostitutes are the target of sexually violent men. During the period from late 1977 to early 1978 a Los Angeles strangler carried out several brutal rape-murders; most of his victims were prostitutes. During the same period of time many street-walkers in northern England were victims of a "Ripper's" mutilation murders.

The prevailing belief that because of the nature of their work prostitutes cannot be raped makes them easy targets for men who assume they can act out their misogyny with impunity. Beating, rape, and even murder are generally considered inevitable occupational hazards. Social attitudes which coalesce around street prostitutes make them and any other women who are identified as prostitutes throwaway women. These attitudes form the basis of many prostitution laws.

THE STATE AS PIMP

Governments have wrestled with the problem of how to handle prostitution for a long time. There is considerable diversity in the laws. But regarding street solicitation most countries fall into a single pattern which involve exploiting and abusing women on the streets and largely ignoring the less visible prostitution. Consistently across societies, street prostitutes are hassled and fined but never to the point of eliminating them from the streets. As long as there is a demand, there will be no major interference with supply. Harassment of street prostitutes is a way of assuring the community that morality is being upheld. As Jennifer James points out, legal definitions of prostitution are based on cash, promiscuity, relationship to sexual partner, and subtlety. "A prostitute is safe in violating the first three aspects of legal concern if she carefully accedes to the fourth—subtlety."[6]

A look at the laws governing prostitution and at their enforcement reveals how the double standard of male morality is implemented and shows the extent to which prostitutes are locked into a moral and legal system that ensures their enslavement even if they can escape their pimp or brothel. Besides assuring the double standard, laws governing prostitution in each country promote the isolation of prostitutes, setting them apart from the rest of society, placing them in a legal or social status that facilitates their exploitation and often prevents them from leaving. Three different systems of prostitution have been distinguished, and all in one way or another set up the state as the first pimp. Those systems either prohibit, tolerate, or regulate prostitution.

1. Prohibition

The prohibitionist system is probably the most overt practice of the double standard. It overwhelmingly punishes the woman while virtually ignoring the men. Statistics from arrest records in San Francisco and New York City are representative of this practice nationwide. In San Francisco in 1977, "2,938 persons were arrested for prostitution and 325 persons were arrested as customers of prostitutes. Although it has been estimated that there are ten times as many customers as prostitutes in San Francisco, 419 persons served time in jail in 1977 for prostitution; not *one* customer of a prostitute served time in jail."[7] Table I compares the number of various prostitution-related arrests in San Francisco for two selected months in 1976.

TABLE I Pattern of Prostitution-Related Arrests for Selected Months—San Francisco, 1976

Arrest	April 1976 Number	%	October 1976 Number	%
Female prostitution	179	82.	157	86.0
Male prostitution	12	5.5	13	7.0
Male customers	15	7.	9	5.0
Pimps (male)	12*	5.5	3	1.5
Total	218		182	

*April, 1976 pimp arrests disposition:
  3 found guilty (N = 3)
  5 cases dismissed
  4 unknown

Source: Based on research conducted by the Women's Jail Study Group, San Francisco, California.

Under the prohibitionist system, as it exists in the United States (with the exception of Nevada) and some other countries, prostitution and pimping are illegal. This system, which most Europeans view as hypocritical morality, socially acknowledges the need for prostitution and the inevitability of it, but makes it illegal. The women who practice it are punished while the men who derive pleasure and profit from it, the pimps and customers, are virtually ignored. Accordingly, those prostitutes who are victims of sexual slavery are seen only as criminals in the sex industry. Even though the laws forbid both pimping and patronizing a prostitute, it is prostitutes who are arrested (a total of 36,093 in the United States in 1977, according to the Uniform Crime Reports).

As in San Francisco, in New York City (and State) pimp arrests are also negligible (see Table II), especially when the testimony of Minneapolis policeman Gary McHaughey is taken into consideration. He estimated that 300 to 400 women annually were taken from there to New York City by pimps. He had specific knowledge of at least 200 pimps operating between Minneapolis and New York City.[8]

TABLE II   Promoting Prostitution (Pimping) In New York City and State 1974–1977*

Offense	Indictment		Dismissal		Conviction		Disposition Unknown	
	NYS	NYC	NYS	NYC	NYS	NYC	NYS	NYC
Promotion of Prostitution—First Degree (promoting two or more women)	26	5	22	4	4	0	0	1
Promotion of Prostitution—Second Degree (coercive pimping or pimping someone under age 17)	71	31	52	23	14	6	5	2
Total	97	36	74	27	18	6	5	3

*First 3 quarters of 1977

Source: New York State Division of Criminal Justice Services

Nevertheless, from January 1974 through the first three quarters of 1977, there were a total of 36 indictments for promotion of prostitution in New York City (97 in the entire state) and 6 convictions (18 in the entire state). Four pimps were convicted of pimping in New York City in 1977.

In 1976 a prostitute worked undercover for the police in a project which resulted in indictments against a dozen massage parlor owners and operators. They had been indicted on felony charges but by the time it came to court the charges were reduced to a misdemeanor. "Justice Irving Lang, who sentenced most of them . . . imposed the following forms of penalties: four weekends in jail and a $500 fine; five years' probation; four weekends and a $250 fine; three years' probation and a $1,000 fine; eight weekends and a $500 fine; three years' probation; conditional discharge and a $250 fine; and a conditional discharge and a $490 fine." The judge defended his actions, saying the pimps got the same sentences any other person without prior arrests would for a misdemeanor.[9]

One inevitable result of the prohibitionist system is that prostitutes, defined as criminals, are reluctant to turn in their pimps and, until they do, prosecution of pimps is virtually impossible. The prostitute with a criminal record has no place else to turn. The system reinforces her already tight dependency on her pimp and virtually locks her into prostitution.

China and Vietnam are probably the only countries in the world that have come close to a truly prohibitionist program. China claims to have completely eliminated prostitution and Vietnam, since the conclusion of the war there, cites significant gains toward eliminating it. But despite their claims, increasingly there are reports of prostitution in some cities in China. It may be that China and Vietnam will follow the same pattern as has been discerned in Cuba and Russia, whose post-revolutionary claims to eliminate prostitution have been reduced to acceptance.

2. Toleration (Abolitionist System)
Toleration is most closely in accordance with the United Nations 1949 convention and has been adopted in many European countries. The system that legally tolerates prostitution makes pimping and procuring illegal. Prostitutes are not criminals by virtue of their work; therefore they have more access to the rights of citizens. Law enforcement is more successful in prosecuting pimps. There is more compassion in the society for the plight of these women as human beings, which is indicated by the relatively larger number of refuge centers for prostitutes found in some countries under this system.

Although there are no laws forbidding the act of prostitution, each country espousing toleration carries other laws on its book which are used to control and/or harass street prostitutes. In France, for example, laws against loitering and soliciting are used against prostitutes, who receive stiff fines when cited for these offenses.

In 1978, according to the French Ministry of Interior, *proxénétisme* (pimping and procuring) was the third largest business in France, with a $7 billion annual profit.[10] *Proxénétisme* is vigorously prosecuted in France; 1,451 cases were handled in 1973 alone.[11]

Proxénétisme is largely organized in gangs known as the *milieu*, and prostitution is only one of several rackets they run. It is said that in many cases of French cities one cannot work as a prostitute on the streets or in hotels without payoff to the *milieu*.[12] While there has been a recent increase in individual or free-lance pimping and procuring in France, the *milieu* still controls many of the 953 prostitution hotels in France.[13]

Proprietors of these *hôtels de passe* are considered *proxénétes*. They reserve some rooms in their hotel to be rented out to travelers or immigrants to avoid being charged with running a closed house. Other rooms are rented to the prostitute on a daily or weekly basis. Prostitutes are required to take between ten and twenty customers (*passes*) daily just to meet room rent. Most proprietors will not rent to a woman without a pimp. The excuse used is that a couple is more reliable for the rent, but this is just a police cover for the tight connection between proprietors and pimps.[14]

There have been charges that police protection and kickbacks have hampered enforcement of laws against *proxénétisme* in France. Vigorous enforcement is restricted by the use of many of those in the *milieu* as established police informers, creating a brotherhood of hotel proprietors, pimps, and police. Laws against pimping, while providing minimal protection to prostitutes, are designed to prevent prostitutes from having friends or lovers. The law, based on habitual behavior, defines as a pimp *anyone* who gives assistance to a prostitute, takes money from her, or lives with her.

In 1975 prostitutes took over a church in Lyon and began a strike that spread to every major city in France. The strike was sparked by a sudden increase in fines (averaging $45 each in 1975) of prostitutes in Lyon. Many women working on the street were getting several fines a night, and they alleged that the police were pocketing the money. While many of the women involved in the strike did not have pimps, it was learned later that one of the main organizers worked for a big-time pimp who encouraged the strike to protest the way his income was being affected by the fines.

The French prostitutes condemned proposals to adopt the German system of prostitution and set up eros centers in France. "We will never become the civil servants of sex," said Ulla, one organizer. The prostitutes denounced the system that would make them functionaries of the State, which then would become the biggest pimp of all.

3. Regulation

Many areas have adopted the regulationist system: South Korea, West Germany, Beirut in Lebanon, Amsterdam in Holland, and Nevada in the United States are some examples. In contrast to the toleration of prostitution by abolitionist countries, regulation *enforces* prostitution, especially through closed houses or eros centers. It is the most direct legal attempt to hide the otherwise visible double standard.

Germany has boasted that its system is the model for regulation of prostitution. Prostitution in Germany may not be banned in cities over 20,000; each city may regulate the practice itself. Pimping and procuring are illegal, and prostitutes, who must be at least 18, are required to have regular venereal disease checks and carry health cards. Income from prostitution is taxed but prostitutes are not eligible for unemployment or social security.[15] In most cities, prostitutes are restricted to a certain section of the city and are allowed to work on the streets, that is, to be visible, only between 8 P.M. and 6 A.M.

But prostitutes resist being hidden away: it has been estimated that only half the prostitutes are registered in some German cities. In 1976 police in Hamburg estimated that there were 2,400 registered prostitutes and 2,500 not registered there. In that year 3,000 prostitutes were registered in West Berlin and 800 in Munich.[16]

It is estimated that 80 to 95 percent of the German prostitutes have pimps,[17] and earlier evidence presented here reveals the prevalence of gangs operating on the prostitution scene. According to Die Arch, a prostitute refuge center in Hamburg, women cannot get into most eros centers without a pimp. Yondorf, who conducted research on prostitution in Germany, found that between October 1, 1974, and July 15, 1975, the following pimp-related crimes were reported in West Berlin alone:[18]

Procurement of minors	9
Procurement of prostitutes generally	127
White slave trade	8
Pimping	85

For the average citizen there is no visible problem of prostitution in Germany. One could live there for years and never
see any evidence of it. Carefully contained within certain
sections of the city, prostitutes, as well as the abuse of them,
are unknown to the rest of the city or the world. Those in
eros centers are further hidden. Realizing the German history for hiding atrocities, I shuddered as I was told by some
women sociologists in Bonn that there was no need to
study prostitution in Germany. This problem, I was told
emphatically, had been solved. Prostitution is regulated,
hygienic, and out of the way.

The United States version of eros centers is found in
Nevada, which boasts of allowing regulated prostitution
throughout the state except in Reno and Las Vegas. One
prostitute described Joe Conforte's Mustang Ranch in
Nevada as "just like a prison." And the fact is that the
security is so tight there that one never knows whether the
iron gates and guard tower are keeping the women in or
troublemakers out. Located in a deserted area outside of
Reno, Mustang Ranch looks and feels like a 1940's style
prison. After confirming by telephone Conforte's invitation
to "come on up," I went there with a friend for a tour and
to interview the women. When we arrived, we were refused
the opportunity to talk to the women working there, then
we were denied a tour of the premises as had been promised, and finally we were mysteriously turned away. We
were given contradictory stories, first told that Joe was out
of town and later that he was busy. We were told to return
to our hotel and that he would call us, but he never did.

In the short time we were there, we observed the central
room which has a large bar and is decorated in red with
several huge sofas. About 50 girls work there at any one
time. There were about 20 working the afternoon we arrived, 15 white women, 3 black, and 2 Asian women,
with a few male prostitutes around.

The place was almost silent, as the girls are not allowed
to talk to each other nor are they permitted to read. They
just sit around until the buzzer sounds. Then they all jump
up, put plastic smiles on their faces, and line up at the
front door. Dressed in body stockings or bikinis, they stand
mute until one is chosen from the lineup by the trick. Five

tricks came in during the fifteen minutes we managed to stay on our short visit there.

According to the prostitute we interviewed (who no longer works at Mustang), a woman coming to Mustang must work a minimum of three weeks before she can leave. She must earn $1,000 a week in the summer and $500 in the winter to stay. The girls work 14 to 16 hours a day, with three weeks on and one off. They don't get out unless they can hustle a date who wants to take them into Reno or unless they get permission to leave for two hours of shopping.

The cut is 50-50 with the house. Extra charges leave the woman with more like 40 percent of the take if she is lucky. She pays 10 percent of her take for room and board (but not more than $10 daily), plus $1 a day to the night maid, $1 to the cashier, $1 for each pair of panties washed, and $2 for each house gown washed. And then there are the weekly venereal disease checkups—$20 for the exam and $2 for each prescription written plus the cost of having the prescription filled. According to the ex-employee we interviewed, almost any kind of drug is dispensed.

Most of the girls at Mustang have pimps. Some people say that prostitutes need a pimp even to get in. Pimps come up weekly (usually from Las Vegas) to collect what is left of their money after the house takes its cut. When the heat is on from the police in Oakland, San Francisco, or Los Angeles, or when a pimp has been arrested, the women are sent to Mustang to work until business on the streets can be resumed as usual.

Despite the prison-like setting and the long working hours, many girls prefer the Mustang arrangement to the streets. Prostitution is legal and Mustang provides minimal protection from customer violence. Local authorities don't interfere with Mustang's own private security system. As they seem to exist outside the law, it is impossible to know the nature and extent of violence there.

In Lincoln County, the closest point of legalized prostitution to Las Vegas, connections have been asserted between organized crime and the brothels, according to one District Attorney there. There are two brothels (or cat houses, as they are called) that are long-term establishments in Lincoln County. Recently a third one opened and immediately was burned to the ground. Murders have occurred that have the stamp of organized crime, with bodies found in the desert.

Regulated prostitution has accomplished nothing it has boasted of. It has not cut down on crime associated with prostitution. According to the police in Reno, the closest city to Mustang, rape there, as everywhere else, continues to increase. Pimps are as prevalent as in any other system of prostitution. Venereal disease checks would have to take place after every client to be effective in controlling the disease. And prostitutes are taxed by the state instead of fined by the courts, but they are not given social security or other benefits normally given to taxpayers. In addition, the regulationist system with legal houses provides both business incentive and legal protection for the traffic in women, as earlier evidence of traffic into Germany illustrates.

Visible street prostitution exposes the double standard that allows masculinist societies around the world to accept prostitution as a needed outlet for men while condemning it as immoral. If prostitution took place only behind closed doors—in brothels, prostitution hotels, and the back rooms of bars—then the double standards which promote and protect prostitution, sexual violence, and sexual slavery would be carefully concealed. Expendable women would be used, abused, and forgotten.

Neither prostitutes nor the pimps behind many of them are amenable to such invisibility. Street prostitution is everywhere. It is the blatant, visible demonstration of the sexual double standard that men try desperately to hide. In some cities the management of hotels, restaurants, and shops complain that prostitutes have gotten so bold that they solicit men who are with their wives. They claim hookers are hurting their business. Many hotel proprietors who provide holding tanks for police to sweep prostitutes off the street, also have informal agreements with bar girls who hook *inside* the hotel.

Visible prostitution is uncomfortable to the tricks who need to have social distance and separation between whores and wives. It is uncomfortable to the police who must uphold morality while still allowing prostitution to exist. And it is uncomfortable to tourists, shoppers, and city dwellers who would rather not see what they believe must be inevitable.

The fact is that patriarchal government has found no system of prostitution that isn't abusive and doesn't exploit women. Each system in its own way locks women into prostitution. In systems in which women are criminals, they can hardly expect justice to turn in their favor or protection to be granted to them. Where prostitution is legally accepted and regulated, the exploitation of prostitutes by pimps and customers is forgotten. Where prostitution is tolerated, as in France, prostitutes are still hassled on the streets and closed houses like the *maisons d'abattage* still exist under double standards of justice. Thus all systems yield to the insistence that prostitution is a necessary social service; at the same time they hate and condemn the women who provide it.

A CULTURAL UNIVERSAL?

It has become popular in some circles to propose that prostitutes be unionized. It is argued that prostitution is a job or profession like any other work. These proposals leave some very major questions unasked. For example, who is management? Neither farm nor factory workers would organize for improved working conditions without a clear delineation of the power structure they are facing. Do prostitutes organize against or with pimps?

The question suggests how liberal rhetoric is based on unspoken assumptions about prostitution. In another example, many groups concerned with the conditions of alienated labor in the society seek to organize workers in the factories and on the farms. Yet while one sector promotes the notion of prostitution as a regular job, the other does not stop to consider that it is likely that prostitutes more than any other group are alienated labor—alienated from their sexual being, their erotic life, their freedom to live without violence.

As a result of the inaccurate designation of prostitution as a profession, women, in light of the politics of feminism, equate the exploitation of housewives with the exploitation of prostitutes, assuming both should be recognized as regular jobs. It is what I think of as the "equality of violence" argument:

Women are beaten and murdered by husbands, boy-
friends and strangers. Generally, the frequency of
prostitutes being abused is not out of proportion when
you consider (1) the number of straight women in
this country who are physically hurt and (2) the stress
factors in the occupation and lifestyle of the prostitutes.[19]

Implicit in this argument is the assumption that violence in
the life of women is inevitable. Prostitute organizations
usually focus on one aspect of the oppression of prostitutes
—the State; that is, laws, police, and courts. Few organizations have addressed the oppression and abuse of prostitutes by pimps and tricks. As a result, prostitution has been
described as a victimless crime, paid sex between consenting adults.

All of these arguments and discussions center around
one theme: prostitution is a necessary and inevitable social
service, a cultural universal. As long as it is here and will
always be with us, we should make the best of it, so the
argument goes. The theme is reinforced through popular
romanticization of "the life."

Romanticization of prostitution, coloring the setting and
the services with glamour, fun, and excitement, legitimizes
it to the public as a social institution and deflects attention
from the violence that surrounds it, the enslavement of
women in it. The romantic view presents a life of expensive
and exotic clothes, first-class travel, indulgent liberated sex,
and lots of money. It is the life of the "happy hooker"—
wherein one "makes love" instead of "turning tricks" and a
client is a "lover" not a "john." It is paid sex where the
customer states his needs and both partners swoon their
way to fantastic orgasms. Big money and constant sexual
satisfaction are disrupted only by an occasional annoying
raid from the police.

Through romanticization, all prostitution becomes synonymous with high-class call girls' work. High-class call girl
prostitution is indeed profitable because it serves the expensive and bizarre habits of our nations' business and political leaders. But life in the brothel is not plush, erotic
excitement. A former call girl, who is now working in a
shelter trying to get young girls out of prostitution, told me
that in her opinion one reason she and all the other call

girls she knew went through their money so fast and couldn't save "for that boutique in the sky" was that to her it wasn't clean money. After six years in the life she left. "When I found myself crying as I turned tricks I knew that I couldn't take life that way anymore."

The "service" provided in prostitution is not just traditional sex but the fulfillment of those sexual demands men cannot or choose not to fulfill in other areas of their life, with girl friend or wife. Their demand is for kinky or perverted and perhaps violent sex. While some clients are looking only for sexual contact, many are seeking an opportunity to experience sexual excitement in the context of humiliation, degradation, beatings, or even torture. In one study, 67 percent of the women interviewed had been seriously injured by customers.[20]

Some customers of high-class call girls prefer sadomasochistic sex where they can assume the role of slave, the tortured one. It has been argued that it is the woman who is in control and who holds the power in these encounters. But Janus and Bess, in their study of *A Sexual Profile of Men in Power*, found that the client is always the powerful one. They are businessmen and politicians who see all life as an exercise of power and are able to rise victorious from their own pain and suffering, having been purified by it, proving their ability to take it and demonstrating a certain kind of martyrdom. The man who demands the painful rituals acts from the "knowledge that as he is directing, casting, and paying for the whole thing, he is completely controlling the situation. In this perverse logic, it is just when all is hopeless and he is seemingly shorn of all power that he is most in command."[21]

Is this a social service that men *must* have provided them, that women *must* perform?

In no other form of slavery are those in power called upon to love those whom they have found to be inferior and despicable. Male domination reduces women to a lower status, holding them in low regard, and at the same time it makes women the object of men's personal need for love, romance, and sex. The oppressors of women carry the unique responsibility of masculinist values to both love and hate women. Some men will be able to reject this contradictory role but others will need to act out its mandate.* Wife-beaters exemplify men who contain the mandate to both love and hate women within one relationship. Other men who do not want to inflict contempt, disgust, and hatred on their loved one may still need to act it out. Prostitution provides that opportunity. It creates a neat and socially sanctioned separation between madonna and whore. This misogyny, the use of prostitutes to act out one's contempt for the lower and degraded sex, is the single most powerful reason why prostitution has always been considered a cultural universal—the oldest profession, the indestructible institution, the necessary social service. It intersects with the domination of women at all levels of society.

* Rich Snowdon from San Francisco-based Men Against Sexist Violence sees this contradictory mandate in terms of fear. "Men are profoundly afraid of women and children, just as anyone who oppresses has every reason to be afraid of resistance and revolt from those they oppress. Men are taught first to fear their victims, and then to react with a desperate, driven anger."

Patricia Hearst: "Did I Ever Have a Chance?"

Patricia Hearst was kidnapped, beaten, tortured, raped, and then herself imprisoned for the crimes that resulted from her victimization. Her case is prototypical of female slavery. When I talked to her in prison in July 1978, I asked her if she saw it that way, too. Her voice was emphatic: "What happened to me happened because I was a young female college student, an easy target. Women are always the easiest targets! It was unique only in the sense that what happened to me happens to many women but for me it was taken to the extreme. I feel that I can identify with many forms of oppression—I have been kidnapped, beaten, raped. I have been a prisoner in both county jails and federal prisons."

Patricia was kidnapped by self-styled leftist terrorists, not by a pimp. She was turned out as a revolutionary bandit, not as a prostitute. The rhetoric of her captors was different from that of pimps but the seasoning that broke Patricia was as calculated as that of the best-trained slave procurers. The social attitudes and legal actions that coalesced around Patricia directly parallel those towards other women in slavery. In the public's mind she became the cause of her own victimization. In the eyes of the law she was a common criminal—not for hooking, loitering, or disturbing the peace, but for bank robbery.

On February 4, 1974, a member of an organization calling itself the Symbionese Liberation Army (SLA) kidnapped 19-year-old Patricia Hearst, an heiress of the Hearst publishing and corporate empire, from the Berkeley apartment where she lived with her fiancé, Steven Weed. Three days later, from a secret hideaway, the SLA announced that Patricia was a prisoner of war and, shortly after that, escaped convict Donald DeFreeze (who called himself "Cinque") set forth a ransom demand for a $6 million food giveaway program for the poor.

It was only a few days after her kidnapping that theories began to develop in radical circles that Patricia Hearst planned her own kidnapping. According to prevailing conjecture, she was a rich kid out for fun, rebelling against the social restrictions of upper-class life. At the time, no one knew much about people in the SLA except that they had taken responsibility for the murder of Oakland School's black superintendent, Marcus Foster, and that they claimed to have revolutionary combat units around the country. While there was not an immediate round of applause from left-radicals for the SLA, there was an instant hatred for Patricia Hearst—a "she's getting what she deserves" feeling. The lines were drawn as the right wing and conservative public expressed pity for the poor young girl and sympathy for her abused father.

Details of Patricia's background, her childhood, school days, and affair with Weed began to come out. The portrayal of Patty as a docile and easily led but rebellious teenager fed both leftist theories and right-wing pity. Public opinion at this point was still malleable, able to shift according to new theories or available gossip—and there was some genuine worry and concern for her well-being.

But the events of April 3 and 15, 1974, changed everything. On the 3rd, a tape recording was released by the SLA in which Patricia announced her decision to join the SLA, and on the 15th she was photographed with others in a robbery of the Hibernia Bank in San Francisco.

Her kidnappers had made her a symbol of corporate abuses and oppression by the rich. The public up to now had been tentative about what symbolic value to attach to these events. Now Patricia became visible in rhetoric and apparent acts of defiance. Immediately the sands shifted and solidified again. Now the left's "I told you so" attitude merged into the right's condemnation as they saw their cherished values being trampled by one of America's formerly finest. Public attitudes expressed a sense of inevitability; they ranged from "what can you expect from the rich" to "there is no way to control these teenagers today." These judgments catapulted into an inevitable hatred of

Patricia; she became everybody's symbol. She was envied, condemned, pitied, or ridiculed for being a spoiled brat or loving daughter, a kidnap victim or a revolutionary, a brainwashed neurotic or a common criminal, a rich kid out for adventure or a helpless victim. Now seen as just a symbol, she was no longer a human being either to the SLA or to the public.

As events passed from the bank robbery to a silent year and a half underground, to her arrest, imprisonment, and trial, people began to complain bitterly about Patricia's taking up so much space in the news and having so much attention paid to her. It was a weird twist of logic, for she had no control over the press that was apparently responding to her newsworthiness. The public had been captivated by her and then hated her for occupying its attention. Her symbolic value had been completed. As she was not a human being to the public, she could be disposed of whenever she was no longer of use. She had once told a CBS news reporter how frightening it was to be with the SLA, never knowing whether the "people you're with (are) going to kill you because you out-lived your usefulness to them." Later, after the trials, after she was out on bail, and when she was finally returned to prison, the public was bored and resentful and in a few cases truly believed justice had been stretched too far in her sentencing.

Patricia was enslaved as much by the public's use of her as a symbol as by the SLA's need for a publicity trip to carry off its version of revolution. I asked her why she thought this was so. She replied: "I think people's own fears about themselves were exposed. People saw in me weaknesses in themselves that they were afraid of—like fears that they could be broken down. It's hard for people to face that. They couldn't stomp that out for themselves. It was cathartic for them to stomp me out."

And stomped out she was. After almost two years underground with William and Emily Harris, the only remnants of the SLA after a Los Angeles shootout, Patricia was arrested with them in San Francisco on September 18, 1976. Usually, when a kidnap victim is forced to commit crimes while with her captors, there is no prosecution for those crimes. Nevertheless, not only was Patricia charged for the Hibernia Bank robbery, but her case was mysteriously moved ahead on the crowded court calendar. The government was taken with a fever to bring this victim to justice, to make a lesson of her.

Patricia was able to explain her participation in the Hibernia Bank robbery only in terms of her enslavement and abuse from the SLA. At her trial she testified that after she was abducted from her apartment, her life was constantly threatened while she was held bound and blindfolded, first in one hot stuffy closet and then in another for 57 days. For two weeks she was allowed to go the bathroom only at her captors' will, and later she would be allowed to go when she knocked on the door. After she had spent two weeks in the closet, her hands were tied in front of her; she was grateful that they no longer had to be tied behind her. Her menstrual period stopped. She was fed periodically, but initially she couldn't eat. When she did, she was often forced to sit blindfolded outside the closet in the humiliation of knowing her captors were watching and ridiculing while she was trying to eat. She was given a bath weekly by her captors, who wore ski masks, while her blindfold was off, and the very removal of the blindfold caused her extreme pain and distortion of vision when the light hit her eyes. From inside the closet either she would hear music continuously playing outside the door or she would hear her captors' guns: "I could hear a lot of clicking and noises; and, it sounded like clips going in and out of guns and sometimes . . . they'd make noises like they were shooting and I could tell like that they were standing right in front of the closet and doing it at me."[1] During her 57-day confinement, the SLA moved from Daly City to a Golden Gate apartment. Patricia was stuffed into a garbage can for the move.

She was told that she had to pay for the alleged capitalist sins of her parents. In pain and humiliation, she was dependent on her captors for air, for food, for the opportunity to urinate, for her life. This dependency was reinforced when she was ordered to make the first taped message telling her family, "Mom, Dad, I'm okay," and asking her father to cooperate with her captors. A tape recorder was brought to her in the closet, and she was given instructions on how to make the first message. Later the SLA women berated her for not doing well enough and reported her to Cinque, who meted out her punishment with sexual abuse.

At one point she was approached in the closet by Angela Atwood. "She said I was going to sleep with William Wolfe," Patricia recalled. Later, according to Patricia, Wolfe entered the closet and raped her. She was raped again by Cinque about a week later. During her trial, Patricia testified to her hatred for Willie Wolfe. Emily Harris called a news conference and denied that Wolfe could have stirred such negative feelings in Patricia, declaring him to be one of the sweetest, most gentle men she had ever known. But Mizmoon, an SLA member who died in the Los Angeles shootout, recorded in her poetry a feeling closer to that of Patricia's:

> Willy . . . I hate him
> I want to scream
> next time he touches me
> Get your God Damned Hand off
>   My Body!
> (but his hands never were)
> damned . . . he's bein' only
> friendly . . . I'm not being
> paid to have him maul me
> Get your damned mind off my body![2]

After 57 days Patricia was allowed to leave the closet, and two days later, she reports, Nancy Ling Perry cut her hair down to one inch all over her head. Prior to leaving the closet, she was probably allowed out occasionally for some exercise and political discussion. During these discussions she realized that the SLA knew more about her father's wealth than she did. She was endlessly interrogated with questions she could not answer and demands for information she did not have. This tactic kept her in the untenable position of trying to meet her captors' impossible expectations while her sense of futility and helplessness increased, engendering in her guilt for the wealth and practices of the Hearst empire.

Probably the pivotal question on which rested the credibility of her word concerned her willingness to join the

SLA. On April 3, 1974, in a tape-recorded communique from the SLA, Patricia's voice pronounced:

> I have been given a choice of, one, being released in a safe area, or two, joining the forces of the Symbionese Liberation Army and fighting for my freedom and the freedom of all oppressed people. I have chosen to stay and fight.

In open court on February 9, 1976, she described the situation in which that decision had been made. She recalled how her captors, as an April Fool's joke, had notified her parents that she would be released on April 1. She testified:

> Well, a few weeks before, DeFreeze told me that the war council had decided or was thinking about killing me or me staying with them, and that I better start thinking about that as a possibility. Then he came in later and said that I could go home or stay with them. I didn't believe them.[3]

Patricia had to make a decision at that moment, a decision that followed 57 days of abuse and torture while confined in a closet. Her decision was not whether to join the SLA and play at revolution or go home to Mom and Dad. Her decision, based on a reasonable evaluation of her circumstances, was whether or not to stay alive. She made the decision of a survivor, but the world saw it as an act of defiance, the frivolity that only the rich can afford.

Whether before the U.S. courts or the SLA war council, Patricia's life was dependent on her word. And in her trial, her word—which ultimately was her only defense—counted for very little. At times it worked against her; it never seemed to work in her behalf.

What would make her word so suspect? Regardless of her recent history with the SLA, she had not proven herself by any standards of criminality to be innately deceptive. It was remembered, of course, that she had evaded an embarrassed FBI for nearly two years, but it was quickly forgotten that her life as a fugitive was spawned by a vengeful kidnapping.

Her kidnapping was of negligible consideration in her trial. Her report of it was the only thing that all parties—defense, prosecution, judge, and jury—accepted. Why? Steven Weed had many times publicly described the kidnapping of his then fiancée, Patricia. He didn't even need to appear in the courtroom or testify at the trial. Male corroboration was enough in order for Patricia, like rape victims or prostitutes, to be believed. For the rest of it—her life as a kidnap victim, as a fugitive—we have only *her* word, *her* testimony.

ON LYING

Did Patricia Hearst tell the whole truth and nothing but the truth, so help her god? It is argued that she lied to save her life; it is not argued that she told the truth to save her life. It is argued that the attorneys gave her a story to fit their strategy; it is not argued that her defense attorneys developed a strategy based on her story.

Who would believe her?

Not the prosecution that overzealously pursued justice against a kidnap victim placed in a bank robbery.

Not the judge who, after her conviction, could have chosen the lenient route of sentencing her under the Youthful Offenders Act, which would have probably given her immediate probation. He instead chose the harshest possible sentencing, giving her a full seven years in federal prison, noting that *her* conduct could not be condoned, that a lesson must be made of *her* to serve as a deterrent to others.

Not her lawyers. The defense strategy used by F. Lee Bailey was, in my opinion, a clear statement to Patricia and to the world of his lack of confidence in his client's veracity. Would he have portrayed her as a mindless, brainwashed victim if he didn't believe she was guilty as charged? I think that by depicting her as hopelessly empty-headed, he not only catered to the stereotyped public image of her, but he also tried to deny the very action she had to take in her own behalf, which was the only key to her survival. He legitimized *his* picture of her by the use of experts. (Patricia told me that she saw about twelve different psychiatrists during the period from her arrest to the trial.) While she was simply a witness in her defense, one psychiatrist after another presented his expertise, attempting to assert or destroy, through that expertise, the credibility of her word. According to this strategy, she did not have to be believed. Legitimized authority assumed that responsibility. Judge and jury were asked to believe not Patricia's words, but the experts' analysis of *her motivations for those words and actions.*

When the Court dismissed the relevance of the experts' testimony on Patricia's state of mind, all that was left for the jury was her word, and they did not believe it. In fact one juror I interviewed summoned considerable respect for Patricia's captors: "It is difficult for me to conceive that all seven of those people were crazy, all mad dogs. . . . These people appeared to treat her in some reasonable fashion." Neither did the jurors believe she was raped. Another man on the jury stated he was not sure: "It could have gone one way or another," and "it was only her word." Another juror, discussing Patricia's confinement in the closet, asserted, "We [the jury] didn't think she had been in the closet that long. . . . In deliberations we felt she had been in the closet *only two weeks.*" [emphasis mine] Clearly most people never think about what it might be like to be locked in a closet—for two weeks or 57 days. The inability of people to put themselves in Patricia's place, to understand what she faced and how she faced it in order to survive, especially when they had the responsibility of judging her, is a clear indication of the extent to which she had become a symbol devoid of any humanity.

Each of the jurors I interviewed described Patricia as listless, empty, pale. In awaiting her answers to her attorneys' questions about the brutality she experienced from the SLA, the jury expected to hear emotional outbursts. But as one juror said of her testimony on being raped, "She described it so calmly and didn't have any emotion in her voice." This led another juror to assert that she had simply been programmed by her attorneys. "She fit exactly what she was portrayed to be—selfless, helpless, defenseless creature." And so, it was reasoned, Patricia was lying through her body as well as through her words. Her clothes, her tone of voice, her complexion, her sad eyes all meant—to the jury and the vigilant public that followed this trial—something other than what they were. In a society that requires women to lie through their bodies with makeup, wigs, bras, girdles, and other affectations, it is assumed that women never look like what they really are. And yet, not to dress in the expected role may bring down the wrath of society on women, causing them to be labeled "loose" or "deviant."

The only voice in this proceeding that credited Patricia's word—a voice that was not officially heard in the deliberations—was that of Mary Neiman, an alternate juror who would have held out for acquittal even if it meant a hung jury. But she never made it into deliberations. Agreeing that Patricia was listless in the courtroom, Mary saw this condition as a result of her experiences and an indication of her truthfulness. In talking to Mary it was clear that her point of reference was a consideration of how any of her daughters would have responded in similar circumstances. "If she were lying, she would have tried to make herself look better," Mary said. While dramatic testimony would have impressed other jurors, Mary was convinced by Patricia's simple statements of what she did. For example, when asked why she wrote on the wall of one apartment in Spanish and signed her name "Tania," she said only that everybody else did it and they expected her to do it, so she did. Surviving couldn't be as simple as that for the other jurors, who, like the public, needed to see violent force from the SLA determining Patricia's every action.

Shortly after her trial, Patricia's lung collapsed, and after surgery her doctors reported that she was generally in a debilitated condition. A legitimate authority on her physical condition finally made her pale, listless state real, even believable. But it was too late. She had already been convicted for lying.

PATRICIA SPEAKS ABOUT SURVIVING

It was not stubbornness but pride that prevented Patricia from giving the jury and the public the dramatic display they were expecting. "I think people wanted to see something dramatic from me. They wanted to see me break down. I did everything I could to hold myself together. It would have been so humiliating to break down after all I had been through."

It was four months from her arrest in San Francisco to the Hibernia Bank trial. She had been broken by the SLA and then kept in their constant companionship for two years. It was hardly surprising that she had not been able to compensate for the effects of those two years in four months. She accounted for her demeanor in the courtroom: "I was still very sick. I had lost a lot of weight. I had malnutrition and had just had pneumonia and the flu. I had not recovered psychologically from what had happened to me and I was very tired. During the trial, I was kept in the holding tank where all the drunks were at the county jail. I never got any sleep with all the yelling and carrying on in cells around me."

Two years after her trial, having been out on bail for eighteen months, Patricia has been able to reflect on why this has happened. In our discussions I was taken by the relativity of her statements when she evaluated her present conditions in terms of her previous enslavement. She was back in prison, having exhausted all appeals in her case. At the time of our meeting she was faced with the likelihood of six more years behind bars, but she could say: "Prison isn't the worst place to be. They try to threaten you with discipline slips here. I never get any, but if I let that little piece of paper have any meaning for me I would never make it. I can't think of it as anything more than a piece of paper. After all, what can they do to hurt me? Nothing! They can't put a gun to my head and threaten to shoot me."

Few of us have ever faced so continuous a threat of being murdered as Patricia has. When the FBI was in mad pursuit of the SLA and the shootout occurred in Los Angeles, Patricia watched the TV with horror as other SLA members were fired upon and eventually the house was burned down, all the time police and newscasters stating they believed she was in the house they were shooting at and burning down. When I asked her what she thought was the single most important thing that she could attribute to her survival, she simply, almost offhandedly responded, "Luck. I was just lucky so many times to not be someplace when I would have been killed, like being in the house in Los Angeles when it was burned down. Everytime something awful happened that could have killed me, I missed it."

Surely, there was more to her survival than luck. Patricia began to open up: "I guess you have to have an ability to do something to stay alive. Some people just give up and don't make it. Staying alive means that you don't give up. You want to stay alive so much that you do anything you have to—it's a selfish state in the sense that you are only able to focus on yourself and how to get through it alive. That is the point in surviving when you feel you have made it at the loss of your self-respect."

It was the shift from living in crisis-dominated moment-to-moment survival to being in jail faced with a different survival that first allowed her introspection on her behavior in a crisis state. "Self-respect is most important to surviving. You have to be able to look at yourself in the mirror in the morning. When I realized the things I had to do just to stay alive, I started feeling confused and guilty about it wondering, 'how could I let myself do this or that.' My psychiatrist helped me a great deal with that guilt."

Patricia described how she had to turn inward and draw from her own reserves in order to survive. She depended only on herself—"No one else can get you through something like this. People are so used to TV programs where, when someone is in danger, there is always someone there in minutes to rescue them. My youngest sister had an awfully hard time facing that I wouldn't just automatically be rescued. When you are held captive, people somehow expect you to spit in your captor's face and get killed."

THE MISSING YEARS:
WAS SHE PATTY OR TANIA?

The way society treats victims of rape is similar to its treatment of victims of female sexual slavery. But the experience of rape is different from that of slavery in one significant respect: time. The period of time for which one is held captive, tortured, and abused, the dependency created over that time, and the effect of trying to survive on one's identity are significantly different for victims of slavery. In this context Patricia's experience sheds light on the experiences of women forced into prostitution. Simply, when one foresees the probability of escape in ten minutes or ten hours, one will behave differently than if, in addition to all the torture and violence, there is no foreseeable probability of escape. In the latter state, the world becomes closed; vision narrows only to present experience. The victim's world is only what is contained in the immediate moment.

When there is a possibility of getting out of a situation, a woman will do what is necessary to survive, whether that be going passive or physically fighting back. Which of those options is chosen depends on the context of the situation, the degree of force used against her, the extent to which she is not immobilized by terror, the training in attitude and physical self-defense she has had. But when there is no possibility of getting out, survival inevitably necessitates redefining oneself to fit the new circumstances.

At the same time, she may be overwhelmed with fear. Males are socialized to fight against fear, to not yield to its force. Females, on the other hand, learn at an early age to accept their fears, submit to them, and then randomly— without design—try to fight their way out. Overwhelming fear increases the sense of terror. Dr. West, one of the psychiatrists who examined Patricia, found this phenomenon to be critical in the violence she experienced: "I would say it was more violent than any military captive, because these, after all, were soldiers and had been trained and gone through various kinds of hardening experiences before they were captured."[4]

Patricia's report of her circumstances, and the reported experiences of other women forced into slavery indicate that enslavement takes place in two phases. First, the victim faces the immediate terror of being kidnapped and physically abused. Like the rape victim, she tries to make sense out of what's happening, to figure it out, to get away. She makes every reasonable interpretation of her captors' behavior that she can from the information she has available to her. She is used to interacting and interpreting the world around her. On the basis of our interpretations, we come to understand, change, and grow. Dr. West found that for Patricia "her usual coping techniques, mobility, independence, autonomy, use of allies, winning the esteem of others by performing well, self-assertion and so on— these were all useless. Her external points of reference for maintenance of her identity had disappeared. All her sources of self-esteem were cut off. At times, the entire situation began to seem unreal to her and, at other times, it was she who seemed unreal or it was another person who was having these unthinkable experiences."[5]

Unlike rape victims, who will eventually get away from their attacker, however shattered they may be from the rape, a woman enslaved cannot physically leave. She must find another way out. It is a common human response when one is faced with tragedy to react with "this couldn't be happening to me." Therefore, when tragedy is unending, when enslavement is total, it should hardly be startling that the conditional is transformed into the permanent: "This *isn't* happening to me." The victim becomes another person, not only as a way to handle the situation but as a result of her captors' forced redefinition of her identity, indeed, her world.

Whether it is with the SLA, through an international ring of procurers, or at the hands of individual pimps, the seasoning of enslaved women enforces a complete dependency on their captors and it makes for them a new identity. Often the question is asked: why didn't she just fake it? The answer is simple and obvious—you don't fake in the presence of murderers, rapists, and torturers. The assumption underlying the question is of course that only a weak, malleable personality would assume the new identity that results from the enslavement. That assumption ignores the impact of female socialization on the ability to survive and it discounts the effects of the seasoning that is purposefully used to destroy a person's identity. Dr. West testified in Patricia's case that after she was released from the closet,

> She was persuaded to take on a certain role and she complied with everything they told her to do. . . . And if she took her part with the group, she just tried to blend in with others and behave in a fashion that she understood was to be accepted. For her, it was be accepted or be killed. Now after they finally went through the sort of little ceremony where she was taken out of the closet after about eight weeks and allowed to take off her blindfold and sit down and eat with the others for the first time as a member, sort of,

sometime soon after that, she was given her name by
Cinque. . . .

Then after she . . . had assumed the role of Tania,
she began to try to be like they wanted her to be—
if she was going to be Tania, that meant writing
venceremos [we will conquer] on the wall with a can
of paint or something, if that's what was expected of
her.[6]

I think Gabel in his study on reification and false consciousness summarized the result of slavery succinctly:
"*Identification with the enemy is the worst form of depersonalization; it is the loss of freedom to be oneself.*"[7]

During Patricia's captivity her social world consisted
only of people who hated her. With them she would be
able to live only in the moment, never knowing and not
having control over what the future would be. Her world
now consisted only of the SLA, their actions, and their
rhetoric. It was an unreal world in that she was cut off
from life as a process, a progression. What we normally
take for granted as life evolving through interaction and
involvement was denied by this group, which lived only in
the context of their rhetoric, not by experience; only by
"correct" positions on issues, not through interaction and
relationships around issues. Patricia could not take into
account a total environment, for she was removed from it
and did not know the world beyond what the SLA told her
it was, what she experienced in the confines of their various hideouts.

Positive change or growth is impossible in a situation in
which time is rigidified into only the present, interaction is
denied, interpretation becomes meaningless. Change normally evolves out of interaction in relationship with people,
one's environment; it is a progression, a movement over
time. When time is halted, progression ceases and the
world is narrowed so as to make interaction almost meaningless. This is the context of the very young child who has
not learned interaction but is totally self-centered, living in
the present moment. Gabel describes this state as the "loss
of the dialectic of the possible and impossible."[8]

In slavery "the possible" is truly denied. The future is
cut off. Life is only in the immediate moment. One does

not think about whether or not to go to a movie, take a certain job, plan a course of study, have a child, or become a revolutionary for lack of anything better to do.

In addition to the torture and imprisonment in closets that inevitably caused her to take on a new identity, the politics and rhetoric of the SLA formed the not-real-world in which she was held. Life for them was an abstraction, a denial of the process of existence. By making their rhetoric into their style of behavior and by assuming a political superiority to the real world, they separated themselves from the real world, living a life based on abstraction which gave them a context to legitimize untold exploitation. That was the world in which Patricia Hearst took on the identity of Tania.

When I first met Patricia two years after her arrest and trial, she was looking well. She had gained weight and recovered her psychological as well as physical strength. But her focus on the present, the immediate situation, was startling to me. She would spend considerable time talking about what happened that day, but when I asked questions that involved thinking about the past or the future, her answers initially were brief, one word. For example:

Q. *What was the most significant factor in your survival since you were kidnapped?*
A. *Luck.*
Q. *What do you want more than anything else in the world?*
A. *Serenity.*

As rapport grew between us and as Patricia started to take time to reflect on these questions, she would on her own initiative come back to the questions with fuller responses, giving substantive, insightful meaning to her initial one-word answer. She was, I think, two years later still filling out that time frame that during the SLA days had been narrowed to the moment. She had a profound understanding of her experiences, how she was treated and how she has been judged, but she sometimes would have to break through the time frame of the present moment to reflect on them.

In an attempt to avoid living her life in reaction to the

past, she has come to deal with it somewhat philosophically:

"I try not to be bitter. All that does is eat away at *me*. It isn't a good way to get back; it doesn't accomplish anything. I mostly try to laugh at the people who threaten me.

"I could look at the last five years as wasted. But it could have been worse. I try to pick the good out of it all. I think there is a lot to be salvaged. I've learned a lot about my strengths and weaknesses. In getting my whole ego and personality destroyed and then building it back up again, I've had an opportunity to get stronger than I was before."

Being in jail does not facilitate rebuilding an ego or redefining identity. After being arrested, she spent fourteen months in solitary confinement "for her own protection," and later she was with other prisoners who hated her either for being rich or for being a snitch. "I feel like I'm becoming a professional prisoner. I'm here. I have to deal with it. The people who run this prison keep telling me this is such a nice place. Like I'm lucky to be here. I feel like saying to them, 'You're no better than the SLA.' I mean, I'm their prisoner. I'm not here because I'm their friend."

One prison succeeded another for Patricia. She had passed from the hands of the SLA to the United States government and became its prisoner. As soon as she was released on bail from the U.S. prisons, she became a prisoner in her own home. This time her captors were her lawyers. The first security company told her she could not leave the house at all, and the restriction was severely reinforced by F. Lee Bailey and Albert Johnson. "They were really overreacting to the possibility of someone else doing something to me.

"Bailey told me never to go out because reporters would be waiting for me. It took me several weeks to figure out that it was all right to go out. Bailey also didn't want me to go to nightclubs, and he told me I couldn't go to Disneyland because someone might try to take my picture with Mickey Mouse!"

But by the time she was released to her parents' custody, she had developed enough strength to assert herself again. She refused to comply with Bailey's attempt to further confine her and insisted on trying to develop a normal life again. "Being out on bail finally put me back into a normal environment where I could have normal interactions with people. Until I could socially interact again, I was not able to assert myself or function the way other people do. That's when I stopped seeing a psychiatrist, even though my family protested, but I figured I could rely on myself then. I wanted to make it on my own."

She went home to people who love her—her parents, her sisters, and her best friend, Trish Tobin. She describes Trish as one of the most significant people in her life over the past four years. "We've been friends since grade school, and Trish is the only person I consider worth having a fight with." She doesn't see many of her other old friends from school. "They weren't part of what happened to me. They didn't have to change as the rest of us did. It's hard to relate to them now, and a lot of people have this thing—they actually are afraid to be around me. Some of my old friends are afraid, their families are afraid, so I just can't put up with them!"

With loving family and friends she was able again to connect the past with the present and the future. Her identity was established in that continuity. When I met with her after she had been returned to the Federal Correctional Institution in Pleasanton, California, she seemed more sure of herself than earlier reports suggested. She had changed lawyers and she herself had taken over decisions and direction regarding the legal issues she faced. Clearly the initiative and the decisions were hers then. Until she was granted clemency, she had to carry the delicate balance between tolerating her confinement and knowing it was unjust, and between seeking release and vindication and not wanting her life to be absorbed in negativism.

FEMINISM AND THE LEFT

From the SLA's inception, theories have been articulated that it was a government-sponsored covert plan to discredit and destroy the left and so-called revolutionary movements. Whether or not that was the case, leftist organizations did not denounce the atrocities carried out by the SLA and consequently those acts were seen as a logical extension of male left revolutionary rhetoric. Tacit approval of the SLA was implied in the silence of groups with whom it was trying to establish a solidarity.

In the beginning, the media in its simplistic way inaccurately lumped feminism with the male left, reporting the SLA to be a feminist revolutionary organization. Having acquired some of the papers left by Nancy Ling Perry in one of the first SLA houses that was burned down, Marilyn Baker (then a reporter for San Francisco's KQED) asserted that "women are the dominant force, the leadership of the Symbionese Liberation Army." She supported this assertion with references to the papers from the SLA house. "The only major editorial correction that appeared in them, again and again, was the reversal of the order of *man and woman*, and *men and women* every time they were typed."[9]

Political ideology is always somewhat of an abstraction, removed from experience. As the experience of oppression is molded and shaped by political theory, its description becomes more and more removed from real, lived experience. Political ideology tends to redefine the experience of oppression into analysis and rhetoric which is aimed at mobilizing action to change that oppressive experience. Self-interest and motivation of the political group determines the extent to which the rhetoric expressing the conditions of oppression is truly representative of the people it claims to speak for. Political movements like the left, dominated by white middle-class males, derive their rhetoric from intellectual theories rather than lived experience of oppression. As a result, their politics are perpetuated more by their self-interest and personal power than by actions that would change the actual conditions of oppression.

Left politics tend to be consumed with theories of class and imperialism carried to abstraction by intellectual analysis that defines rather than reveals the experience of oppression. It superimposes theory on experience instead of taking actual experience and developing theories based on it. In contrast, responsive social movements like the women's movement, the black movement, or the farm workers' movement derive their theories and analysis of oppression from the actual experience of oppression. The male-left's model for understanding the terms and conditions of oppression leads to correct-line politics which can be noted in the personalizing tendency in the women's movement. While the description of the oppression of women has been formulated from personal testimony of women on many issues, some groups have used that personalizing practice only to cultivate rhetoric and correct political lines—reflecting the shallowest understanding of the real political nature of women's oppression.

The SLA belonged to that group of political people whose connection to oppression was intellectual, abstract, and self-serving. While proclaiming themselves to be in support of feminism, the SLA violated in the most dangerous and vicious way the basic principles of feminism by *kidnapping a woman to punish her father* and justified it because she was from a privileged class. Behind the shabby "feminist" rhetoric of the SLA we actually find *men against men over the body of a woman.*

To the women of the SLA, feminism was a kind of self-improvement ideology, one that would take them from passive roles to active ones, improve their language patterns, and allow them to achieve recognition legitimately from the men in their group. But feminism was never seen as a force that must confront patriarchy. That is why the SLA did not recognize the threat Patricia Hearst's change in identity represented to the patriarchal establishment. To the FBI and the general public, she was dangerous and threatening, not simply because of some abstract identification with another class, but because as a woman she was defying—for all the world to see—the sex role traditions in which she had been reared. She had been a loving daughter, but after her change in identity she was a woman trampling on all the female virtues to which she had been so carefully socialized. She appeared openly to reject wealth, her family, her fiancé, and the protection of the FBI. There were few female roles that tradition begs us to play that Patricia didn't challenge as "Tania." What was assumed to be her ungratefulness and defiance angered the public and enraged the establishment.

It was not just because Patricia defied sex roles that this wrath was brought down on her; it was the further implications of her role rejection. In a patriarchy set up to protect and thereby confine women, Patricia as Tania appeared to turn her back on rather elaborate offers of protection—her father's wealth and the FBI's support (even though accepting could have meant her death). Try as they might, Emily

Harris, Camilla Hall, Patricia Soltysik, Angela Atwood, or Nancy Ling Perry could never have rejected so much, for they never had so much combined patriarchal love, support, and protection offered to them. As a child of wealth, Patricia had inherited the Great American Dream for womanhood. The other women were only on the fringes of such patrimony. But Patricia could have had it all. It was her apparent rejection of this inheritance, her defiance against the offerings of patriarchal protection, which brought down the wrath of the FBI in the form of an anti-feminist backlash. The backlash was directed against Patricia, who was at that time a feminist not intentionally, but through her involuntary involvement with the SLA—a group that, ironically, had no genuine commitment to feminism.

LOYALTY

From the time she was kidnapped, society across the spectrum from right to left expected Patricia to vindicate herself. To the right, vindication meant fighting to her death or at least being able to walk away from her captors and into the hands of the FBI even after witnessing on television the massacre in Los Angeles. She was expected to be able to extricate herself from her fear for her life at the hands of either her captors or the FBI, and to undo the dependency that had been cultivated with great calculation by her captors. To vindicate herself to the SLA, to the American left, and to the other self-proclaimed revolutionary movements, she was expected to espouse to death (her death) the cause of violent revolution through murder. Had she refused to testify in her own behalf, she could have secured the support of the "revolution." Had she in martyrdom submitted herself to the fate of her captors, she would have at least garnered the pity of the rest of the population.

Considering all this, as a woman, I am forced to ask myself what it means to have to be dead to prove yourself honorable in a masculinist society.

What, after all, is loyalty, that quality which has been so sorely tested and judged and found wanting in Patricia Hearst by all sides? Loyalty is first a dedication, a faithfulness, an allegiance to something—to one's country, to one's employer, to one's family. One is loyal to that which is in one's best interest, which is consonant with one's values. When loyalty is asked, certain rewards and privileges are given. In return, one adheres to a particular system of values and beliefs. Patriotism is loyalty to the fatherland for the rights and privileges it guarantees its citizens. On the other hand, measures of political correctness are used to determine loyalty to male left ideology and politics which are in opposition to the legitimized fatherland. Above all, loyalty is patriarchal—it is the granting and protecting of rights and privileges to men, by men, for men. It is the bonding of the brotherhood.

Loyalty is amoral for men. As the men of Watergate, the CIA, the corporate structure, and the brotherhood of johns, pimps, and rapists all demonstrate, loyalty to government, the job, family, all encompass room for violence, deception, swindling, and fraud. The brotherhood of patriarchy is confirmed in double and triple standards. Loyalty to one's wife is not inconsistent with beating a prostitute any more than loyalty to one's government prevents one from defrauding it in the name of protection of freedom.

Consider the question of female loyalty in the brotherhood of patriarchy, for that is where all women live. When I began to explore the problems of loyalty that Patricia Hearst has faced over the last several years, it became immediately clear to me that I could not speak from first-hand experience on the subject of loyalty except within the context of personal relationships. I could not speak of the privileges I have been granted or the protection I have been afforded for being loyal to a country, to a job, or to a political organization. As a woman, I simply can never receive from patriarchy that which has been set up for the brotherhood. There are no institutions, no politics, no government where those of my sex have not been dominated, subdued, and robbed of our potential and talents as we are excluded from patriarchal privilege. What then does it mean for a woman to be loyal in patriarchy? It means allegiance to a country that systematically denies women equal rights with men, or to a revolution that promises to replace one group of men with another. It means allegiance to a medical establishment that has maimed and mutilated women with hysterectomies, mastectomies, and estrogen therapies. It means allegiance to a virility cult that asks the women jurist not to convict young male rapists and thereby damage their chances for a prosperous future. It means allegiance to a motherhood cult which raises that experience onto a pedestal and yet knocks it to the ground when there is no male present to validate it. It stems directly from the linear thinking which always allows for only two opposite sides. It assumes that loyalty to one patriarchy means disloyalty to another. In male linear thought, the world is ordered in dichotomies where there are only two sides of everything.

When we talked at the prison in Pleasanton, California, I asked Patricia how she felt about loyalty now. Her response was immediate and firm: "To thine own self be true!" This is the "selfish state" she referred to earlier in our discussion and I think it marks the passage from victim to survivor. Yet it is not freedom. That lies beyond merely surviving and beyond prisons. She was not there yet; she was still in prison, looking forward to being released and to beginning a life that is not lived in reaction to the past.

PART III

The Politics
Of Sexual
Domination

CHAPTER 8

Sex Colonization

Many women and girls directly experience female sexual
slavery without ever going out of their homes. For them
home replaces brothel; they are wives or daughters who are
the victims of husbands or fathers instead of pimps. I am
speaking, of course, of wife battery and incest, practices
which make the private family instead of the public street
or "house" the location of female sexual slavery. In certain
cultures these practices take the form of forced marriage,
polygyny, veiling, and seclusion of women.

In most nations it is evident that family loyalty super-
sedes loyalty to one's country. Across cultures the family is
the basic unit of individual male power. Whether in the
tribal hut, rural cottage, city apartment, or government
mansion—each man's home is his castle. And each man's
home is private. It is in that privacy that female sexual
slavery flourishes.

I am defining female sexual slavery in the family in the
same way I defined it in prostitution in Chapter 3: "Female
sexual slavery is present in *all* situations where women or
girls cannot change the immediate conditions of their existence; where regardless of how they got into those conditions they cannot get out; and where they are subject to
sexual violence and exploitation." In addition to being cautioned against the invasion of man's privacy, arguments of
cultural relativism are used to discourage examination of
the similarities in female sexual slavery as it is practiced
through the family across cultures. Cultural relativism asserts that the practices within any specific culture are
unique to the values, systems, and practices *within* that
culture. For the cultural relativist there are no universal
standards and the morality and values of one national culture cannot be compared to that of any other. Cultural
relativism dominates social, political and academic thought
today and it serves as a justification of many inhuman

social practices. If one questions the principles of cultural relativism, one is charged with ethnocentrism. Ethnocentrism assumes that the judgments made about another culture stem from the assumption of the superiority of one's own culture.

These attempts to respect the cultural integrity of different societies, well intentioned though they may be, serve to separate and isolate women in their common experience of sexual domination.

There is nothing unique across cultures in the practices of the enslavement of women except perhaps the diversity in the strategies men employ to carry them out. Female sexual slavery is a global phenomenon. As a form of oppression, it cannot be subject to either the respect or protection given to those cultural practices which mark a culture as distinct from any other, or those that insure privacy to the family unit. Applying the same standard or value to human life across all national cultures lifts considerations of female sexual slavery above arguments of ethnocentrism. Wherever female sexual slavery is practiced and condoned, particularly when it spans across many cultures, no culture can be deemed superior to another.

Curiously, when we discuss prostitution internationally, the arguments of cultural relativism are silenced and cultural universals are asserted. The result is that the sexual slavery practiced within the family is protected and defended by one set of standards—those based on family privacy and cultural uniqueness—while sexual slavery in brothels and through pimps is supported by the opposite standard, the cultural universal that is based on the assumption that all men in all cultures through all time must have access to prostitutes.

The contradictions between, on one hand, cultural universals which justify slavery in prostitution and, on the other, cultural relativism which protects slavery in the family within diverse cultures, create circular arguments that mystify consciousness. Accordingly, many Africans argue that polygyny is superior to monogamy because it allows men legally to take several wives whereas monogamy allows them to have only one wife while at the same time maintaining illicit relationships with other women. The argument ignores the fact that the results are the same. In each culture men are socially if not legally sanctioned to have access to several women at a time.

Circular arguments accept slavery as a condition of women, something culturally or socially if not biologically determined. Once slavery is accepted, then relative freedoms are used to defend it. Arguments over which culture provides more opportunities for women within slavery are somewhat like the distinctions Malcolm X made between house nigger and field nigger—both equally enslaved, but one assuming that privilege within slavery lessens or removes the conditions of slavery. There is no such thing as good slavery, or better slavery. The fact is that each form of slavery is dependent on the others.

INTERDEPENDENCY OF SLAVERY

Recalling that as recently as 1970 a slave auction of European women for Arab harems was witnessed in Zanzibar, and that INTERPOL in its 1974 report documents a continuing traffic in women between France and Senegal and the Ivory Coast, and that when international rings of procurers are broken up one finds that many young girls have been purchased from rural areas of Third World countries, the linkages between family sexual slavery and international forced prostitution reveal a highly interdependent system.

Where daughters are sold into marriage through practices of dowry or brideprice, we have both the preconditions to and the practice of sexual slavery. Where marriages are arranged through dowry paid by the girl's family, daughters present an economic burden to their families. Particularly in conditions of poverty, they are less welcome into the world than sons, and such a position creates a higher likelihood that they can be taken easily by procurers who pose as employers or potential husbands who will take these girls out of conditions of poverty.

The practice of polygyny creates a market for prostitutes. The fact that some men have many wives in polygynous societies results in a shortage of women for other men. Consequently, the surplus population of unmarried men tend to migrate to the cities and seek out prostitutes. "Widespread prostitution or adultery is therefore likely to accompany widespread polygamy."[1] Where polygyny also includes the seclusion of women behind the veil and in their homes, there are few women on the streets of the cities to be companions of young, unattached men. Prostitution tends to flourish in areas where women are secluded and where female virginity is highly valued.[2]

Such prostitution is also a means of escape for girls who try to avoid forced marriages and migrate to the cities. Where sex discrimination creates few employment opportunities for women and women are kept uneducated, prostitution is a likely alternative. This is not to suggest that all women who migrate to the cities alone or escape arranged marriages find prostitution as their only alternative. But given the high illiteracy rates among women in these societies and their low participation in the labor force, it remains for many as the only alternative. In such situations forced marriage, polygyny, prostitution, and economic discrimination form one highly interdependent system.

The interrelatedness and dependency of prostitution and marriage in Western society is evident in the findings that a significant proportion of street prostitutes come from wife-battering, child-abusing, incestuous homes. Many were the object of their father's incestuous assault and/or other physical abuse. Female sexual slavery is a family condition and a precondition to forced prostitution. Other connections can be suggested but need considerable study. For example, of those men who claim they cannot receive sexual satisfaction from frigid wives, how many are wife beaters whose wives sexually withdraw from them after the beatings? Are these some of the men prostitution is designed to service?

ALL IN THE FAMILY

Wife battery and incest are forms of female sexual slavery that have hitherto been lost under the general rubric of "domestic violence." Sexual violence in the home, resulting in conditions of slavery, is consistently underplayed in research, in police reports, and by social service agencies.

Although female sexual slavery in the family is directly linked to forced prostitution, the interdependency of these two forms of slavery is hidden by the traditional argument that domestic violence breeds domestic violence. This thinking dominates research, police response to calls, and the way social service agencies handle cases. Thus it amounts to justification and self-perpetuation of the practices.

The theory assumes a circular pattern to domestic violence participated in by all members of the family without distinguishing between aggressor and victim. Many wife beaters and beaten wives, according to the circular theory, come from homes where they suffered child abuse or witnessed one parent's abuse of the other and they in turn react to their own children with physical abuse.

Maria Roy studied 150 women who sought aid in an American shelter for battered women and found that in 45 percent of the cases when the mother was beaten at least one child was also.[3] This finding is consistent with Gelles's study, *The Violent Home*. He does not distinguish between wife and husband battery, but found that 50 percent of those who physically fought with their spouse had observed this violence in their own home as children and over 50 percent had experienced frequent violence from their parents.[4]

This leads to the startling figure that in one year some 1.8 million wives are beaten by their husbands.[5] Steinmetz estimates that only 1 out of 270 incidents is reported to authorities.[6] The FBI finds that wife battery occurs three times more frequently than rape, and rape is estimated to take place every twelve minutes in the United States.

The incidence of wife battery is directly linked to the prevalence of child abuse through the violence-breeds-violence theory. It is estimated that there are 100,000 victims each year of incest and child sexual abuse. Approximately 10,000 children are *severely* battered every year. The Department of Health, Education and Welfare indicates that 90,000 children are subjected to some form of physical abuse.[7]

According to the preceding statistics, many but not all of these boy children will grow up to be wife beaters (or perhaps pimps whose behavioral pattern is similar to that of abusing husbands). And many but not all of the girls will grow up to be beaten wives, prostitutes, and/or drug abusers; some will have children who will be abused, and so on, and so on. . . . Neckes and Lynch in 1978 found that 80 percent of the 30 San Francisco street prostitutes they interviewed came from homes where they were sexually and/or physically abused. (See Chapter V, section on Escaping the Brotherhood.) Densen-Gerber and Wathey found that where fathers had offered their daughters token sums of money (twenty-five cents to a dollar) at the time they sexually abused them, "the correlation was .85 indicating that the young, usually prepubescent female who is encouraged to allow her body to be used for monetary exchange will later engage in prostitution."[8]

Analyzing the horrifying extent of "domestic violence" in traditional violence-breeds-violence terms creates the sense of a vicious self-perpetuating circle and therefore a hopelessness in reversing the upward spiral it creates. As long as the specific experiences of violence within the family are generalized under the rubric of "domestic violence" and are accepted as private family matters, the political dimensions of it are inaccessible and therefore cannot be challenged or changed.

The very fact that the feminist movement made wife battery an issue of sexual politics, through their opening of shelters for battered women around the world, has made this violence a public issue. The deadly, hopeless circle has been interrupted, but shelters and supportive services are only the beginning.

As battered women are escaping to shelters and are beginning to speak of their experiences, we are learning the true dimensions of "domestic violence." For example, the directly causal links made by social scientists between spouse battery and child abuse ignore the fact that many wife beaters are not from violent homes. In the Gelles sample, 40 percent of his respondents were *not* abused as children and over 30 percent *never* witnessed abuse of their parents.[9] Wives *don't* seek out abusive husbands because they themselves were abused: according to Roy's survey, 66 percent of the wives had not experienced parental violence as children. And in Gayford's study of 100 battered wives, only 23 percent of the women had been exposed to violence as children, while 51 percent of their husbands had.[10]

It is not necessarily violence that breeds violence. It is

the fact that sexually abusive men—pimps, husbands, or fathers—many of whom learn violence at an early age as a means of problem solving, still receive sanction for their behavior. Hopelessness doesn't stem from an inescapable pattern of violence into which all members of the family are locked, but from social sanction that results from not punishing the offenders but blaming the female victim.

1. Family Slavery Is Sexual

Until women began describing their experiences of battery in marriage and feminists made rape an issue of sexual politics, wife battery was viewed as physical aggression but not as *sexual* violence. Likewise, through in-depth interviews with victims, incest is now known to be another form of family sexual violence carried out by the father or other male in authority in the family. As such, both wife battery and incest are forms of female sexual slavery.

Marital rape is a relatively new concept, although hardly a new practice. Most women who are raped by their husbands do not yet know that their ordeal is something other than wifely duty. Marital rape generally does not exist as a crime in law, public attitudes, or private perceptions, yet it is practiced in fact. The laws are beginning to change in a few states. Under a new law in Oregon, wives can now prosecute their husbands for marital rape. In December 1978 the Rideout case created national attention when Greta Rideout separated from her husband and had him prosecuted for a rape which she alleged took place after he beat her. After he was acquitted, the couple reunited, and finally Greta filed for divorce some months later. At the time they were reunited, her husband claimed to have reformed and to have become more sensitive as a result of the trial.

Many supporters of women's rights had watched this case hoping it would be a breakthrough for women. But as Greta Rideout vacillated after the court decision, she became defined by the standards of victimism. The political demand for a "pure victim" led many who supported this case to ultimately denounce it. Yet Greta Rideout's vacillation is part of the familiar wife battery pattern. Women who have become fearful, intimidated, and dependent in marriages where they are battered and raped keep returning to the marriage out of fear and from hope that this time the reform is real and the dreams that created the marriage can be found again. In their return they may feel they can momentarily escape the madness of a society that refuses to acknowledge the family as the location of slavery or husbands as abusive. Far from being inappropriate, the Rideout case appears prototypical of the wife battery experience.

Lenore Walker, in her study, *The Battered Woman* (New York: Harper and Row, 1979) found that most of the women she interviewed reported they had been raped by their batterers. In Roy's study of battered women, 20 percent of the 150 women reported sexual abuse in combination with other physical abuse. In another study of 40 battered women, 32 percent reported they were sexually abused.[11] In some cases, marital rape takes place after a husband beats his wife and sex is offered as an attempt to make up. Other times it is simply a further demonstration of authority in the whole context of beating and abuse. Some husbands become sexually stimulated by beating their wives. In a study of 100 victims of wife battery in Erin Pizzey's shelter for battered women in London, 15 percent of the wives reported that their husbands "seemed to experience sexual arousal from the violence—since the demand for sexual intercourse immediately followed the assault."[12] Women are rarely stimulated by violence and consequently battered wives have a tendency to withdraw from their husbands sexually. This behavior, in turn, becomes another excuse for continued battery and rape.

Closely related to the reported incidence of marital rape in wife battery is the significant increase in physical abuse of pregnant wives. Gayford found in the study of 100 wives at Chiswick Women's Aid that pregnancy heightened the tirade against women.[13] And Gelles indicates that a husband's sexual frustration during his wife's pregnancy, along with family stress and an increased defenselessness on the part of the wife due to the pregnancy, account for an increase in battery.[14] Being kicked in the abdomen during pregnancy is reported by wives and prostitutes alike.

Incest is the other family crime of sexual violence. It is generally estimated that 95 percent of all incest is in the form of father- (brother-, uncle-, grandfather-) -daughter

assaults. The incidence of incest is probably the most difficult to estimate as it is one of the most hidden crimes
against females. It spans all ethnic groups, religions, and
economic classes. In California the Santa Clara County
center for incest victims and families handled 30 cases in
the first year of operation in 1971. In this middle-class
county of one million people, that caseload expanded to
600 by 1977. One study, surveying Chicago court cases,
found that 164 were father-daughter incest and 2 were
mother-son incest. Another study from Germany reported
90 percent of the cases involved girls with fathers, step-
fathers, and grandfathers. "Fathers and sons accounted for
another 5 percent. Incest between mothers and sons occurred in only 4 percent of the cases."[15]

2. Family Slavery Is Inescapable

The victims of both wife battery and of incest, although
experiencing it somewhat differently, are enslaved. They
are held in situations they cannot change and are exploited through forced sex and/or physical abuse. Battered
wives repeatedly explain how they have felt trapped in their
situation: in a study by Prescott and Letko, 68 percent of
the women reported feeling trapped and 55 percent said
they felt helpless.[16] In Roy's study of battered women,
"over 90 percent of the women thought of leaving and
would have done so had the resources been available to
them."[17] They gave the following reasons for staying: (1)
hope for reform, (2) no place to go, (3) fear of reprisal,
(4) children, (5) economic dependence, (6) fear of loneliness, and (7) divorce as a stigma. One recognizes the
common fears of prostitutes and wives. Some wives never
leave: in 1977, 10.6 percent of all homicides were husband-
wife murders, in 55 percent of the husband-wife murder
cases wives were murdered by their husbands, and in 45
percent of the cases wives killed their husbands.[18] Many
were likely to be driven to killing as an act of self-defense.
Del Martin explains in her book, *Battered Wives*, that
women are motivated by self-defense seven times more
often than men.[19]

Parental authority is the condition of enslavement for
girls subjected to sexual violation by their fathers or other
male relatives. In a study of adult women who had been

incest victims, Herman and Hirschman noted that the victims rarely expressed their anger toward their fathers but that it was instead internalized to "feelings of fear, disgust, intense shame about the sexual contact, and [they] stated they endured it because they felt they had no other choice."[20]

This particular study highlights a profile of incest experience:

> The majority of the victims were oldest or only daughters and were between the ages of six and nine when they were first approached sexually by their fathers or male guardians (nine fathers, three stepfathers, a grandfather, a brother-in-law, and an uncle.) * The youngest girl was four years old; the oldest fourteen. The sexual contact usually took place repeatedly. In most cases the incestuous relationship lasted three years or more. Physical force was not used, and intercourse was rarely attempted with girls who had not reached puberty; the sexual contact was limited to masturbation and fondling. In three cases, the relationship was terminated when the father attempted intercourse.[21]

Although incest is clearly an act of forced sexual aggression, the child-as-seducer theme pervades the literature. Good research is still scant in this area, but two kinds of sexual assault by fathers of daughters have been delineated in recent studies. The first is initially nongenital and gradually develops into overt sexual aggression. The other corresponds more closely to the profile of wife battery; the attack is direct when the father becomes aware of the sexual development of his pubescent daughter. These sexual attacks may be accompanied by heavy drinking.

In either case, based on the rape paradigm, the attention is focused on the child, who is accused of seduction, rather than on the responsible father who forced the sexual act. Guilt is placed on the daughter as she internalizes her

* Densen-Gerber found the majority of incest victims studied in her Odyssey House population were under the age of 12 when first assaulted.

anger. Her father forces her to keep his transgressions a secret. She is in a situation in which she depends on both her mother and father for her well-being—the fear of losing either or both confirms her silence and his protection:

> . . . the daughter who has been molested is dependent on her father for protection and care. Her mother is not an ally. She has no recourse. She does not dare express, or even feel, the depths of her anger at being used. She must comply with her father's demands or risk losing the parental love that she needs. She is not an adult. She cannot walk out of the situation (though she may try to run away). She must endure it, and find in it what compensations she can.[22]

Not only must the girl carry within her the insecurity about parental reaction and the realistic fear of being blamed and abandoned, but she is also too young to be able to understand these circumstances or the sexual experiences forced upon her by her father. In a situation that is forced but not necessarily physically violent, she may (although she may not) experience for the first time erotic feelings that she neither understands nor knows how to handle.

3. Family Slavery Is Justified

The traditional reasons given, both by researchers and by the men and women involved, for men beating their wives and for fathers sexually assaulting their daughters are not only inadequate explanations for these forms of female sexual slavery, they are justifications. The most commonly reported reasons given by wives for why their husbands beat them is (1) arguments over money, (2) jealousy and sexual problems, and (3) alcohol.[23] These reasons amount to justifications for assertion of power through physical and sexual abuse. The central theme in women's reports of why their husbands beat them is the total control their husbands have over them due to their virtual imprisonment in their homes. In Davidson's study of women at Erin Pizzey's shelter in London, 66 percent of the men beat their wives because of jealousy while 83 percent of the wives insisted that they were faithful to their husbands.[24]

Jealous husbands who beat their wives prevent or discourage them from going out of the house and usually the wives comply, not wanting to reveal evidence of battery.

In research one of the two major explanations given for incest is a confusion in the family over role allocation when daughters often take on responsibilities of the mother.[25] As Sandra Butler in *Conspiracy of Silence* points out:

> In some homes the mothers were partially or totally physically handicapped; other mothers had recurring histories of mental illness and either lived within their homes as invalids or frequently were absent from them during periods of hospitalization. Some were borderline alcoholics, while others simply chose to recede into the background of family life by withdrawing emotionally, taking jobs or becoming involved in activities that took them out of the home for long intervals.[26]

I shall return to the mother-daughter relationship under these circumstances later in this chapter.

The other explanation which is used to justify incest assault is the male's lack of impulse control. It is the same lack of control that is at the root of all male sexual violence against women. One notes in the language of fathers interviewed by Butler an absence of responsibility as if the self were acting separately from the person describing what he did. After describing the first incident of forced sex with his daughter, one man explained, "but *it happened* again a few months later. After that second time, *it just kept happening* more and more often. Every time I would drink and get to feeling angry and depressed, *it would just happen.* It's ironic because she was just the same as my wife. She'd lie there and cry the whole time." (emphasis mine)[27]

4. Family Slavery Is Enforced and Sanctioned
Of the women in Roy's study who had left their violent husbands, one third never tried to get help from the police. They feared reprisals from their husbands or social disgrace and they reported they lacked faith in the police system's ability to respond. That lack of faith was substan-

tiated by the two thirds who did call the police: 90 percent of them reported that the police made no arrests, 70 percent reported the police were not helpful at all.[28] Other research on battered women shows that fewer than 10 percent reported being battered to the police.[29] This pattern is similar to that of rape. However, after seeking support from other women through rape crisis centers or a battered wives shelter, women are able not only to report the incident to the police but to demand the action to which they are entitled. Yet little is forthcoming from this system in their behalf.

Inaction or noninterference is justified by the police on the same grounds that police don't interfere with pimps beating their prostitutes—often wives, like prostitutes, are initially ambivalent about seeing the man they love taken to jail. Instead of recognizing and dealing directly with the extent of the terror behind their ambivalences, the police withdraw, leaving the violence to the privacy of the couple.

The problem in reporting incest begins with the age of the victim: a child cannot easily go to authorities on her own. If she is not significantly estranged from her mother, the little girl may try to turn to her. But mothers, whether through jealousy or personal guilt over the situation, react with disbelief or denial. Or the mother, caught between loyalty to her husband and to her daughter, may take the husband's side and refuse to believe he could do such a thing. More often than not, girls sense on some level the precarious situation they are in and don't say anything. Behind a mother's reaction is enormous fear:

> . . . fear of not being able to handle such an enormous problem alone, fear of financial problems that will result if their husbands (often the only wage-earners) are removed from the home; fear of brutal retaliation by the husbands if they report the offenses; fear of stigmatizing the family in the eyes of the community and fear of becoming entangled with the law and its terrifying labyrinth of agencies.[30]

Very few incidents of incest assault are reported, but when they are—what happens? One police officer told Sandra Butler that of the few that are reported, 80 percent

never come to trial.[31] Other agencies as well as medical
and social services could intervene, but they dislike naming
an act incest. When victimization of girls is rarely even
named, it cannot be recognized. As with forced prostitution, the refusal of those in authority to acknowledge the
female's victimization reinforces the victim's inability to
name as a crime what her father has done to her.

> The child's ambivalence about testifying, the pressure
> placed on the child not to testify by others in the
> family who want to protect their reputation, the child's
> credibility as a witness in the eyes of the legal system,
> the child's inexperience with legal jargon, the need
> for endlessly repeated testimony and the presence of
> the sexual offender, often shackled, in the courtroom
> are reasons that prosecutions seldom make it through
> the court system to trial and sentencing.[32]

While men hide behind these justifications, the social order
presents constant validation for their action. Florence Rush
points out in her work on child sexual abuse that historically there has in fact been "no specified taboo forbidding
father-daughter incest" as there has been against mother-
son incest. According to Rush, "though all states carry
penalties for incest (from six months to 50 years imprisonment) judges and juries are very reluctant to punish an
incestuous father." While we are generally inclined to think
of incest with horror, when it comes down to looking at it
in terms of how society treats it, father-daughter incest is
implicitly sanctioned—primarily to protect the father.

Court decisions reflect the extent to which rape and
abuse in marriage and the family are legally condoned:

> *In 1977 one of the first indictments for marital rape*
> *was handed down by a grand jury in Essex County,*
> *New Jersey. A 27-year-old New Brunswick man was*
> *charged with raping his estranged wife. He was*
> *acquitted.*[33]

Cohabitation is acquiring the same sanction of violence as
marriage has.

*In February 1979 a Bridgeport, Connecticut, judge
acquitted a 33-year-old man of raping a 24-year-old
woman who lived with him. The court found that any
sexual behavior is permitted between cohabiting persons.*[34]

On the other hand, there have been some landmark decisions in recent years freeing wives who murdered their
husbands after prolonged periods of abuse from them.

*In Michigan, November 1977, a woman was acquitted
in the murder of her husband. The jury found her
innocent by reason of insanity for murdering her husband who had beat her regularly over several years.*[35]

*In California, December 1977, a woman was found
innocent of murder after she shot her husband as he
was going after her again. She was afraid he would
kill her.*

In both cases the innocence of the women was determined
only on the basis of there having been many long years of
continuously horrible violent assault. What these cases
show is not that women have the right to murder their
husbands, but that husbands can expect to carry out abuse
over many years before fearing retaliation.

The legal and social sanction to batter one's wife extends
far beyond actual practices of wife battery or incestuous
assault. The casual abandonment by husbands of wives
with children, the arrogance with which some men regain
access to their family at will, the irresponsibility or default
in child support, vengeful kidnapping of children when a
wife seeks separation or divorce*—these are but some of
the privileges that extend to men from the sanction of
female slavery.

Wife battery and incest practices illustrate how the fam-

* See Anna Demeter, *Legal Kidnapping* (Boston, Beacon
Press, 1977), for one woman's account of the nightmare of her
children's being kidnapped and ill-treated by their father.
Demeter's account of her search for her children is also an
account of the patriarchal sanction granted to men to carry out
such crimes.

ily institutionalizes male power and authority. Exploitative and violent use of that power in the family is sanctioned and justified through inadequate laws to protect women, through poor law enforcement of existing laws, and by keeping the abuse of women and girls in the home private, and therefore inaccessible to scrutiny. Considering the number of women subjected to wife battery, the numbers of daughters incestuously assaulted, the socialization in the family that encourages these practices, and the physical and sexual abuse of children which are preconditions to forced prostitution, the family can no longer be accepted as a neutral social institution but instead is seen as an institution which frequently promotes and protects female sexual slavery.

INTERNATIONAL FAMILY SLAVERY

The family as an institution of sexual slavery and one that cultivates preconditions to slavery is a condition for women throughout the world, in every patriarchal order. Many women's common experience of female sexual slavery across cultures is doubly protected from exposure: first, it is hidden in the privacy of the home and second, it is justified and protected as culturally specific and therefore a culturally unique practice.

The practice of marital sexual slavery in non-Western societies is imbedded in cultural customs and laws governing marriage. Yet in the massively circulated development studies conducted by organizations like the United Nations there is silence on such practices as seclusion, arranged marriage and brideprice, polygyny, and genital mutilation. Despite the silence in this research, these conditions are of serious concern to many Third World women.

It is beyond the scope of this work to present a full, international documentation of the different cultural practices and social customs that create conditions of female sexual slavery for women in marriage. Instead, I will highlight some examples of how sexual slavery works in the family in some non-Western cultures. I will look first at the practices that result from the cultural definition of honor in the Mediterranean world and then I will discuss the practices that are designed to insure female chastity and

fidelity in parts of black Africa below the Sahara dominated by an agricultural economy. Both systems represent
overt practices of female sexual slavery with well developed
ideologies rooted in the customs, religion, and laws of the
societies. While different cultural practices may seem remote and even extreme to the Western reader, the systems
described here actually represent an explicit statement of
what is implicit in the values and practices of sex slavery in
Western society. These examples describe the conditions of
slavery of Mediterranean and African women and illumi-
nate those values which are common to all patriarchal
practices.

Honor in the Mediterranean World

Ideals of honor: Honor is a code of conduct, a way of life,
and an ideal of the social order which defines the lives,
customs, and values of many of the peoples in the Mediterranean world. For people of Mediterranean countries like
Spain, Greece, Italy, and numerous Arab countries, honor
defines a total system of morality which permeates every
aspect of social life, and affects all levels of individual
behavior. "Honor and shame are two poles of an evaluation. They are the reflection of the social personality in the
mirror of social ideals."[36] Honor is deeply ingrained in the
lives and values of people. ". . . the sentiment of honour
inspires conduct which is honourable, the conduct receives
recognition and establishes reputation, and reputation is
finally sanctified by the bestowal of honours."[37]

Honor is not just important as a reason for an individual
to be able to recognize himself as honorable; its significance lies in the social recognition of others, how he is
seen in others' eyes. "The man of honor . . . is essentially
faithful to himself . . . and this is revealed in the care he
takes to be worthy of a certain ideal image of himself."[38]

Honor is culturally specific even though those who live
by it assume that they aspire to universal ideals. What is
honorable will vary from one region or culture to another.
For example, honor for Bedouins is determined by the
nature of their existence:

> To undertake a raid, within prescribed rules, is honor-
> able. To refuse participation in a raid is dishonoring.

> To defend one's livestock against raiders is honorable
> . . . To own livestock is honorable. Hospitality and
> generosity are matters of honor. To be inhospitable
> or ungenerous is shameful. It is honorable to have
> pure Arab blood, on both one's father's and one's
> mother's side. It is honorable to exhibit a strong sense
> of kin group adherence.[39]

Status and power of individuals and groups are derived
from the act of determining what is or is not honorable
and in defining how honor is achieved. Honor establishes
the superiority of men over women. While both sexes are
bound to be honorable, women are also the objects through
which men's honor is determined. Honor includes a sexual
ideology which defines women as weak, innately promiscuous and therefore capable of bringing dishonor to men.
The Arab distinction between the general concept of
honor, *sharaf*, and the special honor that is binding on
women and tied to sexual behavior illustrates how honor
establishes women in an inferior status to men.

Patai explains that *sharaf* is "something flexible: depending on a man's behavior, way of talking and acting, his
sharaf can be acquired, augmented, diminished, lost, regained, and so on."[40] But women are bound to a specific,
inflexible honor, *'ird*, which determines their proper conduct and upon which men's honor, *sharaf*, depends:

> *'ird* is a rigid concept: every woman has her ascribed
> *'ird*; she is born with it and grows up with it; she can-
> not augment it because it is something absolute, but
> it is her duty to preserve it. A sexual offense on her
> part, however slight, causes her *'ird* to be lost, and
> once lost, it cannot be regained. It is almost as if the
> physical attribute of virginity were transposed in the
> *'ird* to the emotional-conceptual level. Both virginity
> and *'ird* are intrinsically parts of the female person;
> they cannot be augmented, they can only be lost, and
> their loss is irreparable.[41]

Consequently when virginity is lost outside of marriage, the
woman permanently loses her *'ird* and the man or men
whose honor is affected by that particular woman will

temporarily lose their *sharaf*. When they avenge that loss, male honor will be restored. The concept of *'ird* and its permanent loss is derived from the same double standard as that of the rape paradigm. It does not account for how that loss takes place, whether the illicit sexual contact was forced or mutual. It assumes female guilt and responsibility in either context.

Sex is rigidly controlled by the code of honor through the control of women and by making marriage the only legitimate context for its expression. Once these social parameters are defined, sex is seen in the Muslim world as a valuable energy. In *Beyond the Veil*, Fatima Mernissi points out that "the Muslim theory views civilization as the outcome of satisfied sexual energy. Work is not the result of sexual frustration; it is the result of a contented sexuality, of a harmoniously-lived sexuality . . ."[42] Mernissi goes on to illustrate the sexual double standard implicit in the Islamic code and aspirations to honor:

> . . . what is peculiar about Muslim sexuality as civilized sexuality is this fundamental discrepancy: if promiscuity and laxity are signs of barbarism, then the only sexuality civilized by Islam is woman's sexuality; the man's sexuality is promiscuous (by virtue of polygamy) and lax (by virtue of repudiation).[43]

This view of only female sexual behavior as potentially promiscuous is consistent with what Mary Douglas refers to as danger beliefs. Danger beliefs view female functions (i.e., menstruation) as those which make women seem dangerous and therefore people who must be controlled. The danger belief, whether it is rooted in reproduction or sexuality, actually functions to order social relations by asserting male superiority and creating separate and unequal male and female social spheres.[44]

By asserting a conception of women as dangerous to men's honor, the code of honor is intricately connected to sexual power and domination. "Virility is one of those overriding qualities which a man will uphold even if he must in the process sacrifice other values."[45] Dishonor brought upon a man by illicit sexual activity (forced or mutual) of his wife, sister, or daughter reflects on the whole family.

Sociologist Constantina Safilios-Rothschild has studied crimes of honor in Greece. As she points out, dishonor falls on a man either when he doesn't behave in a masculine way or his wife or female relatives are dishonored; "Men are considered to be masculine and honorable only when they can control their wives and all female relatives in such a strict manner that the women behave appropriately and never acquire a dishonorable reputation in the community."[46] Traditionally in Greece, women's honor can only be restored through suicide. Men defend their honor by killing both the dishonored woman, if she doesn't commit suicide, and the male responsible for her dishonor.[47]

Rothschild studied incidence of crimes of honor in Greece from 1960–63 and found they are still committed in rural areas and among lower and working classes in small and large cities.[48] In urban areas they most frequently take place as a result of divorce or desertion.[49]

The situation is similar in the Arab world. An Arab woman testified before the International Tribunal on Crimes Against Women in Brussels in 1976 that "If an Arab woman commits adultery, either her husband, her father, or even her own brother will kill her, because she has brought disgrace upon both her husband's family and her own family. The killing of women is called 'the honor debt.' Her dead body will restore honor to the family name."[50]

Crimes of honor represent the ideal of patriarchal values, the male fantasy of what the perfect society would be like if women were completely subdued. In actual practice, crimes of honor are beginning to recede. Urbanization, technology, and development have disrupted the pure code of honor in the Mediterranean world. But as Rothschild's research on Greece illustrates, crimes of honor, although practiced in their most literal interpretation less frequently now, coexist with modernization especially in the peasant and lower classes. Whether or not they are literally carried out, they represent an idealized value; that which inspires satisfaction of the honor debt is still dominant in Mediterranean culture.

How honor functions as a social control of women and a condition of family slavery can be best illustrated by reference to practices of it in the Arab world. There it finds expression in Islamic teachings as well as governmental law.

By illustrating the extreme situation it is possible to trace the ideal principles it represents compared to other widespread practices. The following report comes from a small village on the Nile. A marriage had been arranged for the sixteenth birthday of a young girl called Fawzia. Her father and brother had been building her dowry. Before her marriage Fawzia accidentally discovered her mother and uncle in an embrace. To ensure her silence, her uncle raped her and her mother then took her to Cairo for a hymenorrhaphy—the surgical restoration of proof of virginity. The marriage took place as arranged. The young girl didn't meet her husband until they were married. Bloodstains on the sheet the wedding night proved her virginity to all.

Some months after she came to know and love her husband and found herself pregnant, she confided to him the terrible rape she experienced. His honor was offended and he threw her out of his house, denying he was the father of her expected child. Journalist Don Schanche, who reported this story, revealed the sequence of events which followed. "Fawzia's brother, Ahmed, returned to the village to be confronted immediately by what he perceived to be a blot on the family's honor. . . . The next day the pregnant girl was found dead. . . . Ahmed acknowledged to the villagers that he had killed her to restore the family's good name."[51] According to Schanche, Fawzia's brother returned to his foreign construction job; her father in Muslim fashion divorced his wife by repudiation, simply denouncing her, and her husband remarried.

It is obvious that if in the modern Arab world total revenge was widely practiced, a large proportion of both the female and male populations would be obliterated. Premarital and extramarital sexual relations as well as rape undoubtedly are as prevalent in Arab countries as they are anywhere else in the world. Yet this incident reveals the practice of honor according to its most literal interpretation.

Honor practices—seclusion and arranged marriage: It is not necessary to resort to such extremes when the control they are meant to exert is self-imposed. Regarding danger beliefs, Mary Douglas points out that "The beliefs are the product of common assent to a set of norms; they express it publicly and visibly, but their power to hold people to a code of behavior is no more than the power of those people's respect for that code."[52] Once those norms are internalized by those they are meant to reduce and control, they are self-regulating.

For Muslim women the code is explicitly stated in the Koran. It is particularly clear regarding seclusion:

> Sura 24, 31: "Say to the believing women that they refrain their looks, and observe continence, and that they display not their ornaments, except what must of necessity appear; and that they draw their veils over their bosoms, and display not their ornaments, except to their husbands, or their fathers, or their husband's father . . ." etc.[53]

Veiling, a form of seclusion, is meant to insure women's chastity by making them invisible to men. Wearing a veil means being wrapped in a long cloak that covers the entire body allowing "what of necessity must appear," which sometimes is the face and hands and other times is only the eyes which must be averted in shyness. To be unveiled is to be considered nude and immoral. The veil is a self-contained prison and effects the total seclusion of girls and women, beginning before or at puberty and continuing throughout their adult life. In a society where clothes signify status, the veil remains a prestigious aspiration for many Arab women.[54] It is seen as a symbolic shelter from sex and aggression.[55]

Women's restricted physical movement and inactivity in Muslim societies can lead to serious health problems for them, as many are rarely exposed to fresh air or physical exercise. This, in part, accounts for the high incidence of tuberculosis among women in societies which still demand female seclusion. In addition, in countries like Pakistan, veiled women can only be seen by female doctors, who are not easily available. In Pakistan, the medical schools have put a quota of 10 percent for admission of women students.[56]

Seclusion requires separate educational facilities. Girls cannot be seen by boys, therefore they cannot be educated with them. Usually this means girls are not educated, which partially accounts for the high illiteracy rate among women in this part of the world. Veiling means that marriage must be arranged, as little or no contact between males and females outside the family is permitted before marriage. It limits women's work potential and severely curtails political participation in the society.

Veiling as a practice is still mandated in many parts of the Muslim world, in the Middle East, and in North Africa. In some countries virtually the entire female population is veiled, while in others like Turkey, where veiling is illegal, the practice is diminished. Yet in other countries like Iran, where attempts were made to discourage veiling, it is now being encouraged as a sign of commitment to Islam.

The veil which is being discarded mostly by women of the upper and middle classes symbolizes the seclusion of women and their segregation from men's space. "The veil means that the woman is present in the men's world, but invisible; she has no right to be in the street."[57]

If a woman leaves her home (for a job, as many modern Arab women do) and she goes into the world of men's space unveiled, she has, according to Mernissi's interpretation, committed two acts of aggression: "trespassing and trespassing in the 'nude.' "[58] Consequently those women who have discarded the veil have to go far beyond that to discard the mentality of female seclusion. They must survive the wrath of men who, seeing women outside their homes and unveiled, consider their behavior exhibitionist assault.[59]

Yet women secluded as objects of patriarchal contempt are not passive victims. Mernissi notes, "Young women be they maids or crafts-women refuse 'SBER' [the sacramental quality of patience and acceptance] as a way of life; their attitude is that of dropping out from the traditional value system altogether."[60] Mernissi has studied the tendency for many Arab women to join religious sects which, although illegal in Islam, afford women an opportunity to fuller expression of themselves. In these sects, women are able to fully participate in religious practices which often involve dance, incantations, and magic.

Women in Islam have also found economic means of adapting to their conditions of confinement:

> . . . the thousands of women in the Middle East who have adapted themselves to the communal practice of not working in the public sector and have still managed to earn income and often to support whole families: who weave or sew or embroider for other families; who take consignments of piecework from factories or shop to finish at home; who cook and sell the products of their kitchen; who care for children or work as servants; who function as *mullah(s)* (religious specialists), *shaykhah(s)*, or *muqaddamah(s)*; who operate as midwives, pediatricians, fortune tellers, and sorcerers; who raise chickens, sheep, goats, or vegetables; who sell raw milk and yogurt from door to door.[61]

Yet even though women have been able to find ways to survive seclusion by making their lives productive, their invisibility in the world of men is the basis for sex discrimination in the labor market. The rate of economic activity of women in countries practicing seclusion reflects their marginal status.

Slavery that results from seclusion and sexual segregation also necessitates arranged marriage. By definition a marriage that is arranged without consent is a situation a woman cannot get out of and therefore constitutes a form of sexual slavery. But the Koran insists that a woman cannot be forced into marriage without her consent: "A woman ripe in years shall have her consent asked in marriage, and if she remains silent, her silence is her consent, and if she refuses, she shall not be married by force. . . ." In actual practice, when women's silence is forced through seclusion, often behind a veil, and through long-term socialization to subservience, consent has quite another meaning as it is obviously not hers to give or withdraw.

TABLE III Economic Activity of Women in Countries Practicing Seclusion, Mid-year 1975

Country	% of men economically active	% of women economically active
Algeria	43.4	1.9
Egypt	51.3	4.3
Iran	48.5	7.8
Libyan Arab Republic	47.7	2.7
Pakistan	48.6	5.7
Saudi Arabia	50.1	2.6
Sudan	55.8	6.7
Syria	45.2	6.0
Yemen (South)	53.6	2.4
Yemen Peoples Democratic Republic	49.8	2.7
Turkey*	53.0	32.1

*Veil outlawed.

Derived from *Yearbook of Labour Statistics*, 1978, International Labour Office, Geneva. From information on population and labor force obtained from national sources, "national data on labour force have been adjusted by the ILO to conform to a standard concept of labour force which is defined to comprise all employed and unemployed persons. It covers own-account workers, employers, unpaid family workers, members of producers' cooperatives and members of the armed forces."

Arrangements for marriage may vary from one situation to another, from a marriage arranged for a daughter at her birth to those marriages arranged between two young adults who know each other. The common pattern, however, is for a prospective bridegroom to inform his mother of a female relative he wants to marry. His mother communicates her son's wish to the mother of the girl. If she receives a positive response, the bridegroom then makes formal arrangements for the betrothal. "More often than not, the girl, if she is being married for the first time, is ignorant of the negotiations that are proceeding, and her parents may promise her to a man she has never seen. It would appear, however, that no young woman well brought up ever refuses a match agreeable to her parents."[62]

It is a practice in Muslim marriages for a male guardian to be appointed to represent the woman. She is not recognized as being able to conclude the marriage contract on her own behalf. The infringement of individual freedom this practice represents is actually a violation of the United Nations Declaration of Human Rights which stipulates that men and women have equal rights with regard to marriage.[63]

Brideprice usually concludes the marriage contract. Payment of an agreed-upon sum by the groom or the groom's family to the bride or her father is often interpreted as a wedding gift or a means of inheritance for women. But when it is realized that part of the detailed arrangements for a marriage are meant to ensure the bride's virginity, brideprice is recognized as a payment for chastity which must be guaranteed by the bride's family. In the past in Morocco, when a bride was found not to be a virgin, she was sent away by the bridegroom.[64]

The Arab witness testifying at the International Tribunal on Crimes Against Women described how chastity must be proven again on the wedding night, in areas where the most literal interpretation of the code of honor is still practiced:

> I will give you a brief example of a marriage which takes place in an Algerian village. The bride who has never met her husband before the wedding day, has the harrowing experience of ritual rape on her wedding night. She is taken into the bridal suite while both the family of the bride and the family of the groom stand outside. The local villagers gather outside the house, beating drums and singing songs for the honor of the families. The bride, who is usually in her teens, is petrified, for if it is not proved that she is a virgin on this night, she will be killed by her father or brothers. The proof of her virginity will be a sheet stained with her blood which the groom will hold up for all to see. Proof that the girl is a virgin will cause great celebration. The mothers of both families will hug each other in joy over this evidence of virginal honor.[65]

Marriage through seclusion, arrangement, and brideprice constitutes a widespread practice of female sexual slavery.

Rights granted to the husband in marriage affirm the slavery conditions of women:

> The duty of the man to command his wife is embodied in his right to correct her by physical beating. The Koran itself recommends such a measure, but only as a last resort. If the wife rebels, the husband is instructed to scold her and then to stop having intercourse with her. Only if these measures fail should he beat her to make her obey.[66]

One other practice to ensure female chastity must be mentioned here—genital mutilation. The physical assault on female sexuality from surgical destruction of female genital organs represents the most extreme acting out of danger beliefs short of murder. Recent evidence indicates that this practice is much more widespread than it was assumed to be. It is also more prevalent in central Africa than it is in the Mediterranean world where female chastity is guaranteed by making women invisible. Genital mutilation of women is still practiced in Islamic countries like Egypt, the Sudan, and South Yemen, but it appears to be a larger practice in black African countries south of the Sahara where women are much more economically active, especially in agricultural work.

Presently it is estimated that over 20 million women in 30 countries are subjected to it. "Excision is practiced by ethnic groups all over East-West and Central Africa in a broad area along the equator and just north of it, from Somalia and along the Red Sea Coast to Senegal."*[67] According to Hosken, infibulation is still practiced in southern Egypt; most of the women in the Sudan are presently infibulated, as are all the female population of Somalia, and women in parts of Ethiopia.[68]

Genital mutilation is an inhumane torture used to ensure chastity in which the primary source of female eroticism is surgically removed by midwife, priest, or doctor. There are

* Among other localities, these take place in Kenya where it is supported by President Kenyatta, in areas in Ethiopia, among the majority of the female population in Sudan, large population groups in Nigeria, Uganda, North Cameroon, most of Upper Volta, Northern Ghana, many groups in Sierra Leone, Mauritania, The Gambia, Senegal, Ivory Coast. . . .

three forms: sunna circumcision, which removes the prepuce; excision or clitoridectomy, which removes the entire clitoris, the labia minora, and other exterior genitalia; and infibulation. Infibulation guarantees virginity, as after excision both sides of the vulva are scraped raw and surgically sewn together, leaving only a small opening for urination and menstruation. These rituals are usually performed at puberty. In some cases the woman has to be opened for sexual intercourse and childbirth after marriage.*[69]

Male circumcision is also a puberty rite in some cultures but one that is a public display of manliness, an assertion of virility. Female circumcision, in contrast, "is typically carried out in private, surreptitiously, the operation calculated to impress the girl with her own inferiority in relation to boys."[70]

Besides ensuring chastity, infibulation has another function. According to Esther Ogunmodede of NOW-Nigerian Organization for Women, the narrow opening which results after the wound is healed "increases the husband's pleasurable sensations during intercourse, even though for the women, sex is nothing but agony, one reason she does not bother to take a lover."[71]

But Soheir Morsy, in her study of a peasant community in Egypt, sees it another way. She recalls the positive role of sex in marriage in Islam and that the wife has a right to sexual satisfaction. And then ignoring the sources of female eroticism, she describes the role of genital mutilation in what she sees as egalitarian sexual relationships:

> It is important to note that clitoridectomy is primarily a practice to safe-guard premarital chastity and virginity. Women's right to sexual gratification within marriage is recognized. Since the clitoris is identified as the locus of sexual excitement, the gypsy who performs the operation is always cautioned against its complete excision. It is said that women who have

* Details of these practices with case histories and accounts of the rituals surrounding them have been documented by Fran Hosken and are available from *Women's International Network News.*

been subjected to complete removal of the clitoris
"drain their husbands of their strength." Informants
note that for such women orgasm is delayed . . .[72]

As genital mutilations are often practiced in rituals, there
are usually no records kept on the practices. In an interview with two doctors from a University Medical School in
Cairo, Fran Hosken was told, "Circumcision is forbidden;
if we get a new case in the hospital we must report it. But
in the rural areas it still continues to be done on girls 5 to 7
years old. Twenty years ago *every* girl in Egypt was cir-
cumcised. Now it is not done in the cities. I estimate about
one third of the population still practice it."[73] In Ethiopia,
for example, Hosken was told by a pediatrician at the
Black Lion Hospital in Addis Ababa that all girls are cir-
cumcised throughout the highlands of that country. It is
noted that it is practiced regardless of religious affiliation,
whether Christian, Moslem, Animist, or Jewish.[74]

For years the World Health Organization tried to ignore
the pressure from groups like Terre des Hommes and from
women's groups to investigate this problem. Finally in
1977 they issued a report: it confirmed that it is still a
widespread practice involving millions of girls.

Organizations like the International Associations of
Women Writers have publicly demanded action from the
World Health Organization, contending that these practices
cannot be defended as cultural traditions. Ogunmodede asserts, "We Africans must get this straight; all practices
which have medically proven to be harmful and dangerous
can no longer enjoy protection by being labeled 'custom
and tradition.' "[75]

The severe, destructive practices that are meant to ensure female chastity and protect honor reflect a very rigid
moral code of double standards. In order to ensure that the
restrictions placed on female existence are not carried over
to men, that code has had to provide a legitimate context
for male promiscuity. Because the patriarchal family is
traditionally recognized as the only legitimate context for
sexual expression, then to be consistent with moral standards of Islam, it was necessary to provide some means for
male promiscuity within marriage to ensure the privilege of
male domination. Polygyny, the taking of more than one

wife, is permitted by the Koran but men are limited to four wives. Polygyny, even though validated by the Koran, has become statistically infrequent in Arab countries. Due to the seclusion of women, their economic contributions to the family are limited. More than one wife is often too much of an economic burden for Arab men.

Undoubtedly, genital mutilation makes polygyny work for men particularly where women have a definite economic value. In African countries south of the Sahara, where women are the agricultural workers, it is a matter of social status as well as income for men to acquire many wives. Because woman's economic value is higher in areas where she is secluded, brideprice often is paid by the husband to the girl's father when a marriage is arranged.

Approximately three fourths of the 136 separate peoples in Africa are characterized by polygynous marriages. Africa has the lowest percentage of monogamous cultures in the world.[76] Polygyny is the highest in Ghana and Sierra Leone according to one survey,[77] while another shows Nigeria to have the highest proportion of polygynous marriages (63 percent of all marriages in that country are polygynous).[78]

In rural areas the agricultural work as well as all domestic work and child rearing is done by the co-wives. Men oversee but participate little in any of these activities. Each wife has a separate room or house for herself and her children. Generally the husband spends two consecutive nights with each wife at a time. In Senegal, for example, "Each family lives in a constant state of stress with three or four women taking each a two-day turn with their husbands, in which case they are responsible for doing the cooking for the entire group. As a result of cooking for two days for up to five adults and ten or more children the women are totally exhausted."[79]

Generally in polygynous families there is conflict among and between the wives for goods and services from their husband.[80] For control over women the optimal number of wives is said to be four. To have one wife is said to be equivalent to having none at all, since her duties are not only to her husband, but to her family of origin; two are competitive, and three may form coalitions.[81]

Genital mutilation also figures into the efficiency with

which polygyny is practiced, as it is calculated to rob
women of their sexual being. Destroying their potential for
erotic feelings precludes the wives from developing amor-
ous interest either in each other or in any other man. They
are thus effectively enslaved by their husbands, whose control over them is not unlike that of a pimp's authority over
his stable.

Polygyny does not decrease with urbanization. In fact,
"the incidence of polygyny in cities tends to increase with
the length of time spent there and with higher levels of
occupation achieved."[82] Clearly polygyny's major function
is not, as many have assumed, to enhance the economic
productivity men can derive from women's labor. It is,
instead, another organization of male sexual power resulting in marital slavery.

Urbanization disrupts rural polygynous arrangements. In
some situations co-wives remain behind in the rural areas
when their husband migrates to the city. Other co-wives
accompany their husband to the city. As the illiteracy rate
is extremely high among women in polygynous areas, when
they do move to the city their economic value is dramati-
cally reduced because they are frequently unemployable.
Clignet found that "In Abidjan, 19 percent of monogamous women were in the urban labor force in 1963 as
compared to 5 percent of the senior co-wives and 4 percent
of their junior counterparts."[83]

Up to 50 percent of the families in Dakar are polygynous and husbands cannot adequately support their families.
Living accommodations are crowded in apartment buildings. Furthermore, as men are trained to see themselves as
being supported by their wives, often when they do earn
money they do not use it to support their family but to buy
another wife.[84]

Female illiteracy keeps women out of the labor market,
reinforcing urban poverty. Yet there is great resistance to
educating girls in polygynous cultures. Clignet found that
education was the only factor that tends to break up
polygyny: "Schooling of the female population is the only
one which had a negative effect on polygyny and has thus
tended to contribute to the disruption of the over-all func-
tioning of traditional family structures. Not only have educated women refused to belong to polygynous families,
even as senior co-wives, but they have frequently been in a

position to force males to change their domestic attitudes and behavior."[85]

SEX COLONIZATION

Sex is power is the foundation of patriarchy, and patriarchy is *rule by male right*. Across all national boundaries, male gender (and the power that accrues to it) is first and foremost the basis for power and authority in society. It defines who controls the social and political order. From male authority flows male rights. Those rights, established through the sex-is-power ethic, are exercised first in one-to-one relationships. It is in the private relationship between men and women that fundamental inequality is established. From individual domination, inequality is incorporated into the larger social, political, and economic order. Institutionalized sexism and misogyny—from discrimination in employment, to exploitation through the welfare system, to dehumanization in pornography—stem from the primary sexual domination of women in one-to-one situations.

Female sexual slavery, in all of its forms, is the mechanism for controlling women through the sex-is-power ethic, either directly through enslavement or indirectly using enslavement as a threat that is held over all other women. This is the generalized condition of sex colonization. Enslavement or potential slavery is rarely seen as such either by its aggressors/potential aggressors or by its victims/potential victims. That is the subtlety of long-term sex colonization.

In 1971 I joined with several other women in issuing the Fourth World Manifesto, which declared "Women, set apart by physical differences between them and men, were the first colonized group. And this territory colonized was and remains our women's bodies." We declared further that "Most males have an individual colonial relationship to an individual female and most males identify with and act on the group colonization of women."

The colonization of a people is not seen by the colonizer as a destructive act. Paternalism conceals and glosses over displays and acts of power. The colonizer sees himself as doing good in taking over the lives, culture, values, and institutions of a people he believes to be innately inferior to himself. The colonizer recognizes that he must use force and exercise power to correct the errors of their inferior ways, that he must destroy lives to remake them in the image he casts for them. The colonizer recognizes no class, no religion, no race within the group he is colonizing as equal to or superior to him. All are subject to his rule. And as a reward for destroying and remaking the lives of people he has taken under his control through physical domination, he extracts cheap or free (translate slave) labor and sex.

Sex colonization is insidious. Not only are women dominated as a group—socially, politically, and economically —but unlike any other colonized group, they must share the homes and beds of their colonizer. In studying national colonization we have been trained to view colonizers as governments instead of individual people. Sex colonization relies on individual colonizers who act in private: the pimp who beats his whore "for her own good," the husband who begs his wife to return after severely beating her, claiming he didn't know what he was doing, the father who would rather have his daughter experience sex from him rather than with "some strangers," the family that has its daughter infibulated to protect her from destroying family honor.

Sex colonization is enforced through sexual slavery in every patriarchal society. Forced prostitution and forced marriage, which includes wife battery, veiling, arranged marriages, and polygyny, confirm the subordination of all colonized women. They remain as a potential if not a present reality for all women and as such are instruments of the colonizer in holding his power.*

Sex colonization through female sexual slavery extends across all male-dominated cultures. It is useless and destructive for women to compare the relative advantages of one cultural form of sexual slavery over another, in an allegiance to a particular national culture. Slavery is a

---

* In this context Anne Summers discusses rape as a political weapon of the colonizer. In her study of the colonization of women in Australia, *Damned Whores, God's Police* (Australia: Penguin, 1975), Summers presents a thorough discussion of the various factors within one culture that contribute to sex colonization. In considering the control men have assumed over female sexuality, birth control, and childbirth practices, as well as in the workplace, Summers is able to illustrate how female socialization is actually an induction into colonial mores.

despicable condition and there is no legitimate argument to assert the practice of slavery in one culture over that in another without condoning slavery per se.

Each male national culture has its own set of beliefs that are contained within an ideology which supports sex colonization. That ideology is perpetuated in the social order through various institutions. Religion often serves as a conduit for ideology. Notions of female promiscuity as illustrated by the rape paradigm stem directly from the Christian ethic in the West. In the Arab world seclusion of women is validated by Islamic law.

But in pluralistic societies, religion is insufficient for the ideology that shores up female sexual slavery. In the West where there is a broad range of beliefs and lifestyles among a vast population, ideology must be conveyed through other forms as well. Pornography will be discussed in the next chapter as a primary institution promoting an ideology of sexual violence. It is the masculinist concept of sexual liberation. It actually can be seen as a kind of "danger belief" in a similar sense as those which view women as uncontrollably promiscuous and therefore a threat to honor.

In pornography women are portrayed as supersexed beings who will devour or destroy men. They are the fantasy of men's fear and loathing of women and as such must be subdued; sexual aggression and violence are the means to bring them under control. In the final analysis, genital mutilation practiced in Africa, crimes of honor practiced in the Mediterranean world, and pornography in the West are equivalent forms, each attempting to control or, if necessary, destroy women through masculinist ideology. Where in the Arab world a woman may be murdered in the most extreme acts of honor, in the West murder of women in snuff films (where women are actually murdered in the climax of sexual pleasure) represents the most extreme condition of the act of male sexual freedom.

NATIONAL COLONIAL REVOLUTIONS VERSUS SEX COLONIZATION

When the colonized internalize the values of the colonizer, colonization is completed through self-enforcement and the colonizer can sit back and accept the fruits of his labor.

Across male national boundaries, women strongly defend veiling, seclusion, genital mutilation, forced prostitution, and marital enslavement. Consequently, even when rebellion against national colonization occurs, sex colonization continues.

Generally there is little evidence that men's nationalistic revolutions against their colonization lessen the practice of female sexual slavery. African nations have freed themselves from the yoke of European colonization by developing a spirit and movement of nationalism—pride in one's own people, society, culture, values, traditions, rituals. The problem this presents for women is that the most valued traditions of the national cultures stem from masculine values, such as male honor, that are oppressive to women. Consequently, practices like veiling and genital mutilation are found in the social values of the colonized male culture. They eventually become the basis for cultural pride of the colonized in the fight against the foreign colonizer. Nowhere was this more apparent than in the Algerian revolution against the French.

Since Algeria's successful socialist revolution against the French, veiling is still widely practiced even though it is not officially required. Many women remain in seclusion. Sex colonization in the context of Algerian liberation was discussed in the Fourth World Manifesto,* where we analyzed Frantz Fanon's defense of the veil as a condition imposed on the woman by herself and therefore a cultural trait to be respected.[86] "His defense of Algerian male culture is every bit as smooth as the French justification of colonial rule. And he denies female oppression under the guise of defending the Algerian national culture from vulture-like attacks by the French. No one will doubt that the French were brutal colonizers of the Algerians, but that does not deny or excuse the equally brutal colonization of Algerian females by Algerian males."[87]

How French and Algerian men used secluded, invisible

* The Fourth World Manifesto was written in response to left-anti-imperialist attempts to co-opt the feminist movement into working for the goals of male national revolutions. In response Barbara Burris presented in the Manifesto a lengthy analysis of the failure for women of the Algerian revolution; it is briefly summarized here.

Algerian women as pawns in their battle against each other for power is best illustrated by the issue of the veil. The French initiated a campaign in Algeria in 1958 to "liberate" Algerian women from the veil. Their interest was less in the liberation of Algerian women and more in creating discordance between women and men. Divide and conquer is a basic strategy of colonizers. One incident in May 1958 dramatized the symbolic value of the use of women in this way: "French women, to applauding crowds, lifted the veils from the heads of a number of Moslem women who gratefully smiled at the cameramen. Behind this drama were the wives of some of the generals and top officers of the French Army."[88] The same French army that wanted to "liberate" Algerian women would carry out massive rapes of these women during the war to dishonor the men.*

The battle of the veil launched by the French just before the revolution hit exactly where it was intended and Fanon articulated Algerian male reaction. "Converting the woman . . . wrenching her free from her status, was at the same time achieving a real power over the man and attaining a practical effective means of destructuring the Algerian culture."[89] The veil was seen by the French as one strategy for holding on to their colonial relationship through divide and conquer in the face of an increasing Algerian population. But the revolution intervened and Algerian rebels made the veil a symbol of their women's patriotism.[90] According to Algerian feminist Fadela M'rabet, in 1964 after the revolution, "a woman unveiled cannot walk anywhere without being stared at and accosted; the dowry has been commercialized . . . in 1964, 175 girls committed suicide to evade forced marriages."[91] Gordon points out that one does see unveiled women working in the ministry offices and welfare centers but there are few women in Algeria in those positions.[92]

A similar campaign was conducted by the French against polygyny. During their colonization the French tried to curb polygyny by discriminating against males who practiced it. Predictably, by the time of the revolution it

* For the most thorough discussion of the use of rape in war, see *Against Our Will* (New York: Simon and Schuster, 1975), by Susan Brownmiller.

too was defended as part of the indigenous national culture.

Despite the gains that accrue to male national cultures from socialist revolutions, those revolutions in many ways reinforce sex colonization with a vengeance. From her interviews with Algerian women after the war, M'rabet summarizes it:

> Not to learn anything, not to see her fiancé before marriage, to be married very young and condemned to *reproduce*; not to have any social life, not to take part in the conduct of public affairs—these are then some of our *traditions*, solid traditions, which long preceded colonialism and continue to survive long after independence.[93]

The practices M'rabet has disclosed continue today in postrevolutionary Algeria. In June 1978 the wealthy family of a 26-year-old Algerian woman who was living with her husband in Montreal arranged to have their daughter kidnapped and returned to Algeria for a marriage that had been arranged at her birth. Dalila Maschino was visited by her sisters and their husbands in her Montreal home, where according to authorities she was drugged and taken by private plane back to Algeria for the arranged marriage.[94]

Revolutions which have freed Arab nations from colonial rule have generally been accompanied by a reaffirmation of Islam. An Islamic fundamentalism is sweeping the Arab and Mediterranean world. Literal interpretation of the Koran increasingly guides governments as well as individuals. In 1976, the constitution of Algeria was amended to note that while it was dedicated to a socialist revolution it is still an Islamic state. One country after another has reasserted the traditional values of Islam and, as they do, the veil is being seen more frequently on women who in some places were beginning to discard it.[95]

The Algerian example of sex colonization in male revolution is played out with only slight variation in Iran today. In early 1979 after years of international campaigning that highlighted the torture of political prisoners in Iran, a revolution swept through the country forcing the deposition of the Shah Mohammed Riza Pahlevi. The overthrow of the

Western-identified Shah marked the return of religious revolutionary leader Ayatollah Khomeini and began the creation of a Muslim nation in government as well as in national religion and lifestyle.

Almost immediately after Khomeini's return, those women who had fought for the Shah's deposition were faced with a test of loyalty. They were told to return to the veil or *chador*. The Shah had been responsible for removing requirements for veiling women. He had also recently introduced co-education and a Family Protection Law (1967)* which gave women some equality in divorce and family property. But the Shah was also known as a tyrannical dictator who, with support from the United States, ruled Iran with the heavy arm of political repression and torture of political prisoners.

During the revolution many previously unveiled women wore the *chador* as a symbolic defiance against the Shah. After his deposition and with the return of Khomeini the women found that the symbol of the veil came to be identified by the new regime as a reaction against all that is Western and therefore politically and morally corrupt.

In the early days of the revolution the Ayatollah denounced co-education, abolished the Family Protection Law, and called for women's return to the *chador*. This attempt to shame women into submission temporarily backfired. During a period when revolutionary "justice" was meted out daily before firing squads, thousands of angry Iranian women bravely took to the streets. On March 8, 1979, the streets of Teheran swelled with women demonstrating against the *chador* with the slogan "In the dawn of freedom there is an absence of freedom." To emphasize that their action was not pro-Shah but instead pro-woman,

---

* It is noted that the Family Protection Law, although a significant departure from sexist tradition, actually represented only a modest reform and a symbolic gain for women. According to Iranian lawyer, Zohreh Majdzadeh, in a report in *Women's International Network News*, Spring 1978, "A woman can obtain maintenance from the man after divorce for only three months and ten days and after that she must fend for herself, even if she is illiterate and has no job or visible means of support. The man is not bound to pay alimony and the courts do not take up this question . . ."

they chose International Women's Day for their protest. Demonstrations which took place over several days swelled at times to a reported 100,000. On March 10, 15,000 women staged a three-hour sit-in at the Palace of Justice demanding the right to wear what best suits them and the country's customs, equal civil rights with men, no discrimination in political, social, and economic rights, and full legal rights for women. Within a few days both Khomeini and Prime Minister Barzargan issued somewhat conciliatory statements and the women stopped demonstrating.

What remains to be seen is the extent to which this articulate minority of women will be able to stand up against sex colonization of the new regime *and* demand that emancipation be extended to all women. Long-term socialization reinforced by powerful religious beliefs threatens to overpower and reverse what had been the beginning of a long-term fight for freedom.

The failure of national revolutions demonstrates that, whatever cultural values are derived from Islam that are important for preservation of the uniqueness of Muslim culture, female sexual slavery in marriage must be judged above any cultural standards. Respect for human life demands that above unique cultural characteristics is the universal principle that every female has the right to live free from slavery, torture, and imprisonment—even when that prison is her home.

DIVIDE AND CONQUER

Sex colonization is global and a global standard is required for recognizing it and for judging the conditions of female sexual slavery contained within it. Colonization begins with the takeover of a people who are physically different from the colonizer, usually by race or ethnicity. Revolution against colonization is made possible when the colonized are able to see others who are physically like themselves living free from colonization. There have always remained some countries in the world not taken over by Western colonization and imperialism where men *could* see others of their race or ethnicity living free, guarding and protecting their culture. But that is not the case for women colonized. Regardless of the national culture they live in, women cannot look to another group that is physically the same as themselves yet is not colonized. Now with the advancement of an international feminist movement, women are increasingly able to reflect on their own cultural condition as they share those experiences they hold in common with other women.

Women's allegiance to the values of male national culture that enslave them is the first illustration of the colonizer's most basic strategy: divide and conquer. The divisions created among women are most severe in situations of sexual slavery. Women are set up to fight against each other while maintaining their loyalty to their individual colonizers and to the male institutions and cultures which colonize them.

Often co-wives in polygynous societies are in a situation of competing for their husband's attention.

Many Arab and black African mothers arrange for their daughters to be excised or infibulated.

Some mothers deny their daughters' claims that they have been incestuously assaulted, leaving long-term bitterness between the females.

Some prostitutes do the procuring for their pimps, bringing young teenage girls into forced prostitution.

Other prostitutes become madams and carry out the enslavement of many women in their own brothels.

Using Summers' description of female socialization as an induction into colonial mores, one notes the subtle forms of colonization that are molded into women's behavior through divide and conquer strategies. Internalizing the values of the colonizer and active participation in carrying out the colonization of one's self and one's sex can otherwise be defined as male identification. Male identification is the act whereby women place men above women, including themselves, in credibility, status, and importance in most situations regardless of the comparative quality the women may bring to the situation. Through male identification, women automatically acknowledge men's authority, word, and actions. Interaction with women is seen as a lesser form of relating on every level. Rather, allegiance to men is automatic.

Male identification is not just a series of specific acts. It is a way of life that permeates existence as much as the air we breathe. It means taking on the values of masculinist ideology, surely the path of least resistance for women in patriarchy. This practice is extended from the highest levels of the business and professional world, where one hears women talk in nonspecific terms of how they'd rather work for a man, to the most personal relationships, where women may deny female friendship to demonstrate their allegiance to a man. We see it in women who will defend men (individually and collectively) in the face of their verbal, emotional, or physical transgression against women. Or, in a more subtle form, we see it in the refusal of women to acknowledge male predatory behavior and to label women who react against it as excessively angry or as man-haters. We see it in the inability of women to put themselves in the place of abused women when, as jurors in rape trials, they usually identify with the defendant, or, as in the trial of Patricia Hearst, they refuse to identify with the victim. The inability of women to put themselves in the place of a woman victimized is ultimately a denial of self living in the conditions of colonization. It results in women then effectively being able to police other women. Sex colonization requires male identification in its most subtle and self-denying forms.

International feminism will find women united through that which is common to the oppression of all women. Such unity is essential if women are to rise above the conditions of sex colonization. But feminists from Western nations have often been guilty of approaching women in Third World countries with an air of superiority which assumes that they will bring liberation to the less fortunate and enlightened. Besides the racism this attitude implies, it also reflects the extent to which Western feminists have not been able to recognize the severity of their own oppression.

Ultimately each separate battle against the unique aspects of sex colonization that define different cultures will have to be fought by the women of that culture on their own terms. To do that without acknowledgment of the dimensions of female oppression common to all women is to remain vulnerable to the mystification that some slavery can be condoned as culturally unique. International feminist organizers must be able to address the manifestations of female sexual slavery in all cultures from common strength and support while not interfering with the efforts of women within their own culture to free themselves.

In addition, as international feminism begins to face the most critical aspects of sex colonization, women from different cultures will be able to learn more about the roles they can play in preventing the intrusion of one male national culture into another that escalates the colonization of the women. For example, the commitment to international feminism would demand response from American feminists to President Carter's appeal for human rights which has proved to be a sham for women the world over. Gloria Steinem called attention to President Carter during his early 1978 trip to Saudi Arabia when he declared he felt at home among his own people while his wife was ordered to walk 10 steps behind him, enter the guest palace through the side door, and sit in her room during the State dinner to which she was not invited, and when she cooperated with these requirements of her, the executive authority of the United States gave support and credibility to those cultural practices in Saudi Arabia which enslave and subjugate women. More specifically, women must be intolerant to the point of action of the United States government's financial and military support to governments that silently sanction the sexual slave trade of women in their countries.

Slavery is a condition of colonization which cannot be challenged effectively without addressing the issues and aspects of life that support it in the whole culture. For women, that necessitates international bonding based on a recognition of the colonization we face within each male-dominated culture.

CHAPTER 9

Pornography:
The Ideology
of Cultural Sadism

pornography—(from the Greek pornè, *a prostitute,* + graphy*) 1. originally, a description of prostitutes and their trade.*

Pornography no longer describes only the sexual activities between prostitutes and their customers. Sexual liberation has brought into the home many of the bizarre sexual activities that men have demanded of prostitutes. Pornography depicts not just what one can do with a whore but with one's lover, one's wife, and even one's daughter. Through pornography, time-honored distinctions of society are now blurring and the gap is quickly closing between love and violence, madonnas and whores.

Sadistic violence and sexual enslavement are not isolated or remote phenomena. Pornography brings them into everyday life. One does not have to look to distant harems or slavery brothels of the world for these practices. One does not even have to see wives being battered, children molested, women raped. Pornography that depicts these acts as erotic is present and available at the nearest adult bookstore, on the local newsstand, or on video tapes to be played in the privacy of one's bedroom. It is precisely because the description of sadistic violence and sex slavery is so immediately available in our lives that it is so difficult to see the threat it poses to the life and safety of women and girls. Against no other group in society could handbooks or blueprints for sadistic violence, mutilation, and even gynocide abound with such safety, support, and impunity.

The representation of female sexual slavery in pornography and through the media is a definite and established part of masculinist culture. It represents a form of sexual violence against women that is built into the structure of societies and the lifestyles of people. I have named this practice "cultural sadism." Cultural sadism is a distinct social form that consists of practices which encourage and support sexual violence, defining it into normal behavior. These practices are woven into the fabric of culture and as such they give cultural sadism its own evolution and history and support it by an ideology that legitimizes and justifies it.

WHAT IS PORNOGRAPHY?

Pornography is a practice of cultural sadism as well as a means of diffusing it into the mainstream of accepted behavior and therefore into private lives of individuals. It is the principal medium through which cultural sadism becomes part of the sexual practices of individuals.

The most prevalent theme in pornography is one of utter contempt for women. In movie after movie women are raped, ejaculated on, urinated on, anally penetrated, beaten, and, with the advent of snuff films, murdered in an orgy of sexual pleasure. Women are the objects of pornography, men its largest consumers, and sexual degradation its theme. There are variations on this basic format which are made to appeal to tastes that become eroded or saturated from repetition. Variations include an escalation of violence and the use of children and animals as "exotic" objects. Homosexual pornography, which acts out the same dominant and subordinate roles of heterosexual pornography, appeals not only to gay but also to straight men. Lesbian pornography is made specifically for the titillation of the male consumer. It is what heterosexual men get off on thinking women do together; generally that pornography holds no interest or appeal to those lesbians who might otherwise be interested.

The use of blacks and other ethnic minorities in pornography is less of an appeal to the minority audience than it is a racist representation of blacks for kinky sex. Pornography, in serving its consumer, relies on some of the most pronounced sexual myths and biases of reactionary thought in American society. Pornography presents the stereotype of supersexed blacks and kinky homosexuality and feeds it to the predominately male heterosexual consumer for his private pleasure. Racism and sexism blend with the other characteristics of pornography to provide entertainment based on sexual objectification, violence, and contempt for women. It is the media of misogyny.

In their 1959 study the Kronhausens noted several common characteristics of pornography: seduction, defloration, incest, use of the permissive-seductive parent figure, and acts profaning the sacred.[1] The first requirement in most pornography is that a setting be established for the action. The setting is used only to establish a mind set for the action; therefore little effort is expended on developing the setting. The situation is defined through a variety of approaches: men planning a rape, women being kidnapped off the street, a pubescent girl home alone with her father, men planning a sex orgy, and so on. Whether it is seduction or abduction, the scene is brief and "the 'victim' is more often than not, a willing collaborator."[2] Frequently the woman or girl is caught by surprise and offers initial resistance. The following excerpt from a Danish publication, "Rape," is not unusual:

> Max and John, two builders, suffered hard in the heat but looked forward to the lunch break. It had all begun when John had caught sight of a dishy bird while he was fitting a window on the tenth floor, and what was more she was sunning herself stark naked on the roof of an adjacent building. . . . John told Max his plan. "First we've got to tie the broad to the downpipe and then instill some respect into her with the stick," he whispered. "We'll soon have her on her knees!" John added.

The action moves quickly into the sexual conquest or what the Kronhausens referred to as defloration, violating the virginity of a young girl and unleashing her overwhelming desire for sadistic sex. Whether or not the girl is a virgin, sexual conquest most frequently involves men in groups and highly sadistic activity. "It is highly charactertistic of these fantasies that no matter what degree of agony is inflicted, the girl invariably disclaims any concern over her pain."[3] Hostility, then, is never a characteristic female response to the sexual conquest. "Rape" progresses:

> Once there was a swish and the stick drew another red weal across her arse cheeks. . . . The hand on Kristina's tits changed the whole situation. Kristina's breasts were highly sensitive, even hypersensitive, and nothing turned her on more than some thorough breast massage. Exhausted, she hung on the ropes and both the fiends could hardly believe their own ears when they suddenly heard a husky, frantic panting that radiated lust.

The sexual conquest is intricately bound to the image of supersexed males and nymphomaniac females. Exaggerated penis size indicates a "man whose potency is almost limitless, and whose sex drive is constantly at record strength," while females are "just as men would like women to be: highly passionate, sensuous, and sexually insatiable creatures who like nothing better than almost continuous intercourse."[4] Such is the way "Rape" concludes:

> Excited, Max continued fondling the nipples, using his free hand on the other breast—and Kristina squirmed, not in pain, but in lust. . . . In this way both boys got what they wanted, panting and shouting with joy and randiness, but Kristina was even happier, having forgotten that she was raped.

Slavery, or bondage and discipline as it is alternatively called, is also a frequent theme in pornography. In slavery, frequent or continual beatings or degradation are meant to break a woman's spirit and make her compliant. With rope and chains women are bound, gagged, and tied into positions which render them totally vulnerable and exposed. The beatings usually precede and then coincide with the sex, mostly oral, which is first forced and ultimately portrayed as being craved by the woman. In *Slaves in Bondage* a husband beats his ex-wife into submission. Finally he releases her:

> It was a long, long night for Mary. When it was
> finally over and Pete didn't have the strength to lift
> the paddle anymore, her body was covered with raw,
> red welts and ugly purple bruises. The skin on her
> pretty face was cut and torn. Pete let her stay tied
> up for a painful hour or two while he hurled insults
> at her.

Sadism is a dominant theme in pornography, whether fully
developed as with Pete and Mary or more subtly ex-
changed. It is the chief mechanism by which fantasy is
created and entertainment is offered.

Distortion of reality is an appeal to fantasy and a form
of entertainment but it is also a political act, an attempt to
create an image of women that is consistent with the way
men want to see and use them. Three such reality distortions are consistent pornographic themes:

First, sexual sadism is presented as a source of sexual
pleasure for women. The male fantasy insists that beatings,
rape, humiliation, and pain turn women on. But pain does
not turn women on and most women report that mutual
tenderness and affection are central to their sexual needs.[5]

Second, sadism is portrayed as the other half of the
sadomasochistic duality in human nature. Pornography assumes that both parties of the supposed duality enter the
act with free will and that the one beaten holds equal
power with the one doing the beating. Sadomasochism is a
disguise for the act of sexually forcing a woman against
her will and it creates a guilt-free environment for those
who seek this entertainment.

Third, sadism involves beatings that result in cuts,
lashes, tears to the skin, and purple bruises; yet, except in
ritualistic sex murders, pornography is careful not to show
any marks, blood, or bruises on the woman's body. Graphically written descriptions of beatings are accompanied by
pictures of unmarred, sexually alluring bodies. In films, for
example, women's pain from violent sexual intercourse or
beatings is edited out by turning off the sound of that scene
and replacing it with music and by not showing the woman's face at times when she would be expressing pain. In
one film in which a woman was simultaneously vaginally
and anally penetrated, she was positioned so that you could

not see her face, and as the penetration took place the chattering of the men in the film was cut off and replaced by music that presumably silenced the screams that must have resulted from the sexual brutality on the screen. For the sexual sadist it is the best of both worlds—beauty and violence together in sex. While the victim becomes invisible, the consumer enjoys the brutality of sadism guilt-free, as he never has to see the consequences of it.

THE PORNOGRAPHIC EXPERIENCE

Pornography is intended for effect; it is intended to produce both sexual feelings and actions in the consumer. Distinguished from art, which in and of itself produces an esthetic experience, pornography instead is a "stimulus *to* an experience not focused on it. It serves to elicit, not the imaginative contemplation of an expressive substance, but rather the release in fantasy of a compelling impulse."[6] Sontag describes this as the emotional flatness of pornography. The arousal of a sexual response in the reader requires the deadpan tone of pornography.[7]

What then is the consumer's experience in his sexual response to pornography? Masturbation is a common behavior that takes place while reading or viewing pornography. The images and stimulation to fantasy and masturbation come in a solitary experience in which the consumer allows himself to be acted upon by the pornographic movie or book. Even though men occasionally may go to an adult bookstore with other men, and even though they see sexual sadism frequently acted out by men in groups, the pornographic experience is basically a solitary, noninteractive one, whereby the self becomes an object.

Theatres and bookstores are set up for privacy. In some theatres live sex shows are viewed from small, private rooms. What is seen or read is unmediated by any other social experiences. If the experience is pleasurable, the substance of pornography is reinforced. The consumer doesn't think about what is being pictured or acted out in front of him; he just responds. He doesn't discuss it with friends. He neither has nor wants a reality check to determine where reality and fantasy are blurred. He doesn't get to believe or disbelieve what is going on; even if there is time to be reflective, the more dominant and prevalent sexual stimulation that is taking place overrides it. There is usually no reality check available or desired in the pornographic experience. Fantasy and reality are blurred and experienced with sexual stimulation in isolation. Distortions presented in pornography stimulate a sexual response which in turn reinforces the enjoyment of distortions. When it is over, the consumer may then choose what to believe and interpret as reality, what to attribute to fantasy, and what to act out. We can be relatively sure that those choices will be based on those things that created the most sexual stimulation and therefore received the most reinforcement.

This is the pornographic experience that is translated into sexual behavior. But usually men do not leave pornographic stores or theatres to act out what they have just seen. Presumably for the moment some sexual satisfaction has been achieved. The pornographic experience now resides in memory, from where it is retrievable to fantasy and then to action.

Fantasy is a key to translating pornography from the book or the screen to human behavior and as such is the next level of the pornographic experience. Fantasy in and of itself is neither positive nor negative behavior. It is a basic, necessary human experience that, depending on its content and the way it is used, can be either a creative adjunct to social reality or a destructive agent of it. The subject matter of fantasy and the way it is used are significant in determining its effects on attitudes, behaviors, and social practices.

Fantasies are very private experiences and sexual fantasies are most private of all. Sharing a fantasy with another may rob it of its excitement and therefore its mystery. Fantasy is essentially an interaction with oneself through images present in the mind. The images may be free-floating, separate entities, may be singular fleeting images, or may form into a story content—a scenario, script, or short vignette. "They exist only for their elasticity, their ability to instantly incorporate any new character, image or idea —or, as in dreams, to which they bear so close a relationship—to contain conflicting ideas simultaneously. They expand, heighten, distort or exaggerate reality."[8] While sexual fantasy is carried out on the daydream plane of one's mind, it is intimately connected to the rest of one's being. It taps our emotions and triggers sexual feelings. Sexual fantasy may be erotic to the point of creating orgasm and often is used as a stimulus to masturbation.

I am speaking here of conscious fantasy or daydreams—fantasy which either enters one's mind unsolicited or is conjured up by the daydreamer, fantasy that takes place when one is awake.

Fantasy is the unspoken life one experiences with one's mind, emotions, and being. Because it is so personal, because it is located in the dreaming expanse of one's mind, question has existed over time as to how fantasy takes place, where the images come from, and what meaning they have for the rest of one's behavior. The ethereal quality of fantasy has provoked us to try to understand more about its nature and effects.

Jung refers to the archetype for an explanation of how fantasy is derived. "It represents or personifies certain instinctive data of the dark primitive psyche, the real but invisible *roots of consciousness*."9 Myths express the archetype which are found in the conscious and unconscious fantasy of the individual. "Archetype" has come to designate behaviors that continually reappear in human conduct over time. It validates them, suggesting that they are functional and therefore necessary parts of human life. This explanation of the source of fantasy as rooted in the recesses of the psyche has been extended far beyond logic or usefulness. The symbol now exceeds the reality it represents. The notion that the sources of fantasy are woven into the fabric of life, constituting part of the psychic history of mankind, requires a kind of determinism that just doesn't stand up to the evidence of social reality.

The fact is that it is impossible to think of any symbol, image, or concept in fantasy if we have no prior knowledge of its existence. Yet it is popularly assumed that fantasy reveals some basic, innate truths about ourselves. But it is in our interaction in the social world that concepts or images are formed or developed. We learn them. We must know about something from our social experience for it to enter our fantasy life. We do not have to know it as a social reality in the same manner, form, or context in which we meet it as a fantasy image, but it must have had in some form a prior social reality to us before it enters our private self-interactive fantasy. Blue does not exist as a color in dreams for those who are color-blind to blue and therefore have no experience of blue. Neither can an archetypal image exist in our fantasy or experience if we've had no social connection to it in our world. Our fantasy life is shaped from the content and substance of social reality. Imagery from the real world is combined with individual creativity to form the unique or at least seemingly unique images, plots, or stories we conjure up as fantasy. In addition to the content of social experience, we bring to our fantasy the emotional import of that experience. Again in fantasy it will not necessarily take the same form as it had when originally experienced. Fantasy is a way of creating a whole different experience of the social reality from which it is drawn.

Fantasy is often the link between one's self and one's sexual life. In the privacy of one's mind one can dream of, fantasize about, or plan out sexual experiences. In the freedom of one's mind those fantasies may be as exotic or erotic as one's creativity will allow. However the images form and are presented in fantasy, they have their source in social reality. The less individual creativity brought into private fantasy, the more closely the fantasy will approximate social reality, the experienced world.

Personal fantasy sometimes enters into sexual interaction with another person. It may precede and prompt a sexual interaction; sexual stimulation from fantasy outside the presence of one's lover may serve as the initiative to be with one's lover. Fantasy becomes part of the sexual interaction between two people in a diverse number of ways. But however fantasy enters a sexual interaction, when sexual experience with another is determined by fantasy, the social-sexual reality of the other person is replaced by the fantasy. The extent to which fantasy dominates sexual interaction with another is the extent to which the other is an object of sexual pleasure. One of the effects of widespread pornography has been to introduce movies, books, or pictures as the erotic stimulant between two people, thereby reducing the need for people to relate to *each other*.

When the images of sexual fantasy that enter interaction

are pornographic, the form of fantasy, the objectification of the other it involves, combines with the content of pornography and the experience becomes a product of cultural sadism. Taken to its fullest form it becomes the literal acting out of private fantasy on to another through force.

Whether or not the pornographic experience leads to sexual fantasies which provoke acting-out behavior, the substance of that experience in terms of contents, emotions, and sexual response remains as a part of one's experience. And like all experience it becomes one of the factors that mold personality, shape behavior, define values, and effect attitudes. Some suggest that pornography is an educational experience. Males between the ages of 21 and 29 are the largest consumers of pornography.[10] Researchers for the U.S. Commission on Obscenity and Pornography noted pornography's instructive value. Gagnon and Simon insist on its usefulness for college males. Stag films "instruct him in sexual technique." And they "primarily reinforce masculinity, and only indirectly reinforce heterosexuality."[11]

Cultural sadism is much more pervasive than pornography; it includes action and behavior as well as the media of sexual violence. Reading or viewing pornographic material does not account for all acts of sexual violence and slavery. Its influence is more widespread than the direct effects it has on its consumers. But pornography is also a crystallization of cultural sadism. As such it is effective in its crystallized state only if it is also diffused throughout the society. That is the role of ideology.

THE IDEOLOGY OF CULTURAL SADISM

Various literary, movie, and media representations of heterosexual love and romance reveal how the cultural sadism of pornography has permeated the whole society. Sex slavery in a variety of forms has become the theme of major award-winning love stories. Lina Wertmuller's highly acclaimed, popular film comedy, *Swept Away By an Unusual Destiny in the Blue Sea of August*, is illustrative of this theme. The device it employs is familiar from sex slavery cases. It uses the "throwaway" woman, the one who is disposed of when there is no other use for her, whether she be a pimp's prostitute or the SLA's heiress. As she is a "throwaway," untold psychological or physical abuse of her is justified as being either what she wants or what she deserves.

In *Swept Away*, as in the SLA saga, the throwaway is a woman of wealth and privilege, the kind of woman who many can enjoy seeing victimized as it provides entertaining catharsis from the oppression of the rich. The heroine of *Swept Away* more than fills the bill as she conveys, in the shrillest of voices, all the arrogance and aloofness that typically is associated with wealth. The movie begins on a yacht in the Mediterranean where she is at leisure with husband and friends. It is as removed as possible from the mundane world, the world filled with danger and terror that women are growing so accustomed to living in. She is beyond the petty daily fears and pressures of survival, physically and psychologically protected by her wealth. She has an almost callous disregard for her safety in her untypical female proclivity to take risks.

Her arrogance and self-sufficiency are all the more grating as she hurls one political insult after another, first at her Communist husband and then at the deckhand when she discovers that he too is a Communist. "I get insulted because I won't be bullied into hiding behind a Marxist mask." But she is more bigoted than political. She taunts her husband's "Vatican Communism" and charges hypocrisy in the Communists who voted down abortion in Italy —abortion that she sees necessary to control the proliferation of the poor. When she learns that the deckhand is a Communist activist, she apparently determines that he will hate and envy her privileges, so she flaunts them at him.

She definitely is not a paragon of virtue but she is a formidable woman and in that sense, like women seen as liberated, she is a challenge—at least that is how Wertmuller sets her up for her "unusual destiny."

The turn of events for her are as abrupt as was the abduction of Patricia Hearst. She and the deckhand become castaways from the luxury and leisure of the yacht to a deserted paradise island. Initially she does not even recognize that she will lose all the protection that wealth had afforded her. Alone with her on the island, the deckhand has the perfect opportunity to right not only the wrongs that she has done in taunting him, but those she represents by exercising the arrogance and privileges of wealth. His physical abuse of her begins slowly, but as he enjoys her humiliation he accelerates it. First, she must wash his clothes, call him Sir, Master. Then he starts pulling her hair, slapping and punching her in the face, and making her kiss his hand. At first he seems to be doing this only to shut her up, to show her her place. Eventually it is clear that to him beating her and humiliating her are pleasures in their own right. When she tries to rebel against his abuse, he turns from slapping to rape. "Now I feel like tearing that pussycat of yours, ramming it and splitting it apart." Abuse will continue until she craves him sexually and accepts his violence. "I've got to become your God." She learns. When she watches him kill and skin a rabbit without any display of emotion she sobs, "I feel like that poor little rabbit." That is the turning point—from then on it is tender romance except for occasional slaps to remind her of his power and of her place.

The climax of romance, the epitome of liberation have been achieved: "I felt swept by a destiny into a sweet mad dream and I don't want it to end." But it does; after the rescue she is turned over from her deckhand lover to her husband. As Patricia Hearst was freed from the SLA and then turned over first to the courts and then to her family, the heroine here is condemned to the prison of bourgeois marriage as she is freed from sexual enslavement. It is at least a poignant reminder of the options women have to sex slavery.

Swept Away—modern romance? sexual liberation? or both? The theme found its way into *Playboy*, which reported in its December 1977 issue that in an informal sex survey of men, 23 percent of their women wanted to be "balled on the beach." Says one: "Thank god for Lina Wertmuller. It seems like every woman in America saw *Swept Away*. Now they want you to take them to the seashore, push them around a bit and then ravage them. . . . Now its chic to be savage. I love it. You couldn't get away with that two years ago."[12] The *Swept Away* fantasy is popular and finds expression in many modes. It inspired jewelry designer David Navarro to create a collection with the sadomasochistic look: "It's a kind of shackle look. A man could walk up and choke her with it if he wanted."[13]

Elsewhere in the world of high fashion, *Vogue* (December 1975) picked up the theme and developed a series of fashion displays in which women were being roughed up. In one a series of photos pictured a beautiful model being beaten while the caption described the jumpsuit she was modeling: "The palest, prettiest tint of peach, in the hottest new pants."

The messages have become clear in recent years. SM (sadomasochism) is not just a weird, fringe sex cult. It is in. It is romance. It is fashionable, chic, fun, and slightly daring. And, its connoisseurs will tell you, it's their right.

Rights are inherent only for the group in power. To be powerless means to be granted only those rights which do not conflict with the interests and goals of the powerful. Rights, then, stem from powerful self-interest. They are derived from the system of beliefs and the ideology of the dominant group; the ideology which in turn defines values and attitudes as it determines behavior.

Sexual domination of women is maintained through the ideology of cultural sadism. Based on male self-interest in patriarchal power, this ideology reifies women, making them into something they are not—the naturally masochistic sexual object existing only for male sexual use and satisfaction. This is not simply the ideology of an elite group but instead something that has been diffused into mass consciousness as illustrated by *Swept Away*. Because woman is represented as one who craves sexual sadism, violent male sexual aggression both equates with and is confused with love and romance. False notions have been created in the mass consciousness in order to justify and legitimize behavior based on these notions. The false consciousness which results is necessary to the ideology of cultural sadism.

False consciousness easily includes both contradictions and incoherence; since its sole function is to maintain itself, it is not answerable to evidence or logic which would reveal the reality that it is obscuring. One pornographer in San Francisco evidenced this when he stated recently that his pornography doesn't promote violence against women: in his pornography he is only into bondage!

Pornography is the means whereby the content of false

consciousness is systematized and structured into the ideology of cultural sadism. Pornography is the explicit "crystallization" of the sexual violence and objectification that precedes it and coincides with it in a diffused and unorganized state. Ideology, because it is organized and systematized, creates an "estrangement from reality," an "impermeability to experiences," what Gabel calls autism.[14] Although it is derived from the actual experience of sexual violence and sexual objectification, by organizing and systematizing it, it appears larger than life and unreal. In addition, it cannot be appealed to with either evidence of social reality or humanitarian sensibility, as its goals are to deny both, since it is based on self-interest and power over the individuals being reified.

The distortions created by pornography, filtered into modern tales of love and romance, cultivated into cultural symbols and images through commodities and advertising, are the result of reifying women and sexuality. Through the removal of women and sexuality from their reality context and the ascribing of selected fantasy to apply to what is removed, the reality of female experience of sex is redefined: sadism becomes a source of pleasure for women, sadomasochism is derived from human nature, and whippings, beatings, and torture don't leave visible marks. Woman is reified and degraded for the utilitarian value she represents as a sex commodity. Men's sexual role has likewise been reified to the powerful, objectifying aggressor. Increasingly, social pressure demands that men accept that socially created definition of themselves.

This is the ideology of cultural sadism that legitimizes and therefore perpetuates sexual violence. False consciousness, the diffuse remaking of reality that underpins cultural sadism, did not happen all at once. It is not unique to contemporary life. With its ideology, it has had a careful historical development, the unraveling of which reveals even more about the ideology circumscribing social life today.

THE HISTORY OF CULTURAL SADISM

Probably the best place to begin looking for the ideological roots of cultural sadism is with its namesake, the Marquis de Sade. While Sade didn't invent sadism, his life depicts one of the fullest accounts of the behaviors with which his name is associated.

Sade's life is a study of violent sexual excess. His family origins cannot be ignored. The level of sexual permissiveness he attained can be directly attributed to the aristocratic privileges he inherited. Sade was born in France in 1740 into the old, wealthy, French aristocracy. As he grew into a young man and as he began to act on his sexual appetite, Sade found that he had the title, wealth, and other resources necessary to carry his sexual drive wherever it would take him. While his aristocratic background did not limit his self-indulgence, the legal and religious systems of his times did. He quickly grew to detest any systems or schools that demanded control of his behavior.

To religion and its restrictive morality he reacted with atheism. To the governments and their legalistic restriction on morality he reacted with anarchism. His principle was that there should be no limit on his ability to act on whatever he chose for his sexual pleasure. Such limitations he interpreted as a thwarting of Nature. His life was based on this pursuit of excess, and later in life when he was penniless and imprisoned, he defended the life of a libertine in his writings. He was, in his own estimation and in the summaries of his biographers, a conscious, willful libertine. He contrasted himself with "congenital perverts" as his life was freely chosen and not biologically destined.

What was the life of an aristocratic libertine, of one who defied social controls and trespassed against moral and legal limitations? Sade was married in May 1763 to a woman who was both docile and devoted to him. By November of that year Sade's extramarital practices had come before the courts. Brothels in Paris were warned by the Police Inspector not to supply Sade with girls for his *petites maisons* because of his excessive violence. It was a common practice for wealthy men to keep several small houses or *petites maisons* in and around Paris where they could be supplied with prostitutes and privately indulge their sexual pleasures. It was known that Sade kept five or six such houses. Complaints from the girls sent to him by brothel keepers led to the warning issued by the Police Inspector. Actual practices in the *petites maisons* that led to this complaint and to others later that year were not recorded.

We learn of Sade's sexual behavior in his *petites maisons* from the Rose Keller affair a few years later. On Easter morning, 1768, Sade was approached for alms by a widow-beggar, Rose Keller. He told her she could earn some money by going to his little house with him. She understood her work to be that of a housekeeper. He claimed that he told her she was to participate in the activities of a libertine. After she escaped, Rose Keller described what Sade required of her. At the house Sade told her to undress, and when she refused he tore her clothes from her. Her deposition states:

> . . . he led her into another room next to that one, and in the middle of which there was a divan of red chintz with a white spot, threw her on the said bed on her front, tied her by the four limbs with hempen cord, put a bolster on her neck. . . . That being attached to the bed he took a birch with which he whipped her, made various incisions with a small knife or penknife, poured red and white wax in a greater quantity on these wounds, after which he began to beat her again, to make incisions and pour wax, all of which ill-treatment he repeated up to seven or eight times.[15]

After her escape from the house, Rose Keller, with the sympathy and support of neighbor women, took criminal action against Sade. Lady de Sade intervened, and through others she arranged to have lawyers pay for Rose Keller's silence. Rose initially protested but finally accepted the money and dropped the case. But it was too late; the case had become publicly known and was too excessive for the courts to drop. It was taken to trial and during the criminal proceedings "The Marquis admitted the principal allegations, but insisted that when she agreed to go with him Rose Keller was not unaware that she was required for a bout of sex play."[16] Another point of dispute in the case was Rose's claim that Sade cut her several times with a knife and poured hot wax on the open cuts. Most of Sade's biographers discredit Rose's testimony as it was contradicted by the testimony of the physician who examined her. It is of course possible that she did add detail to the horror of her experience in order to get the courts to take her seriously—a frequent behavior of women escaping sex slavery knowing that what they just experienced is invisible to the world. It is equally possible that the aristocratic title and fortune of Sade allowed him the opportunity to pressure or pay off the physician (just as his family had tried to do with Rose Keller herself) to get him to testify that he found no evidence of such torture. It is not unimaginable that Sade did exactly what Rose described, but even if he didn't pour hot wax on open cuts, the violence to which he subjected her is enough to condemn him, a point his biographers and philosophical defenders have chosen to ignore.

For this crime, Sade spent a total of 59 days in confinement. Between 1768 and 1801 Sade was in and out of jail for similar offenses and indebtedness, serving sentences that ranged from one week to two years. His wealth ran out supporting his life as a libertine, and in jail he turned to writing for continued expression of his sexual life. In 1801 he was arrested for the publications of *Justine* and *Juliette* and he remained in jail until his death in 1810.

Sade's biographers consistently defend him in the Rose Keller case. Gorer points out that Rose Keller had been paid off.

> The magistrates threw themselves with enormous gusto on to the case, with an enthusiasm which needs explaining. They made sure that it received the maximum publicity; although it was known to them that de Sade was in prison in Lyons, they had the public town-criers of Paris call for his apprehension.[17]

Gorer argues that Sade was made a scapegoat, "for the populace was angry that even more flagrant misbehavior went unpunished from people nearer the throne."[18]

Sade the scapegoat! It is true that the treatment of Sade in this case was a reflection of the hypocritical behavior of the times. It is probably equally true that justice was not pursued because violence had been committed against a woman, particularly a beggarwoman. Before one accepts Gorer's defense of Sade, a few other considerations must be made about the justice rendered in this case. While it was undoubtedly true that Sade was punished while other aristocrats and royalty went unpunished for similar behaviors, what is obscured is that rape, beatings, and torture do not characterize men only of a particular class or caste.

The truth is not just that royalty get away with it. Most men from every class who committed these acts have gotten away with it throughout the ages. It is the license of patriarchy. Within the spectrum of male power, men can select the justice they will implement in order to further their own ends. In the Rose Keller case, biographers redefined the problem to one of inequality in the punishing of perversion and thereby diminished the significance of what actually happened to Rose Keller. The actual events of violence were obscured by the creation of false issues to cover them. Historically and contemporarily, ideology has justified almost every kind of sexual violence against women.

In all likelihood Sade was prosecuted in the Rose Keller case because instead of hiding his practices he flaunted them. Instead of carrying out his life of sexual excess in secrecy, he admitted to it, justified it, and encouraged it. Flaunting the behaviors of a libertine revealed to the public what those behaviors were and are—that sexual freedom was more than simple mutual sexual relations. It was not, as Gorer suggests, that Sade was made a scapegoat in an uneven distribution of justice, but rather that the behaviors he flaunted are usually kept invisible so as never to be brought to justice. By making his sexual life with prostitutes public knowledge, Sade threatened the exposure of untold numbers of men who were engaged in similar practices and relied on secrecy and privacy to carry them out. It must have been a nervous time for all those men whose families and reputations would have been ruined if their private sexual excesses were known. If definite steps were not taken to denounce his actions formally, Sade's open flaunting of such behavior could have been construed as socially acceptable. Prosecution of Sade served that purpose. Neither this case nor any others brought against Sade were ever prosecuted as an attack on the social conditions that encourage using women for men's sexual excesses.

The spirit of Sade's time was dominated by the French

Revolution, the cult of Individualism, the Age of Reason. He took advantage of the prevailing philosophical and social context as much as he was influenced by it. Politically, he was opposed to all those noxious controls that the State has over individual liberty and simultaneously he sought individual liberty in all aspects of behavior. Consequently, he opposed capital punishment but insisted individual murders should not be controlled or punished. He opposed the right to private property by the rich but insisted that the State should not interfere with the actions of a thief. He opposed all forms of slavery, in which he included marriage, but insisted that there should be no interference with individual acts of rape or incest or prostitution.

His logic on the last point is most pronounced and speaks to all his other political goals. As always, Nature was his guide. To provide each citizen with full opportunity to vent his passions according to Nature's dictates, Sade proposed:

> Various health establishments, vast and suitably furnished, and secure in all points, will be erected in the city; there, all sexes, all ages, all creatures possible will be offered to the caprices of the libertines who wish pleasure; and the most complete subordination will be the rule for the individuals offered.[19]

But of course this will happen in a context where life is free from slavery:

> Never can an act of possession be carried out upon a free being; it is as unjust to possess a woman exclusively as to possess slaves; all men are born free, all are equal in law.[20]

These two points, his proposals and his condemnation of slavery, appear contradictory as he cannot have women served up to his sexual appetite under their "most complete subordination" and have them free, too.

> It appears beyond contradiction that Nature has given us the right to carry out our wishes upon all women indifferently; it appears equally that we have the right

to force her to submit to our wishes, not in exclusivity, for then I would contradict myself. . . . It is beyond question that we have the right to establish laws which will force woman to yield to the ardors of him who desires her; violence itself being one of the results of this right, we can legally employ it. Has not Nature proved to us that we have this right, by alloting us the strength necessary to force them to our desires?[21]

TAKING NATURE IN

The problem with Sade's scheme was that it was too obvious. While his proposal for health establishments bring to mind the eros centers of Germany or legalized brothels of Nevada, and while they are instituted to provide free and unlimited sexual expression to men, his justification of violence based on physical superiority and therefore Nature's dictates just doesn't wash. His proposal was too explicit.

By the late nineteenth century Freud would provide the necessary construct. Freud was not alone in this work. It took the nineteenth-century sexologists to create a condition in which Sade's sexuality and his writings could be understood and assimilated into a theory of sexuality. The variety and extent of sexual perversions described by Sade were catalogued and described again a hundred years later by sexologists like Richard von Krafft-Ebing and Havelock Ellis. Both relied on case studies from their work and from popular armchair anthropology, stories from different cultures brought to England and Europe from contemporary explorers. Their extensive documentation did not improve the list developed by Sade but it placed it in a "scientific" context. What Sade had defined as sexual behavior decreed by Nature, Ellis and Krafft-Ebing were able to assert as cultural universals from their extensive cross-cultural documentation.

In addition, Krafft-Ebing named the behavior that is the object of sadism, "masochism":

By masochism I understand a peculiar perversion of the physical *vita sexualis* in which the individual affected, in sexual feeling and thought, is controlled by the idea of being completely and unconditionally subject of the will of a person of the opposite sex; of being treated by this person as by a master, humiliated and abused.[22]

Havelock Ellis was particularly attentive to the role of pain in sexual relations. He undertoo a detailed study of the psychology of sex in which he was able to catalogue almost every reported sexual behavior and custom. He rooted each practice in animal behavior, thus defining it as natural, and then provided as many cross-cultural illustrations as he could record. His procedure was descriptive and classificatory. In his volume on *Love and Pain*, Ellis locates the key to pleasure. It is pain: "Among mammals the male wins the female very largely by the display of force. The infliction of pain must inevitably be a frequent indirect result of the exertion of power."[23] Having documented Nature's plan in the animal world, he then supports it through cross-cultural analysis of social customs. Finally he generalizes on the nature of male-female relationships and this takes him logically to sadism:

Within the limits consistent with normal and healthy life, what men are impelled to give women love to receive. So that we need not unduly deprecate the "cruelty" of men within these limits, nor unduly commiserate the women who are subjected to it.[24]

Again from his observations Ellis determines that sadism is specifically limited to sex: "We have thus to recognize that sadism by no means involves any love of inflicting pain outside the sphere of sexual emotion, and is even compatible with a high degree of general tenderheartedness."[25]

Both Krafft-Ebing and Ellis rested their cases on two major assumptions. The first was that each kind of sexual behavior is instinctual. One is instinctively driven to sadism, masochism, homosexuality, or fetishism. The second was that pleasure follows directly from instinctive behavior, that instinct determines a particular sexual role or pattern of sexual behavior. Delineating sex as an instinct is the first step in bringing Sade's externalized concept of Nature into the very being of the person and yet it follows Sade's reasoning in retaining sex as a determinant of behavior.

Sexual practices are no longer dictated by the natural world. Now they must be clearly derived from the innate, innerworld of man himself. The growing ideology of cultural sadism necessitated a sexual determinism that dictated behaviors from the depths of *human* nature.

Sigmund Freud, building on the work of his contemporaries Krafft-Ebing and Ellis, provided that description. He brought all sexual behavior, including and especially sadism, into the very psyche of man through his concepts of the libido and the unconscious. The libido, as the storehouse of sexual energy, interacts with other psychological systems within the person to create certain behaviors. In the libido are found all sexual objects and aims. Freud distinguished between aim and object: the person who elicits the sexual attraction is the sexual object and "the action toward which the impulse strives [is] the sexual aim."[26]

Aim and object designated by the libido are acted on or formed through unconscious processes that begin in infancy. According to Freud, the first sexual instincts of the individual occur in infancy with the parent as object. But the aim of the sexual instinct cannot be achieved because of the incest barrier.

> A restriction has thus been laid upon the object-choice. The sensual feeling that has remained active seeks only objects evoking no reminder of the incestuous person forbidden to it; the impression made by someone who seems deserving of high estimation leads, not to a sensual excitation, but to feelings of tenderness which remain erotically ineffectual.[27]

Since he is not able to have his mother, his affections of tenderness and love are separated from the sexual instinct, which thenceforth is unlikely to find fulfillment where it also has tenderness and love.

> The erotic life of such people remains dissociated, divided between two channels, the same two that are personified in art as heavenly and earthly (or animal) love. Where such men love they have no desire and where they desire they cannot love.[28]

Psychological repression takes place. The incestuous object of sexual desire has been repressed and the result is a kind of impotence. Later sex objects become a substitute for the original, the mother. If a man loves and respects his later sex object, he will not be able to fulfill his sexual needs with her, just as he couldn't with his mother. Freud reasoned that his need is for an additional "sexual object of a lower type." From analyzing men who claimed problems of impotence in general, Freud characterized the "behavior in love of the men of present-day civilization":

> The man almost always feels his sexual activity hampered by his respect for the woman and only develops full sexual potency when he finds himself in the presence of a lower type of sexual object.[29]

And once with his sexual object of a lower type:

> As soon as the sexual object fulfills the condition of being degraded, sensual feeling can have free play, considerable sexual capacity and a high degree of pleasure can be developed.[30]

Freud housed in *human* nature not only the sexual instinct but all behaviors that accompany sexual excitement, including sadism. His assertion could not be questioned, as the root of sexual behavior is inaccessible to the person, being in the unconscious, which is by definition "the unknown." Furthermore, sadism is no longer the perversion of a few but a basic psychosexual characteristic of all:

> The roots of active algolagnia, sadism can be readily demonstrable in the normal individual. The sexuality of most men shows an admixture of *aggression*, of a propensity to subdue, the biological significance of which lies in the necessity for overcoming the resistance of the sexual object by actions other than mere *courting*.[31]

As Freud's theory goes, the separation of love and tenderness from sex and degradation of the sex object is rooted in infantile behavior which gets repressed and remains in the unconscious. Freud also explains acceptance of pain. Here he leans totally on the unconscious:

a) Sadism consists in the exercise of violence or power upon some other person as its object.

b) This object is abandoned and replaced by the subject's self. Together with the turning round upon the self the change from active to a passive aim in the instinct is also brought about.

c) Again another person is sought as object; this person in consequence of the alteration which has taken place in the aim of the instinct, has to take over the original role of the subject.[32]

Voilà! "A sadist is simultaneously a masochist," says Freud. He has taken a behavior attributed primarily to men, acted out primarily by men, combined it with the pain rendered to the victims of sadism, and has made both the victim and the sadist part of the same dynamic.

Freud's theories of sexuality and sadism are totally deterministic: people act from an undefinable instinct and an unknowable unconscious which was determined in unremembered sexual drives of infancy. The responsibility for behavior is moved from the individual to the instinct and the unconscious. Both sadistic and masochistic behavior are defined in terms of unconscious instinctual *needs*. The concept of unconscious instinct precludes morality and divorces psychology from the concept of victim or assailant. The social situation or milieu, the conditions that give rise to sexual violence have been reduced to a discussion of internal psychological mechanisms.

Freud is only a short step beyond Sade. Except for initial sexual sublimation, he finds that men will follow the dictates of Nature, but Nature is redefined as internal psychological motivations that are transformed through the unconscious. Sadomasochism is now a basic psycho-sexual dynamic, and Freud, unlike Sade, justifies the object role of sadism as well as the acts of its perpetrator as inevitable (but not necessarily desirable) consequences of psychological processes.

Freud affirmed the ideology of cultural sadism and raised it to a level of higher sophistication. His theory of the unconscious, while hailed as a major breakthrough in understanding human psychological makeup, became much more than a statement of psychological process. When it was combined with his notions about sexuality and sadism, a new reality was formed and Freud named this reification *sadomasochism*. The philosophy of determininism does far more than affect individual behavior; it actually creates social reality. Instead of interpreting reality, psychological theory often results in creating a new reality. As Berger and Luckmann point out, "Psychologies produce a reality, which in turn serves as the basis for their verification."[33] Once these theories are accepted, neither logic nor proof nor consistency is required in defining social reality. This dynamic, this reification of the unconscious, has been popularly adopted by mass culture and used to interpret or actually redefine behavior. New realities are created which serve to obscure the underlying fundamental social and political conditions.

For example, the explanation of why a woman stays with a pimp or husband who beats her is attributed to unconscious motivation. As long as the motivaton is unconscious, the woman does not have access to it or control over it and she cannot see it. She is stuck with it. She must accept other persons' *interpretations* of her behavior. That interpretation of her reality usually follows the line that the woman stays with the pimp or husband who beats her as a result of a sublimated need for punishment. That interpretation creates a whole new reality, i.e., a sublimated need for punishment. That explanation is now the reality context in which the woman and her experience are understood. No longer is the fact that she is being beaten regularly by a pimp or husband the reality that gets the attention.

In the same psychoanalytic tradition, Robert Stoller provides a contemporary explanation of cultural sadism:

> . . . hostility, overt or hidden, is what generates and enhances sexual excitement, and its absence leads to sexual indifference.[34]

He asserts this from a review of fantasies that get people sexually excited; "The theme present in scripts that produce sexual excitement is the desire to harm someone."[35] According to Stoller, a host of factors contribute to sexual excitement: "hostility, mystery, risk, illusion, revenge, reversal of trauma or frustration to triumph, safety factors and dehumanization."[36] For him, sex is a battlefield and the experience of it is an act of war.

In Stoller's view, hostility is acted out through the unconscious. Dehumanization or fetishism is the key to the generation of sexual excitement. The fetish, created through fantasy, stands for the human being; it replaces a person. It may be a part of a person like a breast or leg; it may even be the whole person "not perceived as him or herself but rather as an abstraction, such as a representative of a group rather than a person in one's own right."[37] It may be an article of clothing or other object that represents the person or it may be an animal. Stoller insists that human attributes are not entirely removed from the person when one is making the person or parts of the person a fetish. They are just reduced. By reducing human attributes, dehumanizing the person, the fetish (which is the person, a part of the person, or a thing) is endowed with a human quality. A fetish is created in order to take out revenge, to right past wrongs, as with the sublimation of the original sexual aim of the infant for his mother.

Now this might get confusing but it means something like this: for a woman being raped (i.e., hostility), the rapist is not really raping the woman. He has just made a fetish out of her to right the past wrongs of being denied sexual intercourse with his mother. This works neatly into an explanation of many social problems such as the myth that black men rape specifically because they can create a fetish out of women to right the wrongs of racial injustice in this racist society. Or lower-class men rape to right the past or present wrongs of poor working conditions and unemployment. As an explanation for behavior it also functions as a legitimization for racism and classism, as the foregoing logic conveniently precludes any motivation for white, nonworking-class men to rape. They are allowed to become the invisible perpetrators of sexual violence.

When the act of making the victim a fetish is completed, Stoller finds:

It is now a fetish, while the human who is being punished has been neutralized and is consciously no longer so important, not seen fully any more as the person he or she is.[38]

As for hostility:

The torture of one's object in fantasy becomes even more exquisite if one degrades him or her into non-humanness or to the status of part object. One does not thus merely obliterate that person, but rather lets him or her continue existing, but robbed of human qualities.[39]

The ability to reduce women to objects, to treat them in cruel and inhuman ways, to assume that they exist for the gratification of men only—these are the things that feminists years ago meant by sexual objectification. Stoller has taken that very same dynamic and put it into the ideological framework of cultural sadism. He has given sexual objectification a special mystical quality, and now rather than being an excessive act of the will, it is there lurking in the never-known but always present labyrinth of unconscious motivation.

By introducing unconscious motivation as an explanatory variable, Freud and subsequent psychoanalysts excessively complicated the seemingly straightforward analysis of biological determinism which explained human behavior through comparison to animal behavior. The newest articulation of deterministic theory, sociobiology, is restoring the biological explanation for human behavior not just through reference to internal instincts but as something programmed in the genes themselves. According to sociobiology it is DNA and not just some elusive drives which mandate our behaviors.

Social life is reduced to a genetic explanation of survival of the fittest. Behavior patterns, like physical characteristics, are subject to the process of natural selection. The emotional control centers in the hypothalamic-limbic complex of the brain are programmed "to perform as if it knows, that its underlying genes will be proliferated maximally only if it orchestrates behavioral responses that bring into play an efficient mixture of personal survival, re-production and altruism."[40] Sociobiology accounts for behaviors like Freud's sadomasochism through genetic de-termination by explaining that in times of stress the hypo-thalamic-limbic center taxes the conscious mind with ambivalences, thus bringing together love and hate, aggres-sion and fear, etc.[41] For women genetic determinism is tied to reproduction:

> In diverse cultures men pursue and acquire, while women are protected and bartered. Sons sow wild oats and daughters risk being ruined. When sex is sold, men are usually the buyers. It is to be expected that prostitutes are despised members of society; they have abandoned their valuable reproductive invest-ment to strangers.[42]

Sociobiology appears to be the next theory to offer justi-fication for sexual violence. In a recent study of mallards, sociobiologist David Barash observed that when a female mallard is raped, her male mate reacts aggressively both to her and to her rapist (unless he acted in a group.) The mate of the victim rapes her again, which according to Barash, is an attempt to insure his paternity: "forcing a copulation with a just-raped female conveys the benefit of introducing his sperm as quickly as possible to compete with those of the rapist, but at the possible cost of weak-ening the pair bond."[43] Barash illustrates the sociobiological implications of his study by pointing out:

> . . . individuals will behave so as to maximize the difference between the benefits and costs associated with any potential act, with both benefits and costs evaluated in units of inclusive fitness. Rape of one's mate imposes a potential cost, in that it increases the likelihood of another individual's fathering her offspring. The response available to a rape victim's mate also carry benefits and costs, and the observed pattern suggests that the mate behaves in accord with evolutionary prediction.[44]

Sexual violence of the animal world is no longer analagous to that in human life but is found to be programmed through and justified by natural selection in social evolution.

Sexual violence simply can't be helped—it's nature—as said Sade, as said Freud, now says Stoller; and to clarify that mandate of Nature, sociobiologists have fixed it in the genes.

YOU SHALL KNOW THE TRUTH . . .

Theory and practice are not always enough to maintain an ideology over time. Ultimately science must confirm what men in their hearts know to be true. In the late 1960's science was brought to the task of systematically studying the beliefs and theories that assert the connections between pornography, sexual behavior, and violence. The prevailing beliefs that were to be addressed were based on the assumption that pornography is an expression of sexual fantasy and as such:

1. It leads only to masturbation.
2. It is a substitute for a sex partner or, for rapists, it is a substitute for a victim.
3. It provides cathartic release, otherwise popularly known as the safety valve theory, accomplished through 1 above.
4. It prevents sexual repression.
5. It leads to boredom and satiation (not to be seen as contradictory to 1, 2, 3, 4 above).
6. It does not lead to sexual violence (not to be confused with 2 above).

This liberal approach to pornography is countered by conservatives who see pornography as a breakdown in the moral order, a threat to the stability of the family, an affront to God, and a cause of sexual violence.

In October 1967 the Commission on Obscenity and Pornography came into existence under Congressional mandate through Public Law 90-100. The Commission, appointed by President Lyndon Johnson, took up the tools of social science research to gather the evidence necessary to fulfill its mandate from Congress. In September 1970 the Commission delivered its report to President Nixon, the Congress, and the people of the United States. The final report with legislative recommendations was a synthesis of a massive amount of research totaling nine volumes (and weighing 13 pounds) to be published later by the Commission.

The four tasks assigned to the Commission were (1) to analyze the laws pertaining to the control of obscenity and pornography, (2) to ascertain the methods of distribution of pornography and volume of traffic, (3) to study the effect of obscenity and pornography upon the public, and particularly minors, and its relationship to crime and antisocial behavior, and (4) to recommend legislative, administrative, or other action.[45] The third mandate, to study the effects of pornography on people's behavior and crime, was the central task of the Commission. Regarding that mandate, the Commission found and reported:

> . . . empirical research designed to clarify the question has found no evidence to date that exposure to explicit sexual materials plays a significant role in the causation of delinquent or criminal behavior among youth or adults. The Commission cannot conclude that exposure to erotic materials is a factor in the causation of sex crime or sex delinquency.[46]

Further, on the basis of these findings the Commission made significant legislative recommendations:

> The Commission recommends that federal, state and local legislation prohibiting the sale, exhibition, or distribution of sexual materials to consenting adults should be repealed. . . .

> The Commission believes that there is no warrant for continued governmental interference with full freedom of adults to read, obtain or view whatever such materials they wish.[47]

The research that led to the above conclusion and recommendation was carried out under the direction of the Effects Panel, one of the four Commission Panels. The Effects Panel consisted of five commissioners, three of whom were sociologists. Two of the sociologists, Otto Larson and Marvin Wolfgang, issued a minority statement objecting to the above recommendation because it did not go far enough as it limited its scope to adults:

> We recommend the repeal of all existing federal, state and local statutes that prohibit the sale, exhibition or other distribution of "obscene" material. . . . There is no substantial evidence that exposure to juveniles is necessarily harmful. There may even be beneficial effects if for no other reason than the encouragement of open discussion about sex between parents and children relatively early in young lives.[48]

A review of the research that the Commission relied on most heavily to support these findings suggests that the liberal bias of the Commissioners flawed the objectivity that should have been brought to their research. It was ultimately the battle between pro and antipornographers that guided commission research and not the study of pornography. Their work became the product of the history and ideology of cultural sadism instead of an actual pursuit of truth. As a result of his testimony before the Commission in 1970, Victor Cline was invited to review the Commission-financed behavior research reports and the final report. Cline found that

> . . . as indicated by their own writings, some were concerned by the behaviors and the views of the antipornographers whom they saw as censors or dangerous authoritarians who, in ominous and repressive ways, might threaten our most basic freedoms.[49]

The author of the study on the availability of pornography in Denmark prefaced his report with a description of the particular group that sees pornography related to sex crime:

> This group, composed mainly of procensorship citizens groups and law enforcement officials, is highly emo-

tional in its approach and generally unable to tender evidence in support of its position.[50]

(One can assume that if antipornographers controlled the Effects Panel research, the judgmental inflammatory language would have been directed at the liberals.)

A closer look at the research reports clarifies how this kind of bias was actually worked into design, methodology, and interpretation of findings of the Effects Panel research. Research reports on sex offenders, satiation experiments, and studies of the Denmark experience were the data that were most forcefully brought together to support the recommendations for lifting the legal restrictions on pornography.

Sex offender research provided the critical link between pornography and criminal behavior. In "Exposure to Pornography and Sexual Behavior in Deviant and Normal Groups," Goldstein and others reported the effects of pornography on sex offenders who were compared with a control (normal) group. The control group respondents, who were seen as approximating the normal population, were matched to the age, sex, and educational level of the group of imprisoned sex offenders; they had to be free from sexual deviation.[51]

The first problem is apparent. Some years ago the FBI conservatively estimated that only one in ten rapes is reported to the police and beyond that a very small percentage actually find their way to court and conviction of the rapist. As a result there is in the normal population a significant percentage of unreported, uncaught, unconvicted rapists. The rapist, it has been found, is not an aberrant person but normal in personality and style. In this research it is difficult to know whether or not convicted sex offenders are being compared simply with a population of men, many of whom rape and get away with it.

Nevertheless, the comparison was made between the two groups and the following areas were considered critical to determining the relationship between sex and violence: the subject's exposure to pornography during adolescence, his recent exposure to pornography, and the sexual excitement he derived from pornography. In Table IV, I have highlighted Goldstein's findings on the subjects' first adolescent exposure to pornography.

TABLE IV   Exposure of Males to Pornography (Photographic Depictions of Coitus) During Adolescence

	Percent of group exposed
GENERAL POPULATION (Control Group)	
White adults	85
Black adults	74
SEX OFFENDERS	
Female-object pedophile*	56
Male-object pedophile	53
Rapists	62

Source: The Report of The Commission on Obscenity and Pornography, Part 3, *Chapter II: The Impact of Erotica, Figure 10.*

* While for sociologists and psychologists the language of sociological and psychological research acts to bring them closer to a sense of participation in hard science, its main purpose in these studies is to obscure reality and to cater to the authors' personal biases through language manipulation. For example, in this table the man who molests and/or rapes little girls is known as "Female-object pedophile" while the man who molests little boys is the "Male-object pedophile."—K.B.

The data are clear. Sex offenders had a fairly high exposure to pornography as adolescents. This fact is particularly significant when one considers that the respondents were from low socioeconomic homes and financially would have more difficulty getting pornography. The fact that all subjects had high exposure to pornography would tend to confirm their sampling problem that was based on the assumption that the control group is free from sex offender behavior. But the Commission gave the following interpretation to these figures:

> These data show that as compared with nonsex offenders, sex offenders and sexual deviants have comparatively little experience with erotica during their adolescence.[52]

While they are lower than the nonsex offender group, 62 percent of rapists simply does not illustrate *little* experience.* Additionally, it is curious that the Commission chose photographic pornography to document its findings, because in its very own national survey the Commission reported that more pornography is consumed through movies than from books, magazines, or photographs. Only 13 percent of the men had been exposed to photographs while 37 percent had seen pornographic movies.[53] The survey noted that the greatest impact on behavior is from movies as opposed to still life books or photos.

The ideological bias in interpretation continues throughout the research. In studies of recent exposure of sex offenders to pornography, similar patterns and interpretations were found. Goldstein gathered information on how much and what kinds of pornography sex offenders were exposed to in the year before their incarceration and compared it with a control group. He reported the following finding:

Rapists—It can be seen that across all stimuli and media the rapists reported less exposure to pornography during the past year.

Male-oriented pedophiles—This group of pedophiles reported generally less exposure to erotica across

* In analysis of similar research conducted by Goldstein in 1973, *Pornography and Sexual Deviance*, Victor Cline found the following problem of underestimation of statistics:

In Goldstein's interviews, he asked his subjects if they had ever "tried out" sexual behaviors depicted during a peak adolescent exposure to pornography. Fifty-seven percent of his rapists replied yes. . . . Yet in his chapter summary, Goldstein curiously comments, "While [the rapists] noting an intense desire to imitate the [sexual] activities shown [by pornography], only rarely did they satisfy it." . . . The use of the term "rarely" to describe the 57% of the rapists who acted out or imitated the pornography modeled for them, then is inaccurate. Their data show that 77% of the child molesters with male targets and 87% of the child molesters with female targets reported trying out or imitating the sexual behavior modeled by the pornography seen during this peak adolescent experience.

Source: Victor Cline, "Another View: Pornography Effects, the State of the Art," in *Where Do You Draw the Line*, ed. V. Cline (Provo, Utah: Brigham Young University Press, 1974, p. 218).

all stimuli and media than controls.
Female-oriented pedophiles—Female-oriented pedophile group indicated generally less exposure to erotica.[54]

These findings were reported by the Commission and supported with data on the sex offenders' exposures to pornographic photographs.

In reporting the findings, the researchers completely ignored their own data on sex offenders' exposure to movies that portrayed sadomasochistic violence. I have analyzed those ignored findings in Table V. Additionally, sex offenders and persons in the control group had more exposure to sadomasochistic movies than to any other form of pornography. Sadomasochistic movies were the only pornography in which the rapists actually surpassed the control group in recent exposure. Yet Goldstein concludes:

It can be seen that across all stimuli and media the rapists reported less exposure to pornography during the past year.[55]

TABLE V   Recent Exposure to Sadomasochistic Movies

	Percent of group exposed
Rapists	78
Control	74
Pedophile, Male target	79
Control	80
Pedophile, Female target	70
Control	90

Source: "Exposure to Pornography and Sexual Behavior in Deviant and Normal Groups," Goldstein *et al.*, U.S. Commission on Obscenity and Pornography, Technical Report VII.

And he further concludes:

. . . the rapists were no more likely to encounter material combining sexuality and aggression (sadomasochistic themes) than were controls; therefore, the idea for the aggressive sexual act did not appear to derive from pornography.[56]

This double-talk means that if rapists did have some exposure to sadomasochistic pornography they couldn't get any
ideas to rape from it because the control group, who are
normal American men, don't rape and they have the same
exposure. Those statements are not only illogical but they
contradict the data. This research and others like it are
cited most frequently in court cases and in other arguments
against censorship of pornography.

Goldstein also studied the reaction of individuals to
erotic material. In general he found the sex offenders all
reported a higher incidence of each of the following activities:

> Excite to masturbate
> Actually looking at [erotic material] while masturbating
> Masturbate sometimes without erotic stimuli
> Excite to sexual relations
> Thoughts present during sexual relations

This neither was highlighted in the researcher's interpretation nor was it analyzed as such in the report of results.
The Commission chose not to include in its final report the
table giving these data; it ignored these findings and gave
the following contradictory interpretation of the data:

> Research shows that sex offenders and other adults
> in the general population generally do not differ in
> their reported immediate responses to reading or view-
> ing erotic materials—substantial proportions of both
> groups report psychosexual stimulation.[57]

It is not a matter of oversight. Deliberate distortion of
evidence is made to support the conclusion that the Commission set out to reach.

Satiation was another effect the Commission studied. In
a study by Howard, Reifler, and Liptzin, 23 college males
between the ages of 21 and 23 were shown pornography
for 90 minutes per day for 15 days.[58] With that kind of
dosage the findings were neither surprising nor revealing:

> Decreased response to stimuli is one measure of sati-
> ation. Although in our study complete satiation in the

sense of total inhibition of response did not occur, we believe that the physiological data unequivocally point toward satiation in terms of diminished response.[59]

Pornography consumers report a much less frequent exposure to pornography. The rate of exposure in this experiment in no way replicates the general pattern of exposure by pornography consumers, so the purpose of this study is questionable while its ideological goal is consistent with that of other research.

With mandate and money from the United States Congress, the Commission on Obscenity and Pornography, through its voluminous research, created both sanction and tolerance for cultural sadism. It opened the way, through pseudo-scientific legitimization, for the escalation of violence and the use of children in pornography. In doing so, it has created an erosion of sensitivity to sexual violence and a wearing down of values. It did this consciously and with forethought by studying and knowing the effects of pornography and by using it as a model instead of a caution.

In the mid-1960's pornographic literature became available without legal control in Denmark and in 1969 all pornography was legalized. Two important trends resulted from the action: (1) the escalation of the subject matter of pornography and (2) the relationship between pornography and sexual violence. The Commission studied both trends and particularly in the case of the latter came up with contradictory findings. Not surprisingly, it chose to report the findings consistent with its own bias.

Ben-Veniste described the escalation of pornography in Denmark in his study for the Commission. The Commission never mentioned it in its final report. Up to 1965 pornography consisted mostly of pictures of nude women. After that "in the new publications, however, models were posed in the most provocative manner—usually full front or rear view with the legs spread apart and often with the model holding open her vagina."[60] By 1967 sales had declined and the magazines provided the consumers with still more sexual explicitness, which usually involved all activity short of penetration of the vulva and anus, and fellatio.[61]

That lasted about a year in popularity and, as sales decreased, hard-core magazines were introduced in which there were no limits on what could be portrayed. Sales excelled and have remained high.

A similar escalation can be noted in pornography in the United States since the early 1970's and it can be directly linked to the pornographic industry in Denmark. The New York State Select Crime Committee has found that the same children who appear in simple nude pictures in child pornography peddled in the United States are pictured in the hard-core pornography coming out in Denmark. Inspector Lloyd Martin from the Sexually Abused Children's Unit of the Los Angeles Police Department has uncovered cases of children from Los Angeles who appear in Danish publications. He noted that the international demand for children in pornography now is for fair, blond-haired, blue-eyed Americans. Many pornographers are supplied photos by child molesters who seduce or abduct children for their own personal use as well as financial gain in pornography.

As some of the same children are pictured in both simple, nonviolent nude pictures and in forceful, violent hard core, the traditional distinctions between hard-core and soft porn appear rather naive. Those distinctions have been made by pornographers to provide a legal cover for themselves, to fully exploit the market, and to maintain an erosion of sensitivity that in turn feeds their market. This erosion of sensibility and sensitivity has even changed the focus of feminist concern. In 1970, feminists were contesting the sexual objectification of women in pornography in the slick men's magazines such as *Playboy*. Now such organizing focuses around protest against the use of children and the portrayal of violence in pornography. The demand that women not be sexually objectified is treated as excessive and hysterical. Tolerance is created when one level of abuse (i.e., sexual objectification) is justified in the face of higher levels of objectification and more severe forms of violence in pornography.

In Denmark pornography has had a definite effect on the attitudes toward sex crimes and accounts for a decrease in reporting of some sex crimes. The incidence of *reported* exhibitionism, peeping tomism, and physical indecency toward girls *decreased* over the ten-year period between

1960 and 1970. Physical indecency toward women refers to "unlawful, physical, sexual interference with adult women, short of rape."[62] Kutchinsky found:

> Concerning three of these types of crimes—exhibitionism, peeping, and (physical) indecency toward girls—it was possible, without restraint or ad hoc constructions, tentatively to explain this registered decrease as being due to the influence on either the victims or the potential offenders of one single factor, namely the development in the availability of pornography . . . the analysis tentatively indicated that the influence of such a change on the victims was the major *reason* for the registered decrease in (physical) indecency towards women.[63]

In its final report the Commission did not refer to this study at all and instead reported contradictory findings more consistent with its biases:

> A survey of Copenhagen residents found that neither public attitudes about sex crimes nor willingness to report such crimes had changed sufficiently to account for the substantial decrease in sex offenses between 1959 and 1969.[64]

In addition, the Commission studied the patterns of rape, but they chose a curious procedure. Printed police statistics showed an increase in rape reports after an initial decrease in 1967. The researcher chose to ignore these statistics and instead had a research assistant review Copenhagen's police records for the period 1958-69. Their statistics show a rather different trend than those reported by Kutchinsky and Danish police records.

In this area of research, causation can never be statistically proven. Correlation between an increase in pornography and in increase in sex offenses can be established but causal assumptions are always those of the researcher. As a result, and from Table VI, it can be said that the increase in pornography in Denmark actually paralleled an increase in rape, and it reduced women's ability to report other sex offenses.

While psychologists and sociologists labor to prove that no relationship exists between pornography and sexual violence, some behavioral scientists are using pornography in both diagnosis and treatment of sex offenders. Their projects vividly demonstrate the influence of pornography on behavior. Some use pornography to redefine the sexual behavior and orientation of sex offenders. There is a long history of misuse of this kind of research reflected in the horror stories that have come from prisons across the country where behavioral modification has been used to straighten out homosexual prisoners whose only offense has been to love another of their own sex.

TABLE VI   Denmark: Comparison of Rapes Reported

Year	Number of Copenhagen rapes	
	Police[1] Records	Commission[2] Research
1959	32	30
1960	21	20
1961	25	24
1962	29	21
1963	22	18
1964	20	16
1965*	24	21
1966	34	28
1967	23	18
1968†	28	23
1969	27	19
1970	31	—

* Year pornography was first legalized.
† Year pornography escalated to massive sales of hard-core pornography.

Sources:
[1] Berl Kutchinsky, "The Effect of Easy Availability of Pornography on the Incidence of Sex Crime: The Danish Experience." *Journal of Social Issues,* 1973.
[2] Richard Ben-Veniste, "Pornography and Sex Crime: The Danish Experience," U.S. Commission on Obscenity and Pornography, Technical Report VII.

When behavior therapy is aimed at reorienting violent sex offenders and that is done in a social learning framework, there is the possibility of seeing at least some relief to the repetition of sexual violence from these men. The focus of the projects here is not only to redirect sexual orientation but to develop strategies of self-control.

At Atascadero State Hospital in California, Richard Laws is working with pedophile sex offenders who have a criminal history of raping or molesting children. After a lengthy sexual history is taken of each child molester, pornography is used first to diagnose the individual—to find out what stimulates him by sex, age, and behaviors. His sexual arousal is measured by a digital pulse strain gauge which acts as a transducer and allows his erection rate to pornography to be recorded. The treatment consists of the individual's fantasizing and masturbating each day to three nondeviant slides (nonviolent sexual activity between adults) and three deviant slides (perverted or violent sexual activity with children). Dr. Laws attempts to restructure a man's nondeviant representations. Fantasies to deviant pictures are interrupted by the staff member while those to nondeviant representations are not interfered with. New behaviors are introduced to compete with old behaviors. It is skill acquisition, a learned pattern of response that involves developing a strategy of self-control. When a particular individual may not be easily moved from being sexually stimulated by deviant pictures to being sexually stimulated by nondeviant pictures, olfactory aversion, the introduction of noxious odors with the deviant pictures, may be used. Treatment is considered successful when the individual gets no more than a 20 percent erection to deviant slides.

If pornography can be used to readjust an individual's sexual orientation, and in this case to change the sexual object from child to adult, then it is reasonable to assume that not only the fact of pornography but the nature of it is extremely formative on the sexual behavior of the viewer. Behavioral researchers have recognized that sexual gratification from pornography is a powerful reinforcer. If one looks at pictures or movies, gets sexually excited, and masturbates to orgasm, the likelihood is high that that person will return again and again to the source of the pleasure and that that source will have more and more influence on his behavior. It does seem so perfectly obvious after a point that one is amazed at the power of ideology in maintaining the illusion that pornography doesn't affect behavior.

Another behavioral researcher, Gene Abel, along with his colleagues at Tennessee Psychiatric Hospital and Institute, has been using audio tapes to diagnose rapists and has found that they can distinguish rapists from nonrapists by the subjects' response to erotic stories. Abel presented first an audio tape describing mutually enjoyable heterosexual intercourse and then one describing a rape; they were presented twice in alternating succession, to rapists and nonrapists. The men were asked to "listen closely; try to visualize in your mind's eye exactly what is being described; try not to get ahead of the description but just try to see what is being described."[65] The men were asked not to masturbate. The nonmanipulated sexual response in erection was measured by a transducer.

> This analysis revealed (1) the rapists showed the same degree of erection regardless of stimulus content whereas, (2) the nonrapists showed significantly ($p < .05$) less erections and report of sexual arousal for both rape descriptions than for the descriptions of mutually enjoyable sexual intercourse. Furthermore, (3) the nonrapists' responses to descriptions of rape were substantially less than the rapists' responses to either set of stimuli whereas, and (4) the nonrapists showed the same degree of erection to descriptions of mutually enjoyable intercourse as the rapists did to all four stimuli.[66]

To illustrate this finding consider in Table VII the average percent of erection to sexual scenes of rape and nonrape.

Abel also investigated the extent to which aggressive force or assault in the context of rape was sexually stimulating to the rapist. Using tapes that alternatively described acts of aggression (without rape) and acts of rape (aggression and intercourse), he found an almost perfect linear relationship between aggression and rape. Sexual stimulation of rapists to aggression and to rape was correlated at .98 ($p < .01$). "Erection to aggressive descriptions was thus directly related to erection to rape descriptions."[67]

This research shows distinctly different patterns of

TABLE VII   Incidence Erection in Response to Representations of Rapes Compared to Nonrapes

| | Mean Percents of Erection to Scenes of: | | | |
| | First Showing | | Second Showing | |
	Mutual Intercourse	Rape	Mutual Intercourse	Rape
Nonrapist	62	17	60	14
Rapist				
Least violent rapist	52	50	58	49
All rapists	60	69	65	54

Source: Gene Abel *et al.,* "The Components of Rapists' Sexual Arousal," *Archives of General Psychiatry*, Vol 34, August 1977.

arousal to pornographic material by rapists and nonrapists. Men who are predisposed to act out sexual violence on women will find reinforcement for that disposition in pornography, and men who prefer mutually enjoyable sexual relations with women will not find reinforcement from sex-violent fantasy.

Beyond their usefulness, these projects demonstrate and foster a level of objectification that is always necessarily present in sexual violence. The men exposed to this material are not having to interact in the sense of taking another person into consideration. They only have to respond appropriately to pornographic stimuli. Those stimuli are, in the final analysis, what are used throughout society to objectify women. While the sexual objectification in these projects does not convey the violence of hard-core pornography, it is nevertheless sexual objectification that is being reinforced as behavior is being redirected. Consider the following excerpt from one of Abel's audio tape descriptions of "mutually enjoyable intercourse":

> You can see her tits. She's big, really big. . . . You can see her. She's got big thighs and a nice ass, a fairly big ass.[68]

Social scientists have been so successful in convincing people that there is no relationship between pornography and sexual violence that behavioral scientists, while demonstrating that very relationship, act as if there were none.

FREE SLAVES

"But where is one to find free slaves?" Simone de Beauvoir in her classic essay, "Must We Burn Sade," poses the problem Sade faced by asking his question.[69] For Sade, in the ideal erotic act "one must do violence to the object of one's desire; when it surrenders, the pleasure is greater."[70] But Sade's scheme was unsatisfactory as he had to pay prostitutes in order to do his violence and then occasionally he got into trouble for his excess.

Two hundred years of cultural sadism have solved Sade's problem by bringing sex-violent actions into the internal psychological nature of being, and by naming those actions sadomasochism, thus defining them as natural. Science has affirmed that the imagery which represents cultural sadism not only is not harmful but may be useful in sex education. The limits hitherto placed on expression of individuals' freedom are lifted.

Freedom does not just coexist with ideology. Ideology determines what freedom means and how it is exercised. As the tool of the politically powerful, ideology perpetuates power by determining people's behavior and their practice of "freedom." Cultural sadism is the ideology of men in power, of the patriarchy. It creates the measure of viewing and valuing women and deftly integrates it into society's basic constitutional beliefs and values which in turn help the ideology flourish. "Life, liberty, and the pursuit of happiness" from the American Revolution and *"Liberté, egalité,* and *fraternité"* of the French Revolution launched the political values of individualism, which have been reduced in language and practice to the twentieth century's less eloquent "Do your own thing." Based on a belief in natural rights, the principles of individualism in democracy required that one could not be interfered with in the pursuit of happiness unless pursuit of happiness interfered with another's exercise of life and liberty.

Democracy asserts an atmosphere of pluralism upon which the ideology of cultural sadism thrives. Diversity of sexual perversion fits neatly into the pluralistic notion of cultural diversity and is reduced to the colloquialism "different strokes for different folks." No one should question, no one should mind how anyone acts on their sexual needs. This society guarantees the right to freedom of expression. Pornography, as the argument goes, isn't hurting anyone else, so if a guy wants it he should have it.

That logic insists that the objects of cultural sadism cannot be persons. The practices of cultural sadism severely interfere with women's life, liberty, and pursuit of happiness, so a conflict of rights would seem obvious. But, in fact, it is claimed that no one is being violated, that no one's rights are being abrogated; therefore, the one who is the object of cultural sadism does not exist as a person. With its objects or victims defined as nonpersons, cultural sadism is a sanctioned right.

The Constitution in guaranteeing rights speaks only of persons. When women give their consent to the status of object, as many apparently do, we have the answer to Sade's dilemma. Sexual liberation is offered through sexual slavery. That is the message of the *Story of O*.

The setting is a French chateau. What takes place there, the principles on which it is run, are basically Sadean—not too different from his proposed health establishment. Libertines are engaged within with a full staff of valets and servants, a definite organized pattern of activity and, of course, free slaves—not the paid prostitute Sade had to rely on but women who because of their submission make their master's pleasure so much the greater. It is not assumed for a moment that mere agreement is submission. Submission is learned by degrees, and as it is learned liberation is achieved. O is taken there by her lover, who leaves her at the front door. Upon arrival, after being prepared she is orally, anally, and vaginally raped by four men whom she doesn't know and is forbidden to look at. Then, tied and bound, she is hung from a hook in a beam for a strenuous whipping. Except for her screaming from the whipping, we hear nothing from her during all of this—no questions, no protest. She is then lectured that she is never allowed to look at their faces. She must wear a costume leaving her breasts exposed and her genitals easily accessible.

> Your hands are not your own, nor are your breasts, nor, most especially, any of your bodily orifices, which we may explore or penetrate at will . . . you have lost all right to privacy or concealment . . . you will never close your lips completely, or cross your legs, or press your knees together.[71]

Only later, when O has been left alone still bound and tied resting on two layers of fur, does the author reflect on O's thoughts. "O tried to figure out why there was so much sweetness mingled with the terror in her, or why her terror seemed itself so sweet."[72]

It is not enough that O be resigned to these experiences. A free slave must give her permission to be whipped or tortured. O is taken at the will of her masters in any way they please. From time to time she has the opportunity to give her consent. After two weeks she is returned to Paris by her lover. She is completely transformed by the time she returns to her work in photography.

The assumption again is that excess is self-regulating. In her discussion of Sade, de Beauvoir says of prostitutes, "If libertines were permitted to molest them with impunity, prostitution would become so dangerous a profession that no one would engage in it."[73] Well?

In pornographic fantasy of the *Story of O*, we are taken beyond self-regulation in sexual violence to plumb the sexual depths of being without any limitations. So, as O is given by her lover to another man, she becomes a participant in her own demise, giving her permission all along the way. Through hideous tortures she progresses toward "total openness," totally enslaved through the last barrier to liberation. When she learns that Sir Stephen is about to abandon her, she asks and he gives his consent for her to die.

In cultural sadism, the question of woman's will is a spurious one. Women exist as objects and as such will be taken if they don't give themselves. While a woman may choose to participate in the practices of cultural sadism, that choice implies neither freedom nor sexual liberation. As a result, sexual slavery will be the same whether or not it is chosen. Personal liberation in a slave state is impossible.

Cultivating contradictions maintains the illusion of freedom. Violence and evil are juxtaposed with pleasure and good—the mystery of sex. Humiliation is transformed into love, pain into pleasure, the grotesque into the beautiful, submission into liberation. By submitting to the sexual instinct, one is taken to depths never known before. De Beauvoir says of Sade that he "was the only one to reveal selfishness, tyranny and crime in sexuality,"[74] as if by breaking through the sexual restraints society had placed upon him, he had discovered some previously unknown truth about human nature.

There is something very seductive about facing the contradictions, plumbing the depths of being, to discover new truths of existence. It may be seductive but in this case it is neither honest nor true. Evil and crime are not innate in sexuality. They stem directly from the political and social support they receive in a sex-violent society. They are the result of an ideology that insists that men must have whatever they desire to fulfill their sexual needs.

Of O, Peter Michelson in "An Apology for Pornography" says, "On the one hand, she is the answer to every man's secret dream. On the other hand, she is an object awful in her implications."[75] And from the masculine perspective, this story "describes a complete liberation of the sexual libido."[76] There is its connection to pornographic fantasy. For women, Michelson says, O arouses intense anxiety "that love for a man will subsume self-identity, and the loss of love will leave her without reason to be."[77] He goes on: the *Story of O* is allegory and O is the *"first Everywoman."* That is enough to arouse intense anxiety. For O is not merely an unachievable sexual fantasy, O is offered for titillation and imitation.

Facing the contradictions again, Susan Sontag describes O's "extinction as a human being" as "her fulfillment as a sexual being."[78] This is problematic; how can one experience the sexual being if the human being has been made extinct? Is this one of those essential contradictions? Says Sontag: "It's hard to know how anyone would ascertain whether there is truly anything in 'nature' or human consciousness that supports such a split. But surely, the possibility has always haunted man."[79] There is philosophical interest and practical value in pushing at the known limits of existence and forcing contradictions to their ultimate conclusion. But when that exploration involves degradation, humiliation, or annihilation of one group, the philosophical question is turned into an excuse for acting out social hatred of that group.

Now I am not one to suggest that there aren't many enigmas in this life, that contradictions don't exist from time to time or that there is no mystery in living. I grant and indeed experience all of this. But I find it intolerable and dangerous for women to incorporate within ourselves the contradictions of an ideology which serves to promote our own extinction. The most immediate and urgent problem we face when accepting as part of human nature the contradictions of love and pain, sex and violence, is that while powerless in this society we cannot control the exercise of that pain, the use of that violence. They remain as options for men to act on. In the name of sexual freedom they are encouraged to self-expression without limits. The logical conclusion of these contradictions is in the final contradiction—life and death, just as gynocide is the final expression of sexual slavery.

To live in a society where blueprints for female enslavement and gynocide abound is intolerable. For women to accept it means, as in the case of O, participation in our own demise. But to demand the elimination of all pornography, as women must, is immediately to be accused of trespassing on the rights of men who have fought so hard to protect the rights they have been granted. Make no mistake: in pornography the right of freedom of speech cannot be separated from the right to sexual access, just as pornography cannot be separated from behavior.

CHAPTER 10 ⸻⸻⸻⸻⸻⸻⸻⸻⸻⸻

From Violence to Values...
And Beyond

Since I began studying sexual slavery I have often been asked: Why do men do these things to women? To speak in general terms of male domination and the oppression of women seems far too abstract when one thinks of the women, individual human beings, whose destroyed lives cannot be either understood or reconstructed from rhetoric. In the face of pain, humiliation, and degradation that comes to women and girls through the sheer contempt of sexual slavery, I am forced to focus the question more precisely. First, what makes some persons capable of the violence of sexual slavery? Second, on a larger scale, how can our society justify rendering individually inflicted pain invisible?

The most painful moments in writing this book have come as I faced the complete invisibility of sexual slaves— knowing the unspeakable violence against young girls and women that no one acknowledges. The teenage girls who disappear and are never known to be missing. The anonymous caller to a woman's shelter who wanted to arrange a meeting to "get rid of a white slave" and then never showed up. It is in moments of facing these realities that I have felt the last vestiges of hope start to slip, almost elusively, away. To see how society accepts that abuse and how it is internalized and accepted by its victims has often left me feeling as if my heart would break—an emotion men condemn as a failure of objectivity. And yet I realize that it is the stifling of such emotion that creates the conditions of violence and slavery. I've come to recognize in a way I've never before known so deeply and powerfully the extent to which emotionless objectivity leads directly to objectification—the starting point of violence, particularly sexual violence.

Why do men do these things to women? Because, in part, there is nothing to stop them. Norms and sanctions are rarely applied against female sexual slavery. And so, like the child who tests every limit he or she discovers until there is adult interference, there are men who will trample on every human value, every standard of human decency, every vestige of respect for human life, beyond almost every taboo.

One overriding characteristic of sexual slavery is that, as calculated and sometimes predictable as many of its practices are, there is, in the moment of abuse, a sense that the pimp, husband, father, or rapist is *out of control with permission*. In his typology of the violence-prone person based on an extensive study of violent men, Hans Toch found that one group of violence-prone men "may be described as comprising people who see themselves (and their own needs) as being the only fact of social relevance."[1] Specifically, this typology includes categories particularly appropriate to cultural sadists:

> *Bullying*: An orientation in which pleasure is obtained from the exercise of violence and terror against individuals uniquely susceptible to it.
> *Exploitation*: A persistent effort to manipulate others into becoming unwilling tools of one's pleasure and convenience, with violence used when the victims react against this.
> *Self-Indulging*: A tendency to operate under the assumption that other people exist to satisfy one's needs —with violence as the penalty of noncompliance.
> *Catharting*: A tendency to use violence to discharge accumulated internal pressure, or in response to recurrent feelings or moods.[2]

I do not know what makes some men adopt the pattern of behavior summarized in this typology while others find human, caring means for expressing their needs and desires.* But the sexual development of all men, the "nor-

---

* I dismiss such arguments as the XYY syndrome in that the pervasiveness of male sexual violence against women cannot be explained even in part by genetic deviations.

mal" male sex drive as it is transmitted through sexual socialization, is undoubtedly of major significance in creating the self-centered, exploitative personality that carries out female sexual slavery. More and more we are recognizing that the extreme condition (acts of rape, beating, torture, incest) represents an ideal type (or typical circumstance) derived from what is considered normal role expectation.

Although many men do not seek violent expression of their sexual desires, the socialized male sex drive presumes personal sexual power, a power that can be reinforced by physical violence and can therefore lead to sexual enslavement of women and girls.

THE MALE SEX DRIVE

Sex drive is considered synonymous with male sexuality. Women are attributed with sexual feelings of a diffuse and subtle nature but it is believed that they do not possess a sex drive outright. On the contrary, so explicitly has the male sex drive been described that the adjectives used are generally those reserved for Fourth of July celebrations. It is explosive, likened to a *time-bomb with a short fuse, a fire burning out of control*, or the *discharge of a bullet from a gun*.[3] It is seen as an autonomous instinct not subject to self-control, one which of its own accord is driven to find release. According to Theodor Reik:

> The crude sex-drive is a biological need which represents the instinct and is conditioned by chemical changes within the organism. The urge is dependent on inner secretions, and its aim is the relieving of a physical tension. The internal stimuli activated by the chemical changes tend to bring about a discharge.[4]

Similarly, Havelock Ellis saw the sex drive this way:

> . . . taking on usually a more active form in the male, has the double object of bringing the male himself into the condition in which discharge becomes imperative, and at the same time arousing in the female a similar ardent state of emotional excitement.[5]

The drive according to these men is so overwhelming that the male is the one to be acted upon by it; thus the sex drive is put out of his control. At the same time it demands a fitting object for release, and thus the female role is defined.

Freud agonized over the issue of whether this powerful drive could be subjected to control, for he felt that civilization is based on that need for control. But he concluded "that the task of mastering such a mighty impulse as the sexual instinct is one which may well absorb all the energies of a human being."[6]

I remember as a young teenager of the 1950's that my mother took care to explain to me some things about boys and their sex drive. Both my family and my church forbade "making out." Nevertheless, at about the age of 14 my friends and I were heavy into necking and if-we-dared-to-be-so-bold petting, too. We stopped short of "going all the way"; "nice" girls just didn't do such things.

Sex was not a subject of discussion in our house but my mother must have realized on some level what I was doing with my boyfriend even though I was careful not to get caught. So she explained to me in as sex-free language as possible that "making out" and petting were like playing with fire, a fire that could easily get out of control. It was *my* responsibility to see that that didn't happen. If I allowed a boy to kiss me and one thing led to another, then I would be getting him all excited and he wouldn't be able to control himself. His "thing" would get hard and then he couldn't be expected to stop. I would no longer be a nice girl. It was my responsibility and not his to make sure that this didn't happen. He would not and indeed could not be held accountable.

One could argue that my home was sexually repressive (and it was), but according to prevailing standards and research findings, my mother wasn't wrong. She was expressing the general belief of the 1950's about the male sex drive—a belief which stands unchanged today.

As adolescent boys learn sexual power through the social experience of their sex drive, so do girls learn that the locus of sexual power is male. Given the importance placed on the male sex drive in the socialization of girls as well as boys, early adolescence is probably the first significant phase of male identification in a girl's life and development. While a girl may learn as a child that men—what they do, think, and are—are more valued than women, for most girls the first dramatic and direct experience of that social knowledge is likely to take place in adolescence when they assume responsibility for and learn to become responsive to the seemingly uncontrollable sex drive of adolescent boys. As a young girl becomes aware of her own increasing sexual feelings, she learns to understand them primarily in the context of the boys' sex drive. In response to the dictates of compulsory heterosexuality, she turns away from her heretofore primary relationship with girl friends. As they become secondary to her, receding in importance in her life, her own identity also assumes a secondary role and she grows into male identification.

Kinsey is one of the first sexologists to see the sex drive as *learned* behavior and not an uncontrollable instinct. He notes that "individual patterns of response may depend at least to some extent on the physiologic equipment," but he hastens to add that "there is, however, considerable reason for believing that some aspects of the behavioral pattern represent learned behavior which has become habitual after early experience."[7] Other evidence suggesting the extent to which the seemingly uncontrollable drive is actually learned comes from work done on premature ejaculation— in clinical settings such as that of Masters and Johnson.

The first definitive experiences of the fully developed, learned sex drive are in adolescence when, according to Kinsey, the time between sexual stimulation and response is shortest.[8] From cultural myths boys readily learn, first, that this drive is one that must be fulfilled because it cannot be contained and, second, that they have the implicit right to take girls and women as objects to fulfill that drive. Sexual power is thereby conditioned in the sex experience of adolescent boys. While boys are experiencing and experimenting with their sexuality, the culture provides them with substantive images of idealized sexual encounter; they often learn that they must live up to pornographic models of sex. As boys, growing into men, experiment with their sexuality free from both restraint and responsibility, that mode of behavior becomes, unchanged, the basis of adult male sexual power.

Learned, impulsive, uncontrollable adolescent male sex drive has become for many men the mode of their adult sexual behavior. It is *arrested sexual development*, which stems from a sexuality that has not grown beyond what was acted out at age 12, 13, or 14. Arrested sexual development defines the context for all aspects of their behavior and is perfectly compatible with Toch's typology of violent men. It explains the self-centered, exploitative, and bullying behavior that characterizes pimps, procurers, rapists, and wife beaters. These men have learned to take immediate sexual gratification and ultimately any other form of gratification in whatever way they choose.

Arrested sexual development stems from the adolescent social situation in which boys learn that sex is power. They act—the other must react. They must find the most desirable route of expression for something they are never expected to control, something they've learned they can't control. They find that the female object they choose for sexual release cannot say no, or that even saying no, she really means yes. This is the learned behavioral style which carries over into adulthood as it is conditioned into the physiological sexual response. Demanding response to a compelling urge dominates behavior even though it has been found that the uncontrollability of erection is contained by adulthood. Some men who are questioning the performance criteria they have been taught to live under and to demand of their partners are suggesting that male sexual satisfaction need not depend on erection but may be a more diffuse sensation.[9]

The sex drive is not simply a physiological response of the sex organ. It is a learned behavior which is experienced in the context of the ideology of cultural sadism. And it provides each man through his adult life with his own private measure of power. Some men will not need to act out that power. It is yet unclear why the sex drive that develops into pleasurable sexual encounter for some will for others remain an arrested sexual development and become an act of male power and aggression over others.

We are asked to be encouraged by the findings reported in *Beyond the Male Myth*, a survey of 4,066 men on male sexuality. The survey reports that things are improving: "An overwhelming number of respondents—about 98 percent of all the men surveyed—felt that it was important for a woman to have an orgasm . . . over half the men were self-critical if their partner did not respond fully."[10] And to help things along: "Four out of five men are making a conscious effort to delay their orgasms as long as possible."[11]

Such self-restraint is so little to ask and it appears from this survey that it is also so little to give, for the other side of this "hopeful" message is the familiar themes of power and performance. "If men were once indifferent to female orgasms, many are now overzealous. Some regard the partner's failure to achieve orgasms as an affront to their masculinity and will press on into the night hoping to generate the heat of passion by the sweat of their brow."[12] Now not only must the male sex drive be fulfilled but women *must* respond according to performance rules—the apparent price for their increased attention.

Sex-is-power can be cast into many forms inluding denying or demanding female response. Both replace mutuality with domination. Sexual domination acted out in one-to-one relationships is the basis for the cultural domination of women and female sexual slavery. Because such domination is expressed in separate, personal, private sexual experiences, and because on that level there is no visibility of collective action, the generalized abuse of women from the sex-is-power ethic has been seen only as individual acts.

As I mentioned in previous chapters, because it is invisible to social perception and because of the clandestine nature of its practices, it is presently impossible to statistically measure the incidence of female sexual slavery. But considering the arrested sexual development that is understood to be normal in the male population and considering the numbers of men who are pimps, procurers, members of syndicate and free-lance slavery gangs, operators of brothels and massage parlors, connected with sexual exploitation entertainment, pornography purveyors, wife beaters, child molesters, incest perpetrators, johns (tricks) and rapists, one cannot help but be momentarily stunned by the enormous male population participating in female sexual slavery. The huge number of men engaged in these practices should be cause for declaration of a national and international emergency, a crisis in sexual violence. But what should be cause for alarm is instead accepted as normal social intercourse!

EROSION OF SENSIBILITY

Arrested sexual development and the ideology of cultural sadism account in part for the conditions of generalized violence as well as the specific conditions of sexual violence we live in.

It is in this state of massive violence that we find that most violent crimes are committed by men. In 1977 "males accounted for 80 percent of the arrests for Crime Index Offenses and 90 percent of the arrests for violent crimes."[13] This has changed little since 1968, when men were arrested for 91 percent of the violent crimes. Looking at two specific violent crimes in 1977, murder and rape, we find that men committed 82 percent of all single-victim/single-offender murders. Men committed 79 percent (N = 6,783) of the murders of other men and 89 percent (N = 2,447) of the murders of women in that year.[14]

Recognizing that rape is one of the least reported violent crimes, we still find the reported extent of this male violence enormous. "In 1977, 57 out of every 100,000 females in this country were reported rape victims, a 10-percent rate increase over 1976. Since 1973, the forcible rape rate has increased 19 percent. The metropolitan areas experienced a risk rate of 68 victims per 100,000 females."[15]

Daily reports of violence that range from petty theft to mass murders bombard our senses from news of the world, the nation, and the local community. Television and movies present ongoing violence as a form of entertainment. People's daily lives are infused with an overload of violence both actual and fictionalized. To cope from day to day, as the incidence of violence escalates, one becomes inured in order to avoid being overcome with helplessness and hopelessness. The result is a state of psychological numbing, a mechanism used to distance ourselves from it all. In addition, through the ideology of cultural sadism, certain levels of sexual violence are accepted as the norm. Cultural sadism grants implicit social sanction to sexual violence. When that sanction is combined with psychological numbing, we have an *erosion of sensibility*, clinically known as *desensitization*.

In November 1978, 3,000 women in San Francisco demonstrated against the continued abuse of women in pornography. The demonstration, which attracted feminists from across the country, was a major event. It was a serious forceful statement against sexual violence. But violent pornography is no longer shocking or worrisome. On the other hand, the first report of 408 murder/suicides in Guyana, which included the murder of children by their parents, stunned the eroded sensibilities of the American public to shock and grief. The toll later mounted to 914, and that, along with the murder of Representative Leo Ryan by Jonestown leaders, turned shock and grief into agony, at least for the moment. The newspapers were splashed with stories of how the victims were forced to take the lethal dose of potassium cyanide and to inject children with it.

News coverage of the Guyana suicide/murders not only overshadowed the large protest of women in San Francisco; local and national papers conducted a virtual news blackout on the demonstration (while, I might add, they carried ads for the very pornography the women demonstrated against). The constructive acts of calling attention to the atrocities that range from rape to murder that are perpetrated against women in and through pornography were as silenced as had been the warnings to the State Department by Jonestown escapees that mass suicide rehearsals were going on there.

Any series of contemporary tragedies would suffice to illustrate the confusion between good and bad, love and hate, that has so permeated this civilization that we appear to have lost our capacity in this state of desensitization to know right from wrong. These events, closely linked as they are in time, are a starting place for unraveling the values and beliefs we have come to accept which provide the conditions for such seemingly inexplicable tragedies and such invisible practices as female sexual slavery.

NONOPTIONS OF LINEAR THOUGHT

From the ideology of cultural sadism, eroded sensibilities seek relief and respite in belief systems. In addition, the overbureaucratization of society and nonresponsiveness of government breed impersonality into everyday life, creating the condition of alienation: the individual is alienated from her/himself as well as from the larger society that seems only to absorb individuals as part of the masses. The widespread violence we are experiencing is in part a reaction of men against that alienation, but for women living under the conditions of male domination, male violence is a further act of alienation and the source of terrorism.

Belief systems emerge to satisfy the alienated, eroded spirit. They are attempts to improve the quality of life. Yet in today's world they do not rationally address the conditions underlying alienation and erosion of sensibility. Instead, they exist as a patriarchal overlay that confuses rather than clarifies problems. Although American society is outwardly pluralistic, containing many diverse social groupings, the actual choices for addressing alienation are ordered in dichotomies. They are derived from the linearity characteristic of patriarchal thought which always sees only two sides to everything—sexual freedom or sexual repression, madonna or whore, heaven or hell, victim or volunteer. Linearity denies the interactive and dialectical. It does not honor change, complexity, and growth. It imposes false categories, offering narrow either-or choices as the solution or escape from current conditions.

In order to find clarity, to see hope beyond sexual slavery, it is necessary to sift through false dichotomies which currently dominate thought. They are the options which are being employed by mass society as it tries to seek some truths, some understanding of the present tragedies. And at the same time they are the options that create the conditions for those tragedies. In general the current options are valueless individualism and traditional morality.

1. Valueless Individualism

Worse than the apathy of the 1950's is the prevailing condition of calculated, valueless individualism. In the 1960's the response to alienation took the form of political protest —individuals reacting against the conditions of alienation with confrontation. Political protest, male-dominated though it was, addressed the problem of quality of life through anti-racist, anti-imperialist politics. Its concern was with oppressed peoples and exploited societies. While there are still genuine political movements concerned with oppression, exploitation, and the quality of life, in the 1970's there has been resurrected an individualism which, flowing directly from the human potential movement, emphasizes taking one's own space, defining one's own reality, taking care of one's own needs. For many, concern over the quality of life is personal, individual, and focused on one's own well-being. Taken to the extreme it leads to shutting out the needs and pain of others, those "bad vibes," by asserting one's needs above all else.

Referring to this preoccupation with self as "psychobabble," R.D. Rosen points out that it "must be seen as the expression not of a victory over dehumanization but as its latest and very subtle victory over us."[16] The original intention was positive—a reaction against the repressiveness of traditional morality and the widespread experiences of alienation. And for many women trying to throw off years of male domination it has become an apparent means to self-definition. But to the extent that this new identity is formed in the context of contemporary individualism many are finding personal solutions to collective, political problems without addressing the overall conditions of male domination, thereby making their solution temporary and inadequate to the problem. This individualism does not eschew the collective, but "collectives" become groups of disconnected individuals whose commitment to each other is based on their common agreement about the importance of private, self-understanding. As such it is a short circuit for real communication and collective change.

Because of liberal motivations, and in reaction to traditional morality, this individualism rejects making value judgments on others' behavior, ideas, or actions. There is no right or wrong. People are free to do whatever they want, in whatever way they want, whether in a religious cult, a traditional family unit, or a sadomasochistic ritual. What was motivated by respect for individual differences in reaction to earlier generations' moralistic judgments on and intolerance of anything or anyone different from the norm, is now for many valueless. And that ethic of value-free acceptance of everyone's actions and beliefs allows individuals to escape into themselves, relieved of responsibility for the civilization in which they live.

This inherently valueless state is institutionalized in governmental and academic practices and in laws. The State Department's refusal to intercede in the Jonestown colony even as reports of slavery and suicide rehearsals reached them, reflects the callous disregard for human life that has become part of the freedom of living in a democracy, a freedom which while called individual liberty oppresses and destroys. Meanwhile, the government gives the appearance of moral leadership through investigations into the Watergate conspiracy or Bert Lance's finances—investigations that sought to protect politics or use of money.

A denial of the basic values of human life is also at the root of many arguments for cultural diversity. In the face of international colonization of women, we are asked to respect male self-determination and the uniqueness of national cultures that veil their women, practice clitoridectomies, hold women in harems, and condemn raped women to death.

Within the halls of academia where objective social science research is carried out, we find some academicians proud of the extent to which they can make their research on human behavior value-free. Without value judgments, some are able to study the voting patterns in small South Dakota towns with the same degree of emotionless objectivity that they study survivors of the Holocaust or victims of wife battery.

Finally, the Constitutional guarantee of freedom of speech for political dissent has in public debate aligned itself with this valueless state—one in which pornography, despite the sexual violence it contains and promotes, is being protected on the same terms as the right to protest the war in Vietnam. In this case valuelessness is the result of the commitment to abstract ideals even in the face of human destruction from overextension of those ideals.

Valuelessness is of course itself a value statement in negation. It is a declaration of nonresponsibility and a proclamation: self-interest above all else. It creates a social atmosphere in which distinctions between good and bad are not only not desirable, they are wrong—that is the value implicit in valuelessness. It is the negative sanction against moral judgment, moral conviction. It states simply: it is wrong to determine right or wrong.

By traditional morality I am referring to that general

system of beliefs and attitudes which is usually associated with right-wing politics and tradition as well as born-again Christianity. In contrast to individualism, traditional morality does offer values and does make judgments between good and bad. yet those definitions are often false appeals to morality and result in confusion in sexual values.

What I am talking about can best be illustrated by the values articulated in the anti-homosexual movement. From Anita Bryant's organizing to defeat the Dade County, Florida, ordinance that would have insured some basic human rights to homosexuals, to John Briggs's unsuccessful attempt to prohibit homosexuals from teaching in California schools, one notes an articulation of values from a large number of people which is based on the hatred of a group of people simply because of their choice of same-sex sexual partner. Homosexuality is viewed as perverse not because it destroys human life but because it deviates from the arbitrarily defined norm—heterosexuality. As a result, for those holding these values, heterosexual violence is less of an offense against the moral order than either homosexual love or violence.

In these terms of traditional morality, what caves were to lepers, closets are supposed to be to homosexuals, and the violation of nature comes from the meaning of being perverse—not from being violent, evil, or dangerous.

Accordingly, sexual perversions are those sexual acts or experiences that are not heterosexual. Rape is predominantly heterosexual, so it is not a perversion; but two women tenderly making love is a perversion. The glorification of rape in *Clockwork Orange* was heterosexual, but Radclyffe Hall's absorbing, tender novel of lesbian love, *The Well of Loneliness*, was declared obscene. Incest is predominantly heterosexual, but, as evil as it seems to many, it is not in these terms considered a perversion. It is, in fact, socially sanctioned. Wife battery is heterosexual, but one court after another declares a woman unfit as a mother because she chooses to live her life with another woman. Western religion does not accept but will tolerate prostitution—except for boy prostitution, which is homosexual and an abomination. The homosexual corruption of little boys, teenage boys, or young men cannot be tolerated; the heterosexual destruction of young girls is inevitable.

This is the confusion of values that the nonjudgmentalists meant to react against. But by reacting without analyzing the ideological self-interest of patriarchy, by trying to react against repression without maintaining principles, by taking the position that anyone has a right to do anything, they only shifted matters into an equally destructive state, from false values to total valuelessness.

Female sexual slavery exists in the vacuum between the disregard for social and political problems that stems from valueless individualism and the confusion of values created by the traditional moralists. The crisis of female sexual slavery demands that we reclaim the need for values—not values as they *had* been, but values that stem from new definitions of what is right and wrong, what is enhancing to human beings versus what is demeaning, and what leads to a positive valuation of life versus what tends toward destruction and dehumanization.

PERVERSION AND VALUES

I propose to get to new values first through a redefinition of perversion, which will lead to a renewed understanding of *good*. Perversion means "a turning away from what is good and right." Perversion is not just that which is wrong, bad, or evil, but that which distorts, devalues, depersonalizes, warps, and destroys the person as she or he exists in time and space. It involves destruction of the human being in fact. Accordingly, neither heterosexuality nor homosexuality are per se perverted. Instead, sexuality that is fostered through the arrested male sex drive which objectifies, forces, and violates, whether it is heterosexual or homosexual, is perversion.

In my mind, *where there is any attempt to separate the sexual experience from the total person, that first act of objectification is perversion*. Although objectification has been considered part of the mystery of sex, I think that in exploring new values we can locate a mystery much more profound, intense, and worth searching for.

In creating new sexual values we must first discard the

assumption that sex, *ipso facto*, is automatically good or bad. Sex is neither good nor bad until it is experienced alone or with another under a given set of conditions. Sexual values involve the whole psychic, social, and spiritual being, not only that which is gender-determined.

In going into new sexual values we are really going back to the values women have always attached to sexuality, values that have been robbed from us, distorted and destroyed as we have been colonized through both sexual violence and so-called sexual liberation. They are the values and needs that connect sex with warmth, affection, love, caring. To establish new sexual values is actually to resurrect those female principles, giving them definition and form in the present context.

Sexual values and the positive, constructive experience of sex *must be based in intimacy*. Sexual experience involves the most personal, private, erotic, sensitive parts of our physical and psychic being—it is intimate in fact.

I think of sexual intimacy in the same way I think of private thoughts. There are those ideas or thoughts that are very private and special to me. They stem from the very depths of my being and in a sense define a very important personal part of me. I share these thoughts with only a few people, those whom I trust and who I want to know me on that level. It is a privileged sharing, as their sharing of private thoughts is to me, an intimate exchange of deeper parts of ourselves than we show to the rest of the world, distant friends or acquaintances.

In this age of nonspecific "openness" where private thoughts are shared equally with everyone, we deprive ourselves of that specialness, that privacy which is the first basis of intimacy.

Sexual intimacy is not something to be given lightly. It is an experience to be *earned* by each from the other. We do not automatically grant trust or respect; they are earned values. Sexual intimacy is not automatic, as depersonalized sexual experience often is. It involves, in the deepest sense, experiencing the pleasure of physical and sexual closeness with another while being able to put oneself in the place of the other, taking on the meaning of the experience of the other, creating not a private but a shared joy. Such intimacy grows and is cultivated from dignity, respect, caring, tenderness. As those things grow, the most personal parts of oneself continually open for more intense and profound sexual experience for heightened erotic experiences. Audre Lorde suggests the power of the erotic:

> The erotic is a measure between the beginnings of our sense of self, and the chaos of our strongest feelings. It is an internal sense of satisfaction to which, once we have experienced it, we know we can aspire. For once having experienced the fullness of this depth of feeling and recognized its power, in honor and self-respect we can require no less of ourselves.[17]

Sexual intimacy, as true sharing, is denied by the values of individualism whereby one is preoccupied with one's own needs. It is obscured in traditional morality where men are neither challenged nor condemned for sexual aggression. True intimacy has been difficult for women to come to terms with, as traditionally it has been the area in which women have lost their power, identity, and centeredness. For many women it has been an experience of male sexual power: men have simply taken what had been defined as theirs to take. Through feminist consciousness-raising women have come to recognize and reject the conditions of powerlessness. Exploited and dominated at this most personal and vulnerable level, women have moved away from intimacy only to find that new problems arose as they escaped from male power into self-centeredness and as they tried to depersonalize their sexual being.

Intimacy is destroyed by depersonalization of this private, sensitive aspect of our being; the self is devalued into an object and deprived of respect, honor, and dignity. That is the living hell of female sexual slavery, the daily, hourly deprivation of sexual intimacy through forced sexual objectification. It wears down the spirit, strips the ego, denies the value of "self." Jeanne Cordelier is one of the few who has dared to expose the hell of prostitution as she lived it. She describes "the first time":

> For me, too, there was a first time. Being a prostitute is like living through an interminable winter. At first it seems impossible. Then as time passes, you start

thinking that "sun" is nothing more than a word thought up by men. . . .

There you are, in a dump that's more or less clean, holding a towel in your hand, looking at somebody you've never seen before. The more you retreat, the more he advances; since the room is fairly cramped, you soon find yourself with your back against the wall. The guy's arms are around you, they're all over your body like slimy tentacles that grope you, strip you, and drag you down as he pulls you over to the bed. . . . For an instant you escape from the nightmare: you're back in the church playground, playing hopscotch. It seems like yesterday. You almost feel good, and you shut your eyes to make the dream last. When you reopen them, after a split second, reality blinds you. Reality has taken the form of a cock, a real family man's wiener, a little soft but still enterprising.

The man pounces on you. His features are drawn. He calls you his little girl, his baby doll, his cherry pie, his quim, his yoyo, his honeyfuck, his tramp, his darling whore. As he penetrates you, he gasps for breath, grinds his teeth and kicks like a mustang. And as he shoots his load, flooding you with a month's abstinence, you lie there in the same position, unmoving, with your arms hanging limp, your legs spread, your eyes staring. You feel soiled, spoiled, destroyed. While he recovers, flopped comfortably on top of you and dripping sour sweat, funny ideas start going through your head. When he deigns to get up, indifferently dripping all over you, you mechanically walk over to the bidet and sit down in disgust . . .

You've almost accepted what you've become.[18]

AND BEYOND

By redefining perversion and by asserting the new values of sexual intimacy we challenge the root of male domination. This is the radical nature of feminist politics. New values are prerequisite to creating a society in which the use of women as Cordelier described it is no longer acceptable or even tolerable. As the first step in breaking the acceptance of depersonalized sex, it is a culture-creating act, the foundation for revolution. According to sociologists Jaeger and Selznick, "The primordial culture-creating act is the transformation of an impersonal setting into a personal one."[19]

New sexual values infuse quality into the most personal and private life. Once we live with new values, we are able to break down depersonalization and create conditions from which new forms of personal power can grow, power that is not arbitrary, capricious, or invested in the control of others. New sexual values assert a different basis for relationships than that of sex colonization. Culture creation "is an effort to make the world rich with personal significance, to place the inner self upon the stage to transform narrow instrumental roles into vehicles of psychic fulfillment."[20]

Of course many people's experience of sex is based in intimacy that does not objectify. However, their values are not capable of transforming culture unless they become political as well as personal, unless they assert dimensions of female power into the private world of sex colonization. When they do, then what begins as a personal experience can extend to encompass all who have been enslaved and colonized. Feminism demands more than private solutions or even private solutions stated in political terms.

Eroded sensibilities must once again become passionate with the need for liberation. This passion—while it looks to a future of new values, new quality of living—should never, for even one moment, forget the present agony of women who are now sexually enslaved. Fierce intolerance of slavery and passionate vision for change are the forces which create among the colonized the united political strength that brings about revolution.

Political change means confrontation with the values, institutions, and individuals which keep women colonized. Sex colonization assumes sex as an automatic right of men, but sexual intimacy precludes the proposition that sex is the *right* of anyone and asserts instead that it must be earned through trust and sharing. It follows then that *sex cannot be purchased, legally acquired, or seized by force* and that women must oppose all practices which promote "getting sex" on those bases.

Marriage and prostitution are experiences of individuals but they are also institutions. They are, in fact, the primary institutions through which sex is conveyed and in which female sexual slavery is practiced. Sex is purchased through prostitution and legally acquired through marriage; in both as well as outside each, it may be seized by force.

Prostitution promotes the cultural value that men should have sexual service provided to them under any conditions and terms they choose. They need not do anything but pay for it.

Marriage, as an institution of legalized love, presumes sex as a duty, a wife's responsibility. Regardless of the mutuality of feeling that may exist when two people enter marriage, it is often the case that after the original basis for relationship breaks down, men still assume sex as their automatic right.

Prostitution and marriage are elusive institutions. Once battery, marital rape, or forced prostitution begin, women are not only locked in brothels or their homes but they are trapped in the intangible institutions that encourage or perpetuate their slavery. Unlike other institutions, in prostitution or marriage there is no one place where collective protest against these institutions can be lodged. Instead, through the colonization of women they permeate the whole society in individual relationships.

One aspect of the radical act involved in women organizing shelters for battered wives is that they bring women together from the separate, elusive, and private situations of personal slavery. In escaping marriage and husbands, women have the opportunity to come together, develop mutual support, and learn to experience relationships that are not based on power, domination, or abuse. Shelters are also a place where the divisions between women born out of our colonization can begin to be healed.

The same support must be organized on a large scale for prostitutes and potential prostitutes, the runaways who pour into the cities every day. Shelters are beginning to be organized in some cities, but it is difficult to get funding for projects to support women who are labeled as deviants and criminals. In European countries where prostitution is tolerated, there are some networks of support that range from assisting a woman to escape or leave prostitution to seeing her through the prosecution of pimps or brothel owners. Yet prostitutes are still society's outcasts. It is that definition which must be challenged.

There are many ways that women can be supported in leaving prostitution or be prevented from entering it. Solutions, though, must not come in fragments the way social services are usually provided—job training here, health services there. Instead, we need a large-scale network of support and services, a network which recognizes the severity of the situation which women are leaving or escaping and brings together a range of support to respond to the needs of the whole person. Those needs will range from practical considerations like a meal and a place to sleep, to emotional support and caring, to realistic analysis of economic alternatives such as a job or educational program, to medical care, to intensive personal counseling. A network providing these and many other services would extend to many levels of operation, including outreach teams or street workers, crisis hot lines and emergency storefront shelters, and long-term live-in centers. This network, like those established for rape victims and battered wives, must be controlled by women and for women, and those receiving service must be actively involved in the operation of the centers. The plan I am proposing here is a general outline, a framework based on successful experiences in providing alternatives for battered wives and on the efforts that are beginning to be made for prostitutes. As this is a whole new area of endeavor in the United States and one that is only minimally functional in countries which tolerate prostitution, it is still too early to know which kinds of programs will be most effective. The most we can do is understand the conditions women will be coming from and try to construct realistic alternatives that will respond to their needs. The thing that we do know is that these women can no longer be ignored.

In 1977 there were 66,158 reported female runaways in the United States—59 percent of all runaways. They increased by 10.4 percent from 1968, while during that period male runaways decreased by 22.5 percent.[21] These statistics represent only a small portion of the runaways, as many parents don't report their children missing either because they don't care or because they fear alienating the child further by involving the police. Nevertheless, these statistics reveal increasing trends of girls ending up in cities by themselves, often with no money and in great need. For many, pimps will be their first contact.

Many prostitutes and runaways have left homes where they were victims of child abuse and/or incestuous assault. Traditionally female juvenile runaways have been treated as criminals; they have been picked up, taken to juvenile hall, and booked for running away. Girls are declared incorrigible and sexually promiscuous. Instead of recognizing the abusive situations many of them are escaping, the police who pick up runaways off the street send them back home if they have not committed any crimes. The case of incest is similar: the commitment of many social service agencies and new projects is to restore the family unit.

No woman or girl should ever be forced or even encouraged to return to the people or person who has abused her. We don't try to unite victims with their rapists; neither should we encourage wives to return to violent husbands, daughters to incestuous fathers, or prostitutes to violent pimps, even if these men promise, as many do, that the days of violence are over. We break the deadly cycle of violence by stepping out of it. Once women and girls are able to escape abuse in marriage and the family or in prostitution, they have the right to live free from those who had enslaved them; they must be encouraged to recognize this right after long years of abuse have kept them from thinking in terms of freedom and self-worth.

More than simply living free from abuse and enslavement women must learn how to break from the self-defeating pattern of male identification that makes them vulnerable to that abuse and denies them a full existence in their own right. Through feminism women are becoming more self-assured, self-directed, and ultimately female(self)-identified. As adult women grow in independence and self-identity, they become models of that behavior for young girls growing up. This kind of modeling is one means of interrupting the process of female socialization which presently cultivates dependency and male-identification. Seeing women defining their own lives and not accepting either definition or authority from men simply because they are men will provide young girls with models of strength and assertion. As they aspire to adopt those behaviors, young girls will become increasingly invulnerable to the befriending and love tactics of pimps and procurers. One young prostitute called me a short time after I interviewed her to tell me that until she met me she had never known any independent women. She was excited with the possibilities of what that could mean for her life. Unfortunately the other supportive resources necessary for her to leave prostitution were unavailable. Role models were not enough.

Practical strategies for helping women leave prostitution must also involve prevention. If female outreach teams or street workers were available, they could try to locate runaways in places like bus stations and train depots, where pimps go to procure naive and needy young women. And they would try to reach women on the street who are "burned out" from prostitution but see no alternatives. If such teams were backed up by emergency refuge shelters, they would be able to offer realistic support and assistance in the form of a meal, a place to sleep, and someone to talk to who can help them determine a direction for their lives other than prostitution.

The Covenant House provides these services on an emergency basis for runaways who flock to the Times Square area of New York City. But as Trudee Peterson, a worker there, pointed out, even though she can convince a young girl to leave prostitution after a night or two in the shelter, there is no place in New York City she can send her for the support and services she needs in order to get out and stay out.

Long-term, live-in shelters removed from the prostitution areas are like second-stage houses where women can live together who are trying to stay away from prostitution and reconstruct their lives. These shelters would provide emotional support, as well as counseling contacts to job-training programs, educational programs, and actual jobs. Most important, they will have a living atmosphere where women can learn new types of relationships that are not based on violence and abuse. One of the most difficult periods in the life of a woman who has decided to leave prostitution and is seeking police support by turning in her pimp is that time when she usually ends up alone in a motel room or with relatives who don't understand or who reject what she has been through. She goes from the intense, exciting, albeit violent life of the streets to seclusion. If she has to wait for preliminary court hearing alone, by the time the pimp comes to trial she has either left town or more likely dropped the charges and gone back with him. Long-term shelters must take into consideration that life a woman is leaving and must realize she will need a lot of attention and activity focused on herself and others around her to fight off the initial loneliness she experiences. In addition to being hooked into violence, some will be hooked on drugs. Neckes and Lynch found that 47 percent of the female street prostitutes they interviewed in San Francisco were drug users.[22] Long-term centers must be connected to detoxification programs.

The children of prostitutes live in the web of violence like those of battered women. Child care centers for prostitutes' children are beginning to be developed; these offer women good care for their children and they can provide therapeutic help to children living in such difficult settings. But they have another and very dramatic potential. Often many prostitutes who have been subjected to beatings by their pimps and abuse from tricks have little regard left for themselves. With shattered egos and destroyed self-images, many accept violence against them as a way of life. The care they should have for themselves they often invest in their children. Like most mothers, they want the best for their children although often they don't know how to go about getting it. Child care centers providing quality attention to prostitutes' children are also a means of reaching the women, of making contact with them and giving them a reference point that is based on caring and respect for their lives outside the life of prostitution. As in marriage, it may be that appeal for the well-being of a prostitute's child will be the first step for her in her own behalf.

In a tightening economy one asks just how are these services to be supported? Where will the money come from? Presently in all American cities there are large budgets allocated to the criminal justice system, which pursues prostitutes as criminals. In 1977 the City and County of San Francisco spent approximately $2 million in enforcing prostitution laws.[23] Almost all that money went to arresting, jailing, and prosecuting prostitutes. Few customers and hardly any pimps were arrested.

To begin, feminists must demand that money be diverted

into increased arrests of pimps and violent customers, *and* into supporting networks of prostitution outreach teams, emergency shelters, crisis hot lines, and long-term shelters. The money presently used to support the double standards of male sexual morality must be returned to women through projects controlled by women outside the bureaucracy of oppressive social services, not just in San Francisco but in every city in the country. In light of the extent of female sexual slavery, all this is still but a modest beginning.

The core of women's oppression in female sexual slavery reveals the interconnection and interdependence among sexual domination, economic exploitation, and discrimination. To refuse sanction to female sexual slavery in all of its manifestations is to directly challenge the patriarchal economic order which has been built on sexual domination. By channeling women into marriage or prostitution, they are kept economically marginal thereby not disrupting male economic and political power. From the practices of sex stereotyping jobs, sex discrimination in hiring, salary and promotion, sexual harassment and abuse on the job, we see how the institutional dimensions of female sexual slavery have been extended to the labor market where women are no longer a reserve, but now are demanding to be an active force.

While female sexual slavery is the core of sexual exploitation, in fighting it we must not skip steps. Challenging the oppression of women will remain ineffective if we follow the simple path from raised consciousness to inflamed rhetoric without insisting on and experiencing necessary value changes. Thus, the feminist values that create personal change will finally be extended to all women and brought into direct confrontation with the colonizers of women. Personal value change requires specific social and political changes.

As long as women who are prostitutes are socially labeled as outcasts, they will be expendable as throwaway women, and legally defined as criminals. A widespread campaign for legal change must address the roles into which society has forced these women, and the changes must provide a way out. Consequently, legal change will mean direct confrontation with the laws that protect and enshrine masculine double standards. Those are the laws that require the public expenditures that are used to implement them.

As illustrated earlier, all forms of prostitution laws—prohibition, regulation, and toleration—are uniform in their harassment of *visible* prostitutes. In addition, regulation supports the institution of prostitution by legalizing it. In turn, legalized brothels, while making prostitution comfortably invisible, provide a cover for the traffic of women procured for sexual slavery.

Decriminalization, which is the basis of the system of toleration, is the only means of taking women out of the *official* status of either criminal or prostitute. But decriminalization must be without reservation and must include street hookers as well as those women in brothels. The ability of most countries in the world to maintain laws against street hookers is based on the expectation that prostitution is a necessary service, although the defenders of morality don't want that fact recognized. They want prostitution practiced in private where abuses are not seen or known. We can no longer afford to support the double standard behind which men have carried on female sexual slavery. As unwelcome a sight as street prostitutes are to many, they cannot either be the subject of double-standard morality harassment, or be hidden away so that we don't have to look at or be affected by what we have socially sanctioned.

Across cultures decriminalization that is aimed at visible as well as hidden prostitution would provide the opportunity for women who have the status of citizens and not criminals to leave prostitution more easily than they can while being locked into it by social stigma and a criminal record.

Decriminalization of prostitution must be accompanied by increased enforcement of laws against pimping, procuring, and involuntary servitude. When women are neither criminals nor official prostitutes, they theoretically have the rights of any other citizen to bring charges of assault, rape, or kidnapping against pimps and customers. Only when value change accompanies legal change will that theoretical right become a reality.

Likewise, prosecution of pimps or violent tricks will not

automatically follow from decriminalization. There will have to be a confrontation with law enforcement officials from the police department to the district attorney's office to the judges and the courts. Men are not as motivated to prosecute other men as they have been to prosecute and harass women.

Decriminalization, if it is fought for in the context of new sexual values and accompanied by efforts to bring women out of prostitution, will not provide social sanction for that institution. To demand decriminalization of prostitution and increased prosecution of pimps and violent customers on these terms is to directly challenge the principles of patriarchy as they are enshrined in law. Law (and its implementation) is the crystallization on one level of the values of a society. In challenging them, we challenge the standards by which female sexual slavery has been carried out.

But, ideally, it should not be the function of law (as it presently exists) to enforce morality or values by making them legal standards under which people must live. New values will revolutionize society only when they are accepted and cherished by the people, not when they are imposed on them. Consequently, as we fight to remove oppressive laws, we must not make the mistake of the oppressor and assume we could or even should impose a new morality through law. In the context of new sexual values, laws are useful only to the extent that they prohibit practices of sexual slavery or sexual violence. They must provide the means for removing the sexual terrorists and enslavers of women from society through arrest, prosecution, and imprisonment.

Individual liberty is the other side of female sexual slavery; it is the goal of feminism. For us now the *means* to liberation is as important as the goal. The means, how we get there, will be the basis for the new society we are trying to create. We can effectively challenge sex colonization only by guaranteeing individual liberty to the colonized. Not to safeguard individual liberty would be to substitute one set of colonizers for another as male revolutions have done to women. Therefore, while we condemn and punish those who carry out female sexual slavery, and while we condemn the institutions which perpetuate it, we must take care not to condemn in law or practice the women who work and live in those institutions. Our respect and caring must extend to not just those who are identifiable victims but to all women under the yoke of colonization.

For that reason, and in espousing individual liberty, we must not interfere with women who freely enter marriage and can leave it just as freely. Neither should we inferfere with women who enter prostitution freely, be they self-employed professional call girls or high-status African prostitutes, as long as they can freely leave their work any time they choose. I assume that this liberty will take place in the context of increasing participation in new values. As new values are actively disseminated through the population, institutions of sex colonization will become less and less attractive. And I assume that we must determine a woman's ability to freely enter or leave institutions of sex colonization based on her actual conditions and not simply on her perception of them or her desire to participate regardless of the conditions.

The liberty that feminists are demanding for women must be granted to all, whether or not we agree with them. But liberty loses its meaning when women are not in fact free to change their situation or when they participate in limiting others' freedom, as when prostitutes acquire women for their pimps, or when wives cooperate with their husbands' incestuous assaults on their daughters.

These changes are only the beginning of a revolution that has never happened before. It is one that will grow out of united strength of women, a strength derived from new values. What is exciting is that instead of adopting a plan handed over to us, as male revolutionaries unsuccessfully attempted by trying to intimidate us, we are charting our own course to liberation. It must ultimately address all levels of exploitation, particularly the economic and the political; but for women colonized both the economic and political are based in the sexual. The challenge is before us, if we dare. . . .

Appendixes
Chapter Notes
Index

APPENDIX A _____

INTERPOL Report

TRAFFIC IN WOMEN: RECENT TRENDS

Document prepared by the General Secretariat of the International Criminal Police Organization (INTERPOL) in 1974 for the United Nations Division of Human Rights

INTRODUCTION

The I.C.P.O.–Interpol General Assembly, during its 40th session in Ottawa in 1971, called on the General Secretariat to make a study of international proxenetism.

Since the most widespread form of international proxenetism is traffic in women, in 1972 the Secretariat sent out to all the Organization's National Central Bureaus a questionnaire to collect information and statistics on the subject. The response to this questionnaire was disappointing and in 1974 the General Secretariat again consulted member countries with a view to collecting further details and information about new trends. The present report gives a summary of the results of both consultations.

On both occasions, the questionnaires made a distinction between traffic in women proper and "disguised traffic."

A definition of traffic in women was obtained by combining the provisions of several conventions on the subject.[1] These texts make it an indictable offence to hire, induce or lead astray a woman or girl—whether she is a minor or has reached her majority and even if she consents —with a view to making her engage in prostitution in a country (state or territory) other than that in which she usually resides.

However, "disguised traffic" was defined as the act of hiring women in one country with a view to making them

[1] The International Agreement of 1904; The Conventions of 1910 and 1933; The Convention of 1949–1950, known as the "Unified Convention."

engage in certain types of employment in another country (as dancers, cabaret artistes, barmaids, etc.) and in conditions in which they are subjected, incited, or exposed to prostitution.

The following countries supplied replies to the questionnaire: Argentina, Australia, Austria, Belgium, Bermuda, Brunei, Burma, Burundi, Canada, Central African Republic, Cyprus, Denmark, Dominican Republic, El Salvador, Ethiopia, Federal Germany, Fiji, Finland, France, Gabon, Greece, Hong Kong, Iceland, India, Indonesia, Iran, Iraq, Ireland, Israel, Jamaica, Japan, Jordan, Kenya, Kuwait, Laos, Lebanon, Lesotho, Luxembourg, Madagascar, Malawi, Malaysia, Mali, Malta, Mexico, Nauru, Nepal, Netherlands, Netherlands Antilles, New Zealand, Nigeria, Norway, Oman, Pakistan, Peru, Rumania, Senegal, Sierra Leone, Spain, Sweden, Switzerland, Syria, Thailand, Tunisia, United Kingdom, United States, Venezuela, Vietnam, Zaire, Zambia.

TRAFFIC IN WOMEN THROUGHOUT THE WORLD: RESULTS OF THE SURVEY

The results of the survey made by the I.C.P.O.–Interpol are given below for each country in alphabetical order. When a country in the above list of those which answered the questionnaire does not appear in the summaries given below, this means that that country's reply did not contain information of use to the survey: either the country stated that traffic in women did not exist there, or that it did not have any information on the subject, or that no denunciations or complaints had been received in this connection.

Where positive answers were given, countries did not always make a distinction between traffic in women proper and "disguised traffic." Consequently, it has not always been possible to make this distinction in the summaries. Sometimes the replies merely indicated that foreign women were prostitutes in the country concerned, without indicating whether or not any of the constituent elements of traffic in women were present: hiring, inciting or leading women astray to make them engage in prostitution outside the country in which they usually reside. In other cases, the replies sometimes allude to intervention by procurers, but did not stipulate whether this occurred before the prostitute arrived in the country concerned or later.

In the summaries below, even these incomplete or fragmentary details have been included, since they refer to questions dealing with the traffic in women, the constituent elements of which had, however, been clearly defined.

The information sent in by the countries has been summarised so as to give just the main points. It merely reflects the facts known to the police and does not pretend to give an exact idea of the actual importance of the phenomenon. The General Secretariat can only reproduce the information it received.

Argentina:

Between 1965 and 1974, only 4 cases of traffic in women ("disguised" or not) were recorded and dealt with by the judicial authorities. 31 persons were implicated in these cases, 16 of whom were women. Because of the difficulty of collecting proof, mainly due to the reluctance of victims to co-operate with the police, persons who commit such offences are often prosecuted on different charges (e.g., failure to comply with police orders, aiding and abetting prostitution, etc.).

Procurers work in small groups and there are no large criminal organisations involved in this field.

It has been noted that women from neighbouring countries enter Argentina with tourist visas valid for 3 months and work as prostitutes. When the visas expire, they return to their own countries and try to obtain new visas.

Moreover, women—mostly recruited in the Argentine provinces and in Chile—are mainly taken to Puerto Rico and Spain but also to Italy, Turkey, and the Middle East. Sometimes they pretend to be tourists. All kinds of women are recruited, whether they have previously worked as prostitutes or not, notably from fashion, dancing, and cabaret circles.

In cases of disguised traffic, the women worked as barmaids, waitresses, or dancers. In one case, the women involved used false identity and travel documents. In another case, the organiser of a dancing troupe confiscated his dancers' passports when they arrived in the Middle East and the women were finally forced to become prostitutes.

Australia:
In 1971, 12 women of Spanish and Italian origin who had visas issued in Uruguay were expelled from Australia for operating as prostitutes in Sydney.

Belgium:
No statistics are available. However, it is known that women from France, the Netherlands, Federal Germany, Argentina, and Uruguay work secretly as prostitutes.

In 1973, a procurer engaged three young Thai girls in Thailand and took them to work as prostitutes in Belgium.

In 1974, two North African nationals kidnapped a young Norwegian woman from a train between Brussels and Amsterdam with a view to making her work as a prostitute. However, the victim was released after being assaulted and raped.

Bermuda:
Since 1965, there have been no convictions for prostitution or allied offences (traffic in women).

It is suspected that women who come to work as bona fide entertainers do also occasionally work as prostitutes. Occasionally, local men bring back one or two prostitutes from the U.S.A. or Canada; these women enter the country as tourists. However, such cases are rare.

Brunei:
There is very little prostitution in the country. Some women from neighbouring countries engage voluntarily in prostitution.

Canada:
No information is available on this subject. Some women, commonly referred to as "call girls," travel between the U.S.A. and Canada, operating in both countries.

Cyprus:
Groups of cabaret artists from the Middle East, Greece, and Spain, and more rarely from Yugoslavia, Hungary, and Czechoslovakia, visit Cyprus. Some of these women probably work as prostitutes but this does not create any serious problems.

Denmark:
There has only been one recent case involving traffic in women. In 1971, a young girl answered an advertisement offering a post to someone to display dogs at shows; she was contacted by three women who drugged and kidnapped her and took her to Germany. There she managed to escape. The intention was to force her to become a prostitute.

El Salvador:
No statistics are available, but there are very few cases of this kind. As for disguised traffic, several cases have been noted, the traffic being carried on between Guatemala and El Salvador.

Federal Germany:
In 1973 and 1974, German nationals persuaded young women from Hong Kong and Ethiopia, by making them false promises, to go to Germany to work as "masseuses" in "massage parlours," or as barmaids in nightclubs.

Finland:
At the time this country replied to the Interpol questionnaire, the police were investigating a case where three young girls were engaged by a man who paid their travel expenses to Italy where they were to keep men customers company in restaurants.

In another case, enquiries into a suspicious advertisement proved negative.

France:
Between January 1965 and March 1973, 75 cases of traffic in women were taken to court: 120 persons were implicated in these cases. The women concerned (350) were mostly French prostitutes who were to be sent to neighbouring countries and to Africa (Senegal, Ivory Coast). In these cases, 510 sentences of deportation, repatriation, extradition, and expulsion were passed.

During the same period, a certain number of cases of disguised traffic concerning approximately 1,000 women were taken to court. The employment "fronts" were mostly those of barmaids, bar and dance hostesses, and unqualified masseuses. A very large number of black ballet dancers of all nationalities are engaged in nightclubs in France. Moreover, many French women are recruited in France to work abroad as waitresses in bars where prostitution is carried on (mainly in Belgium and Luxembourg), or as ballet dancers (mainly in the Middle East).

Since March 1973, several important cases of traffic in women, disguised or not, have been solved and taken to court. For example:

1. A network of procurers was broken up. The network, composed of 6 Guadeloupe nationals and 2 Germans, had recruited about twenty young women from Pointe-à-Pitre to make them work as prostitutes in Paris and in the "Eros Centres" of Düsseldorf and Essen (Federal Germany).

2. A procurer was prosecuted. He had sent prostitutes on a "tour" of various countries in Europe (Germany, Belgium) and Africa (Ivory Coast, Senegal), and had correspondents among the owners of certain establishments in those countries. He and his women had used false identity documents.

3. Twelve persons were charged after enquiries were made about a network of procurers who had recruited about thirty prostitutes in France and sent them as barmaids with a 6-month contract to Dakar (Senegal) where they were working as prostitutes in a bar.

In several cases, procurers who had engaged young French women for brothels in Federal Germany, were prosecuted. In addition, several cases concerning French prostitutes employed in Belgium as barmaids or "hostesses" were solved.

Hong Kong:

Between 1965 and 1971, 15 cases of traffic in women were tried by the courts; 18 persons were convicted. The prostitutes implicated in this kind of case come mostly from Thailand and the Philippines where they are recruited by a representative of a "syndicate" who lends them money for their travel expenses. These prostitutes usually work in brothels in the tourist area. All their initial earnings are put aside to offset the capital expenditure, and thereafter they share their earnings on a 50–50 basis. When they arrive in Hong Kong, these women often pretend to be tourists or artistes. In past years, it has been estimated that at least 80 women from the Philippines and 40 from Thailand have been so engaged in Hong Kong at any one time.

In the same period, a certain number of cases of disguised traffic were reported to the judicial authorities. However, there are no statistics on these cases. It is estimated that in 1971 approximately 600 women from Thailand and 100 from the Philippines were engaged in prostitution under cover of employment as waitresses, barmaids, or masseuses in places of entertainment.

Apart from this, women from Hong Kong left the territory to work in nightclubs abroad, where they are exposed to prostitution.

Since 1972, the surveillance carried out by the immigration authorities has made it possible to break up most of the networks of procurers and the number of foreign prostitutes in Hong Kong is now decreasing.

According to recent information (May 1974), 18 Thai women have been located by the police; 17 of them are prostitutes and the 18th is known to recruit women in Thailand. In these cases, it has been established that prostitutes who had been sent back to Thailand sometimes return to Hong Kong—some even several times—using forged passports.

India:

According to certain information, women from India are thought to go to Persian Gulf countries to work as chambermaids; some of them are apparently forced into prostitution.

Indonesia:

Since 1965, no cases of traffic in women have been reported.

However, 17 cases of disguised traffic came to the attention of the authorities between 1966 and 1974. These cases involved 93 women, most of whom came from Java and travelled to towns in Sumatra near Singapore and Malaysia. Some of these women were apparently going to Singapore to "work." Police investigations showed that there is an organised ring of traffickers who have bases in various other countries.

Iraq:
Some foreign women cabaret artistes have been suspected of being prostitutes, but it was impossible to obtain proof.

Israel:
On occasion, investigations are made into apparently suspicious advertisements asking for young women to work abroad. However, there are no statistics in connection with traffic in women.

Japan:
There is no information, except in connection with a case in which four Japanese brought 4 young Thai girls to Japan on tourist visas. The girls operated as prostitutes while working in a club as hostesses.

Kuwait:
Between 1965 and 1973, approximately 1,300 prostitutes were arrested. Most of these women came from neighbouring countries and were expelled from Kuwait. Sometimes women who enter the country to work in certain establishments eventually work as prostitutes.

Laos:
Between 1965 and 1973, two cases of traffic in women were brought before the courts. Four persons were implicated in these cases. The women concerned were from Thailand.

Lebanon:
This country sent in the statistics drawn up by the appropriate department, giving the number of prostitutes and procurers arrested during the period from 1965 to 1974. These list the arrests of 1,186 foreign prostitutes, 480 of whom were Egyptian, 386 Syrian, and 116 women of Palestinian origin. The others came from many different countries. Of a total of 454 procurers arrested, 245 were foreigners.

Tolerated brothels exist; but there is also some clandestine prostitution. Most of the owners of places of entertainment exploit the prostitution of the artistes or barmaids who work there.

Luxembourg:
Between 1965 and 1973, 25 cases of traffic in women were taken to court; in these cases, 38 persons were implicated. The women concerned (286) were nationals of European countries: 253 of them were French. 2 Luxembourg women were taken to Italy by their procurers.

In 47 other cases of traffic in women, judicial proceedings could not be instituted due to lack of evidence. 38 procurers were deported.

Traffic in women is often handled by organised network. Usually, the women—in possession of tourist visas—arrive with their procurers. They stay for a month and then leave the country, only to return six months later. When a prostitute stays for a long time, her procurer usually takes on a job such as waiter in a café or taxi driver as a cover.

As for disguised traffic, it was not possible to take any such cases to court; however, 75 establishments are suspected of being places where prostitution is carried on, the women being employed in various jobs as a cover, such as waitresses, barmaids, artistes, etc. Between 1965 and 1972, 525 suspect women and 40 procurers were recorded. Most of these women (80%) were French; the others came from various European and South American countries.

Malaysia:
Only one case of traffic in women was recorded, in which 7 persons were implicated. They were Thai women who stated that they had been forced to become prostitutes.

Mexico:
Between 1969 and 1972, 5 persons were prosecuted for proxenetism. 50 persons were expelled for engaging in prostitution.

Nepal:
From 1965 to 1974, 41 cases of traffic in women were recorded. The authorities received no information about disguised traffic.

Netherlands:
Between 1967 and 1974, 4 reports were drawn up on cases

of traffic in women, but the sentences passed on those involved were passed for other charges.

Netherlands Antilles:
On the island of Curaçao there is a brothel housing women from Colombia and the Dominican Republic. This establishment is approved by the Government in view of the large numbers of sailors, since the island is a world harbour.

New Zealand:
Certain New Zealand women were suspected of working as prostitutes in Hong Kong and Singapore, but there was no evidence to indicate that traffic in women was involved.

Peru:
No details are available concerning traffic in women, whether disguised or not. Certain suspicions about cases of disguised traffic could not be confirmed.

Senegal:
After a network of procurers in France was broken up in 1973, it was possible to close a bar used for prostitution and expel the woman manager and two prostitutes, all of whom were French.

Also in 1973, the destruction of an organisation of procurers in Uruguay made it possible to expel from Senegal the French woman owner of a place of entertainment and a Uruguayan prostitute; two other persons implicated in this case left the country of their own free will. Here, the prostitutes claimed to be working as barmaids.

Spain:
Since 1965, 18 cases of traffic in women have been handled by the courts; in these cases, 54 persons were implicated. In 7 other cases (involving 28 persons), the evidence was not sufficient to enable the offenders to be sent before the courts. In such cases, the offenders are generally expelled. The women concerned came mainly from France, Argentina, and Uruguay. The countries to which the women were to be sent were: Australia, Liberia, Japan, Morocco, Mexico, and the Middle East.

There were 19 cases of disguised traffic (implicating 49

persons and concerning 63 persons) which had been dealt
with by the judicial authorities: e.g., waitresses from Trini-
dad and Tobago and Australia were engaged by an English agency; Moroccan women were recruited as cabaret
artistes; 2 women (one English, the other French) were
engaged as waitresses for a nightclub in Ivory Coast. In
other cases there was insufficient evidence (Spanish women
recruited by "artistic agents" to work in Tangiers and in
Africa south of the Sahara, dancers recruited for work in
the Middle East where their passports were confiscated to
force them to become prostitutes, etc.).

Switzerland:

Between 1965 and 1973, two cases of traffic in women, one
of which was disguised traffic, were sent to court. Eight
persons were implicated in these cases. The women concerned had been sent to Ivory Coast (5) and to France
(1). In the first case, they had been recruited through an
advertisement asking for hostesses to work in a bar in
Abidjan, and it was made clear to them that they could
increase their income by becoming prostitutes.

Thailand:

Police records were destroyed by fire in 1973. Statistics are
therefore only available from 1st January 1974. 83 procurers, 34 pimps and 767 prostitutes have been recorded
since that date. In 741 cases examined, 90% of the prostitutes came from the north of Thailand.

Tunisia:

No cases of traffic in women have been discovered since
1965.
    As far as disguised traffic is concerned, this may involve
hostesses, mostly recruited outside the country, who may
finally allow themselves to be persuaded by their employers
or certain customers and work discreetly as prostitutes,
especially outside working hours. However, due to lack of
evidence, no law enforcement action can be taken.

United Kingdom:

A very small number of women who were already prostitutes in their own countries were able to enter the United
Kingdom and, by making marriages of convenience, ob-

tained British nationality so that they could work as prostitutes without being expelled.

From 1965 to 1973, there were no convictions for cases
of traffic in women, whether disguised or not. However,
2 cases of traffic and 9 cases of disguised traffic came to
the attention of the authorities but proceedings could not
be instituted because of lack of evidence. In the cases of
disguised traffic, 18 persons were implicated; the women
involved had been sent to Lebanon, Federal Germany,
Italy, and Nigeria as barmaids, receptionists, or croupiers.

United States:
Between 1965 and 1972 there were 8 cases where judicial
proceedings were taken against people who had taken foreign women to the U.S.A. for immoral purposes (prostitution, etc.).

Venezuela:
No cases of traffic in women have come to the attention of
the police.

It has been observed that some foreign women of South
American origin come to Venezuela to work as independent prostitutes. When this is suspected, the women are
expelled from Venezuela.

Waitresses in bars also prostitute themselves, but there
are no statistics on this.

PREVENTIVE MEASURES

In the questionnaires sent out by the Interpol General Secretariat, member countries were asked to describe the preventive, legislative, or other measures they had adopted in
this connection.

The following countries indicated that they have penal
provisions to suppress and prevent traffic in women: Ar-
gentina, Austria, Bermuda, Brunei, Burma, Canada, Cy-
prus, Denmark, El Salvador, Ethiopia, Federal Germany,
Finland, France, Hong Kong, Iceland, India, Iran, Iraq,
Israel, Japan, Laos, Lesotho, Luxembourg, Malaysia, Mali,
Mexico, Nepal, Netherlands, Nigeria, Oman, Pakistan,
Peru, Rumania, Senegal, Spain, Switzerland, Thailand,
United Kingdom, Venezuela, Zaire.

Since some of these countries only stated that their penal law covers traffic in women, others merely gave legislative references, and only a very small number of countries actually sent in copies of the relevant texts, it is very difficult to evaluate the preventive value of these penal measures.

Even when adequate texts do exist, one question still remains: that of knowing whether a penal law covers only traffic in women proper or if it also covers the behaviour of intermediaries in disguised traffic, since the latter are often not procurers in the strict sense of the word, but merely agents of employment agencies; the answer to this question frequently involves a problem of interpretation of the law. Moreover, it is not always clear if special provisions exist for traffic in women or if this traffic is only punishable indirectly through other penal provisions (e.g., those governing offences of living on immoral earnings, pimping, etc.).

It should be remembered that certain legislations also cover acts committed outside the national territory of the country concerned (e.g., Spain, United Kingdom).

It is, in fact, practically impossible to evaluate the preventive influence of penal legislations on this subject since the information received was very incomplete.

Some countries stated that administrative measures have a preventive effect with regard to traffic in women, whether disguised or not.

For example, special permission to leave the country or to work abroad is needed by: young girls who are minors (Greece, United Kingdom); women who work as artistes in places of entertainment in certain parts of the world (Greece); women in general (Indonesia and Zaire).

In other countries special licences are required by: persons who wish to purchase or run bars, hotels, etc. (France, Luxembourg); persons who wish to set up and run employment agencies (Finland, United Kingdom); women who wish to work as barmaids (Luxembourg, Senegal).

Several countries stated that:
—they try to prevent foreign prostitutes and their procurers from entering the country by using the measures which could be applied by their immigration services (refusal of visas, deportation);

—police checks are carried out in places of entertainment and on the public thoroughfare;
—they register cabaret artistes who visit the country;
—they have large-scale campaigns against vice, etc.

The United Kingdom emphasied the role played by voluntary organisations for the welfare and protection of women and young girls in the prevention of traffic in women and prostitution.

This list of preventive measures, drawn up on the basis of information sent in in reply to the Interpol questionnaires, is obviously not exhaustive.

CONCLUSIONS

The following conclusions have been drawn from material which is far from complete. They are therefore to be treated with all necessary caution.

A. There are hardly any cases of traffic in women in which the victims have been forcibly kidnapped in one country and taken to work as prostitutes in another country. Nearly always the women concerned are apparently consenting—most of them have already worked as prostitutes in the country in which they are recruited.

B. Disguised traffic in women still exists all over the world.

Here again, a certain number of victims are more or less consenting, and when they accept various kinds of employment abroad, they probably know what is expected of them and occasionally engage in prostitution to supplement their income. However, in this field, there are a certain number of naive women who are attracted by the promises made to them by some employment agencies or by organisers of artistic tours, etc., and who eventually find themselves in a situation where they are forced into prostitution and may finally think that this is the only way they can earn their living.

In this respect, the I.C.P.O.–Interpol can only repeat the proposals made in its report on "International traffic in women under the cover of employment exposing them to prostitution" (1965), a copy of which was sent to the United Nations at its publication.

C. With regard to the networks involved in traffic in

women, whether disguised or not, the replies received reveal that these are concentrated in various geographical areas, or follow certain routes.

1. South American women—mostly Argentine women or women who have visited that country—are "exported" to Puerto Rico, to the European Mediterranean countries, or to the Middle East.

2. There is a European regional "market," mainly in French women who "work" in neighbouring countries, mostly in Luxembourg and Federal Germany (in "Eros Centres"), but women from South America and other countries are sometimes also involved. There are links between this "market" and other regions, notably the Middle East.

3. Some traffic networks apparently recruit women in Europe and send them to certain African countries which have reached a point in their development which allows the international exploitation of prostitution (Ivory Coast, Senegal).

4. There is an East-Asian market which recruits women —mostly from Thailand, but also from the Philippines —and sends them to other countries.

5. The statistics received from Lebanon give reason to believe that there is a concentration of prostitution in this country. The women involved come mainly from other Arab countries, but also from many other countries. The situation would appear to be the same in Kuwait.

6. The replies received reveal that, apart from the networks and those areas where such activities are more or less concentrated, women from all countries may be found as prostitutes in any country other than that in which they usually reside, but it is impossible to determine whether or not they have been victims of traffic in women.

D. It may be supposed that the number of cases of traffic in women which have never come to the attention of the authorities is quite high and this is easy to understand. In most cases, the victims refuse to cooperate when the police try to gather the necessary evidence to convict

offenders implicated in these activities. There are various
reasons for this behaviour; sometimes consenting women,
or women who have become consenting, want to carry on
operating as prostitutes, or they themselves may have
committed an offence, or finally, they may be threatened
by their procurers and dare not confide in the police. The
police and judicial authorities, however, need proof and
witnesses' evidence to build up a case; they cannot take
effective action without the co-operation of the public and
of the women concerned.

E. It would appear that the "facts" observed in connection with procuring often take the form of a collection of
different elements for which it is difficult to find precise
legal definitions. At first glance, these "facts" are open to
different interpretations. There is a whole range of acts and
situations: for example, a foreign prostitute may have been
recruited by her procurer in the country where she usually
resides, or later in another country in which she works and
to which she had first come on her own initiative; different
types of employment may appear as a cover for a prostitute recruited in the country where she usually resides in
order to make her work from then on as a prostitute in
another country, but they may also be activities carried on
within the framework of disguised traffic and which may
ultimately have led the woman concerned to become a
prostitute.

APPENDIX B

Convention Signatories

Ratifications of and Accessions to the Convention for the Suppression of the Traffic in Persons and of the Exploitation of the Prostitution of Others

State	Signature		Ratification, accession (a)	
Albania			6 November	1958 a
Algeria			31 October	1963 a
Argentina			15 November	1957 a
Belgium			22 June	1965 a
Brazil	5 October	1951	12 September	1958
Bulgaria			18 January	1955 a
Burma	14 March	1956		
Byelorussian SSR ..			24 August	1956 a
Cuba			4 September	1952 a
Czechoslovakia			14 March	1958 a
Denmark	12 February	1951		
Ecuador	24 March	1950		
Egypt			12 June	1959 a
Finland	27 February	1953	8 June	1972
France			19 November	1960 a
German Democratic Republic			16 July	1974 a
Guinea			26 April	1962 a
Haiti			26 August	1953 a
Honduras	13 April	1954		
Hungary			29 September	1955 a
India	9 May	1950	9 January	1953
Iran	16 July	1953		
Iraq			22 September	1955 a
Israel			28 December	1950 a
Japan			1 May	1958 a
Kuwait			20 November	1968 a
Liberia	21 March	1950		
Libyan Arab Republic			3 December	1956 a
Luxembourg	9 October	1950		
Malawi			13 October	1965 a
Mali			23 December	1964 a
Mexico			21 February	1956 a
Morocco			17 August	1973 a
Norway			23 January	1952 a
Pakistan	21 March	1950	11 July	1952
Philippines	20 December	1950	19 September	1952

Poland			2 June	1952 a
Republic of Korea .			13 February	1962 a
Romania			15 February	1955 a
Singapore			26 October	1966 a
South Africa	16 October	1950	10 October	1951
Spain			18 June	1962 a
Sri Lanka			15 April	1958 a
Syrian Arab Republic			12 June	1959 a
Ukrainian SSR			15 November	1954 a
Union of Soviet Socialist Republics			11 August	1954 a
Upper Volta			27 August	1962 a
Venezuela			18 December	1968 a
Yugoslavia	6 February	1951	26 April	1951

Additional signatories since 1980:

Bolivia
Congo
Cyprus
Djibouti
Ethiopia
Italy
Jordan
The Lao People's Democratic Republic (Laos)
Niger
Senegal
United Republic of Cameroon

Note:

The American reader should note that the United States has not signed this Convention and that the laws regarding prostitution in that country are in violation of the Convention. (See Chapter 6.)

CHAPTER NOTES _____

Chapter 2   Josephine Butler: The First Wave of Protest

1. Vern Bullough, *The History of Prostitution* (New Hyde Park, N.Y.: University Books, 1964), p. 167.
2. Josephine E. Butler, *Personal Reminiscences of a Great Crusade* (Westport, Conn.: Hyperion Press, 1976), p. 2.
3. Judith Walkowitz, "The Making of an Outcast Group," in *A Widening Sphere, Changing Roles of Victorian Women*, ed. Martha Vicinus (Bloomington: Indiana University Press, 1977), p. 82.
4. Butler, *Personal Reminiscences*, p. 13.
5. *Ibid.*, pp. 112–13.
6. Glen Petrie, *A Singular Iniquity: The Campaigns of Josephine Butler* (New York: Viking Press, 1971), pp. 16–17.
7. Josephine E. Butler, *Some Thoughts on the Present Aspect of the Crusade Against the State Regulation of Vice* (Liverpool: Brakell, 1874), p. 18.
8. Josephine E. Butler, "Sursum Corda: Annual Address to the Ladies National Association" (Liverpool: Brakell, 1871), p. 7.
9. *Ibid.*, p. 35.
10. Josephine E. Butler, "Address Delivered at Croyden," Ladies National Association, 1871, p. 10.
11. Josephine E. Butler, "State Regulation of Vice," 1898, British Committee, Leaflet No. 108b, July 1910, p. 3.
12. Walkowitz, "Making of an Outcast Group," p. 73.
13. *Ibid.*, p. 85.
14. *Ibid.*, pp. 86–87.
15. Petrie, *A Singular Iniquity*, pp. 102–4.
16. Edward J. Bristow, *Vice and Vigilance: Purity Movements in Britain Since 1700* (Totowa, N.J.: Rowman and Littlefield, 1977), p. 80.
17. Charles Terrot, *Traffic in Innocents* (New York: Dutton, 1960), p. 35–36.
18. Alfred S. Dyer, *The European Slave Trade in English Girls* (London: Dyer Brothers, 1880), p. 7.
19. Bristow, *Vice and Vigilance*, p. 88.
20. Maurice Gregory, *The Suppression of the White Slave Traffic* (London: Friends Association for Abolishing State Regulation of Vice, 1908), p. 9.
21. Petrie, *A Singular Iniquity*, p. 22.

22. Bristow, *Vice and Vigilance*, p. 91.
23. Petrie, *A Singular Iniquity*, pp. 235–41.
24. Ann Stafford, *The Age of Consent* (London: Hodder and Stoughton, 1964), pp. 134–35.
25. Josephine E. Butler, *Rebecca Jarrett* (London: Morgan and Scott, 1886), pp. 28–29.
26. Terrot, *Traffic in Innocents*, p. 160.
27. *Ibid.*
28. *Ibid.*, p. 168.
29. *Ibid.*, p. 171.
30. Bristow, *Vice and Vigilance*, p. 110.
31. Stafford, *Age of Consent*, p. 214.
32. Butler, *Rebecca Jarrett*, pp. 54–55.
33. David J. Pivar, *Purity Crusade Sexual Morality and Social Control, 1868–1900* (Westport, Conn.: Greenwood Press, 1973), p. 158.
34. Butler, "Sursum Corda," p. 12.
35. Walkowitz, "Making of an Outcast Group," pp. 90–91.
36. *Ibid.*, pp. 73, 91.
37. Spending and containment are discussed by G. J. Barker-Benfield in "The Spermatic Economy: A Nineteenth-Century View of Sexuality," *Feminist Studies*, Summer 1972, pp. 45–74, and developed more fully by him in *Horrors of the Half-Known Life* (New York: Harper & Row, 1976); and by Steven Marcus in *The Other Victorians* (New York: Basic Books, 1964), Chapter 1.
38. Sofie Lazarsfeld, *Women's Experience of the Male* (London: Encyclopedic Press, 1938), p. 437.
39. International Agreement for the Suppression of the White Slave Traffic, May 18, 1904, London, Her Majesty's Stationery Office, 1905.
40. Teresa Billington-Grieg, "The Truth About White Slavery," *English Review*, June 1913.
41. *Ibid.*, p. 445.
42. *Ibid.*, pp. 445–46.
43. Ernst A. Bell, *Fighting the Traffic in Young Girls* (Chicago: G. S. Bell, 1911), p. 160.
44. Maude Miner, *Slavery of Prostitution* (New York: Macmillan, 1916), p. 116.
45. *Ibid.*, p. 104.
46. Carol Green Wilson, *Chinatown Quest* (San Francisco: California Historical Society, 1974).
47. Bristow, *Vice and Vigilance*, p. 179.
48. Christabel Pankhurst, "The Government and White Slavery," Pamphlet reprinted from *The Suffragette*, April 18, April 25, 1913.
49. Emma Goldman, *The Traffic in Women* (Washington, N.J.: Times Change Press, 1970), p. 20.

50. *Ibid.*, p. 26.
51. Pankhurst, "The Government," pp. 7, 8.
52. Goldman, *The Traffic in Women*, p. 27.
53. Pankhurst, "The Government," p. 11.

Chapter 3 Victims and Survivors

1. William Ryan, *Blaming the Victim* (New York: Vintage Books Edition, 1972) p. 7.

Chapter 4 The Traffic in Sexual Slaves

1. Michael Lofchie, *Zanzibar: Background to Revolution* (Princeton, N.J.: Princeton University Press, 1965).
2. Sean O'Callaghan, *The White Slave Trade* (London: Robert Hale, 1965), p. 58.
3. Stephen Barlay, *Sexual Slavery* (New York: Ballantine Books Edition, 1977), p. 242.
4. Dr. S. Venugopal Rao, "International Approach to the Problems of Traffic In Women: Efforts of the ICPO-Interpol," Report of the 25th International Congress of the International Abolitionist Federation, New Delhi, October 4–7, 1972, p. 76.
5. "Traffic in Women: Recent Trends," United Nations Economic and Social Council, Commission on Human Rights, Sub-Commission on Prevention of Discrimination and Protection of Minorities, Document E/CN.4/Sub. 2/362, June 20, 1975, p. 13.
6. *Ibid.*
7. *Ibid.*, p. 1. The Convention was approved on December 2, 1949, and it entered into force on July 25, 1951.
8. *Ibid.*
9. *Ibid.*, p. 12.
10. *Ibid.*, pp. 3, 4, 5.
11. Mohamed Awad, *Report on Slavery* (New York: United Nations, 1966) p. 309.
12. Barlay, *Sexual Slavery*, p. 31.
13. *Ibid.*
14. "Suppression of the Traffic in Persons and of the Exploitation of the Prostitution of Others," United Nations Economic and Social Council, Commission on Human Rights, Sub-Commission on Prevention of Discrimination and Protection of Minorities, Working Group on Slavery, E/CN.4/Sub.2/AC.2/5, June 16, 1976. (The Working Group was established in 1974 by resolution of the Sub-Commission.)
15. Patrick Montgomery, "The Anti-Slavery Society in 1973," *Contemporary Review*, vol. 223, no. 1291, August 1973.
16. "World Plan of Action," from United Nations World

Conference of the International Women's Year, E/Conf. 66/5, p. 30.

17. United Nations Social and Economic Council, Commission on the Status of Women, E/CN.6/NGO.267, September 16, 1976.
18. "Traffic in Women: Recent Trends," p.2.
19. *San Francisco Chronicle*, June 5, 1978.
20. Opinion, John M. Cannella, U.S. District Judge, Southern District of New York, April 18, 1978, Perlita Diza Winthal and Natividad Diza, Individually and on behalf of All Others Similarly Situated versus Ruben Mendez, Mrs. Ruben Mendez, I. G. Patel, and Mrs. I. G. Patel, and All Other Members of their Class.
21. Gilberto Olmedo Sanchez, ed., "El Paraguay Libre," New York, August 1, 1978.
22. Jack Anderson, *Daily News*, December 20, 1977.
23. *Le Matin*, March 18, 1978.
24. Susan Brownmiller, *Against Our Will* (New York: Simon and Schuster, 1975), pp. 93–95.
25. Roland-Pierre Paringaux, *"Vietnam, Conséquence de la guerre," Le Monde*, June 2, 1977.
26. Awad, *Report on Slavery*, p. 198.
27. Alan Dawson, *55 Days* (Englewood Cliffs, N.J.: Prentice-Hall, 1977), p. 267.
28. *"La réhabilitation des anciennes prostituées au Sud Vietnam," Femmes et Mondes*, Clichy, France, no. 36, 1977.
29. Tom Weber, *San Francisco Chronicle*, April 20, 1976.
30. Bernard Fall, *Street Without Joy* (New York: Schocken, 1972), p. 133.
31. *Le Monde*, June 2, 1977.
32. Matsui Yoyori, "Sexual Slavery in Korea," *Frontiers, A Journal of Women's Studies*, II, no. 1 (Spring 1977), pp. 27–28.
33. *Ibid.*, p. 24.
34. *"Prostitution au Senegal," Femmes et Mondes*, Clichy, France, no. 23, 1973.
35. *"La Côte D'Ivoire et le Cameroun . . .," Femmes et Mondes*, no. 24, 1974.
36. *Ibid.*
37. Loretta Schwartz, "The Plight of America's Five Million Immigrants," *Ms.* magazine, June 1978, p. 66.
38. *Ibid.*, pp. 66–67.
39. Elizabeth Vorenberg and James Vorenberg, "The Biggest Pimp of All," *Atlantic*, January 1977, p. 36.
40. Victor Marchetti, John D. Marks, *The CIA and the Cult of Intelligence* (New York: Dell Books, 1974), p. 133.
41. *Ibid.*, p. 134.

Chapter 5   Pimping: The Oldest Profession

1. Stephen Barlay, *Sexual Slavery* (New York: Ballantine Books, 1975).
2. Iceberg Slim, *Pimp, The Story of My Life* (Los Angeles: Holloway House, 1969), pp. 11–12.
3. *Ibid.*, pp. 74–75.
4. From papers confiscated from a pimp in 1977 in a San Francisco police raid.
5. This and following quotes between pimps and Mary Christenson are derived from transcripts of tape recordings made while Mary was working undercover, usually at the San Francisco bus station, May 1977.
6. Testimony to the New York State Select Committee on Crime, Public Hearing—Children, Pornography, and the Illicit Sex Industry, November 14, 1977.
7. Mark Schorr, "Blood Stewart's End," *New York*, March 27, 1978, p. 54.
8. *Ibid.*, p. 56.
9. Testimony to the New York State Select Committee on Crime, Public Hearing—Children, Pornography, and the Illicit Sex Industry, November 14, 1977.
10. Christina Milner and Richard Milner, *Black Players* (Boston: Little, Brown, 1972), p. 90.
11. *Ibid.*, p. 94.
12. *Ibid.*
13. *Ibid.*, p. 95.
14. News release from New York Senator Ralph Marino, December 29, 1977.
15. Gail Sheehy, *Hustling* (New York: Delacorte Press, 1973), p. 123.
16. Testimony to the New York State Select Committee on Crime, Public Hearing—Children, Pornography, and the Illicit Sex Industry, November 14, 1977.
17. Testimony to the New York State Select Committee on Crime, Public Hearing—Operation of Massage Parlors in New York City, January 26, 1978.
18. *San Francisco Chronicle*, October 29, 1975.
19. *San Francisco Chronicle*, August 1, 1978.
20. "Report to the Attorney General on Child Pornography in California," Attorney General's Advisory Committee on Obscenity and Pornography, California, August 16, 1977, p. 16.
21. Sean O'Callaghan, *The White Slave Trade* (London: Robert Hale, 1965), p. 38.
22. Patrick Montgomery, "The Anti-Slavery Society, 1973,"

Contemporary Review, vol. 223, no. 1291, August 1973.
23. *Variety*, June 27, 1973.
24. Lloyd Shearer, "Intelligence Report," *Parade*, Sunday, November 11, 1977, p. 12.
25. Brian Eads, "Package Tours That Provide a Wife," reprinted from *London Observer*, San Francisco Chronicle, June 9, 1977.
26. *Ibid.*
27. *San Francisco Chronicle*, December 8, 1975.
28. *New Women's Times*, January 5–18, 1979, p. 11.
29. *Detroit News*, April 1972.
30. Interviews with Judie K. in 1977 and recollection from her autobiography in progress, *Sunday, Snakes and Serenity*.
31. Barlay, *Sexual Slavery*, p. 12.
32. *Hartford Courant*, September 16, 1977.
33. *London Times*, April 7, 1976.
34. *Sacramento Bee*, Friday, March 9, 1973.
35. *Detroit Free Press*, August 28, 1972.
36. *Chicago Sun Times*, January 18, 1972.
37. Testimony before the Grand Jury of the City and County of San Francisco, State of California, Investigation of _____, April 19, 1976.
38. Marilyn Neckes and Theresa Lynch, "Cost Analysis of the Enforcement of Prostitution Laws in San Francisco," Women's Jail Project, research sponsored by the Unitarian Universalist Service Committee, 1978.

Chapter 6   Throwaway Women

1. *San Francisco Chronicle*, September 18, 1975.
2. *San Francisco Chronicle*, March 6, 1979.
3. Statement of Susan Heeger, New York Civil Liberties Union, September 1978.
4. Jeanne Cordelier, *The Life, Memoirs of a French Hooker* (New York: Viking Press, 1978), p. 258.
5. Homicide Analysis/Office of Management, Analysis of Crime Section, New York, 1976.
6. Jennifer James, "Women as Sexual Criminals and Victims," in *Sexual Scripts: The Social Construction of Female Sexuality*, ed. Judith Long and Pepper Schwartz (Hinsdale, Ill.: Dryden Press, 1976), pp. 179–216.
7. Theresa Lynch and Marilyn Neckes, "The Cost-Effectiveness of Enforcing Prostitution Laws," San Francisco, December 1978, Chapter III, p. 29.
8. Testimony to the New York State Select Committee on Crime, Public Hearing—Children, Pornography, and the Illicit Sex Industry, November 14, 1977.

9. *New York Times*, March 12, 1978.
10. Interview with staff of *Équipe d'Action*, Paris, March 1978.
11. *France-Soir*, November 1974.
12. Dominique Dallayrac, *Le Nouveau Visage de la Prostitution* (Paris: Robert Laffont, 1976), pp. 92–93.
13. Interview with staff of *Équipe d'Action*, Paris, March 1978.
14. Dallayrac, *Le Nouveau Visage*, pp. 92–93.
15. Barbara Yondorf, "Prostitution as a Legal Activity: A Policy Analysis of the West German Experience" (unpublished paper, Seattle: University of Washington, School of Public Affairs, 1977).
16. *Ibid.*, Table I.
17. *Ibid.*, p. 16.
18. *Ibid.*, p. 11.
19. Jennifer James, *The Politics of Prostitution* (Social Research Assiciation, 1975), p. 46.
20. *Ibid.*
21. Sam Janus and Barbara Bess, *A Sexual Profile of Men in Power* (Englewood Cliffs, N.J.: Prentice-Hall, 1977), pp. 96–97.

Chapter 7 "Did I Ever Have a Chance?"

1. Transcript of *The Trial of Patricia Hearst* (San Francisco: Great Fidelity Press, 1976), p. 163.
2. Fred Soltysik, *In Search of a Sister* (New York: Bantam Books, 1976), p. 230.
3. Transcript, p. 62.
4. *Ibid.*, p. 256.
5. *Ibid.*, p. 257.
6. *Ibid.*, pp. 257–58.
7. Joseph Gabel, *False Consciousness* (New York: Harper Torchbooks Edition, 1978), p. 231.
8. *Ibid.*, p. 226.
9. Marilyn Baker, *Exclusive* (New York: Macmillan, 1974), p. 57.

Chapter 8 Sex Colonization

1. Ester Boserup, *Women's Role in Economic Development* (New York: St. Martin's Press, 1970), p. 44.
2. Boserup, *Women's Role*, p. 100.
3. Maria Roy, "A Current Survey of 150 Cases," in *Battered Women*, ed. Maria Roy (New York: Van Nostrand Reinhold, 1977), p. 33.
4. Richard Gelles, *The Violent Home* (Beverly Hills: Sage Publications, 1972), pp. 173–74.
5. Reported by Professor Murray Straus, University of New

Hampshire, to U.S. Commission on Civil Rights, in *New Women's Times*, Rochester, N.Y., January 5–18, 1978.

6. Suzanne K. Steinmetz, "Wifebeating, Husbandbeating—A Comparison of the Use of Physical Violence Between Spouses to Resolve Marital Fights," in Roy, *Battered Women*, p. 65.
7. Margaret Varma, "Battered Women: Battered Children," in Roy, *Battered Women*, p. 265.
8. Richard Wathey and Judianne Densen-Gerber, "Incest: An Analysis of the Victim and the Aggressor," Odyssey Institute, 1976, p. 8.
9. Gelles, *The Violent Home*, pp. 173–74.
10. J.J. Gayford, "Wife Battery: a Preliminary Survey of 100 Cases," *British Medical Journal*, 1 (1975), p. 196.
11. Roy, "Current Survey," p. 28; and Suzanne Prescott and Carolyn Letko, "Battered Women: A Social Psychological Perspective," in Roy, *Battered Women*, p. 81.
12. Terry Davidson, *Conjugal Crime* (New York: Hawthorn Books, 1978), p. 31.
13. Gayford, "Wife Battery," p. 196.
14. Richard Gelles, "Violence and Pregnancy: A Note on the Extent of the Problem and Needed Services," *Family Coordinator*, January 1975, p. 82.
15. Judith Herman and Lisa Hirschman, "Father-Daughter Incest," *Signs*, 2, no. 4 (Summer 1977), p. 736.
16. Prescott and Letko, "Battered Women," p.84.
17. Roy, "Current Survey," p. 32.
18. Uniform Crime Reports, U.S. Government Printing Office, 1977, derived from table, "Circumstances by Relationship, 1977," p. 12.
19. Del Martin, *Battered Wives* (San Francisco: New Glide Publications, 1976), p. 14.
20. Herman and Hirschman, "Father-Daughter Incest," p. 747.
21. *Ibid.*, p. 743.
22. *Ibid.*, p. 748.
23. Roy, "Current Survey," p. 40.
24. Davidson, *Conjugal Crime*, p. 31.
25. Herman and Hirschman, "Father-Daughter Incest," p. 745.
26. Sandra Butler, *Conspiracy of Silence: The Trauma of Incest* (San Francisco: New Glide Publications, 1978), p. 110.
27. *Ibid.*, p. 89.
28. Roy, "Current Survey," p. 35.
29. Lenore E. Walker, "Who Are the Battered Women?" *Frontiers: A Journal of Women's Studies*, II, no. 1 (Spring 1977), p. 52.
30. Butler, *Conspiracy of Silence*, p. 124, quoting from Yvonne Tormes, *Child Victims of Incest* (Denver: American Humane Association, Children's Division, 1968), p. 35.

31. Butler, *Conspiracy of Silence*, p. 154.
32. *Ibid.*, p. 163.
33. *San Francisco Chronicle*, April 27, 1977.
34. *New York Post*, February 12, 1979, p. 2.
35. *San Francisco Chronicle*, November 1977.
36. J. G. Peristiany, ed., *Honor and Shame* (Chicago: University of Chicago Press, 1966), p. 9.
37. Julian Pitt-Rivers, "Honor and Social Status," in Peristiany, *Honor and Shame*, p. 22
38. Pierre Bourdieu, "The Sentiment of Honor in Kabyle," in Peristiany, *Honor and Shame*, p. 211.
39. Raphael Patai, *The Arab Mind* (New York: Charles Scribner's Sons, 1976), pp. 90–91.
40. *Ibid.*, p. 120.
41. *Ibid.*
42. Fatima Mernissi, *Beyond the Veil* (Cambridge, Mass.: Schenkman, 1975), p. 13.
43. *Ibid.*, p. 15.
44. Mary Douglas, *Implicit Meanings* (London: Routledge and Kegan, 1975), p. 62.
45. Patai, *The Arab Mind*, p. 91.
46. Constantina Safilios-Rothschild, " 'Honor' Crimes in Contemporary Greece," *Toward a Sociology of Women*, ed. Constantina Safilios-Rothschild (Lexington, Mass.: Xerox, 1972), p. 84.
47. *Ibid.*
48. *Ibid.*, pp. 89–90.
49. *Ibid.*, p. 90.
50. Diana E. H. Russell and Nicole Van de Ven, eds., *Crimes Against Women: Proceedings of the International Tribunal* (Millbrae, Calif.: Les Femmes, 1976), p. 101.
51. Don A. Schanche, "Her Uncle Raped Her, Her Brother Killed Her," *Los Angeles Times*, reprinted in *San Francisco Chronicle*, September 17, 1977, p. 13.
52. Douglas, *Implicit Meanings*, p. 63.
53. Robert Roberts, The Social Laws of the Qorân (London: Curzon Press, 1925), p. 13.
54. See Mernissi, *Beyond the Veil*, p. 84 and Hanna Papanek, "Purdah in Pakistan: Seclusion and Modern Occupations for Women," *Journal of Marriage and the Family*, August 1971, p. 522.
55. Papanek, "Purdah in Pakistan," p. 518.
56. *Ibid.*, p. 525.
57. Mernissi, *Beyond the Veil*, p. 84.
58. *Ibid.*, p. 85.
59. *Ibid.*, pp. 85–86.
60. Fatima Mernissi, "A Particular Aspect of Women's Contribution to the Economy: Crafts, Past and Present," from

Women in Pre-Colonial Morocco, Changes and Continuities (UNESCO, 1978), p. 90.

61. Elizabeth Warnock Fernea and Basima Qattan Bezirgan, eds., *Middle Eastern Muslim Women Speak* (Austin: University of Texas Press, 1977), Introduction, p. xxvi.
62. Reuben Levy, *The Social Structure of Islam* (London: Cambridge University Press, 1957), p. 108.
63. Mernissi, *Beyond the Veil*, p. x.
64. Levy, *The Social Structure of Islam*, p. 115.
65. Russell and Van de Ven, *Crime Against Women*, p. 101.
66. Mernissi, *Beyond the Veil*, p. 61.
67. Fran Hosken, "Genital Mutilation of Females in Africa: Summary/Facts," *Women's International Network News.*
68. *Ibid.*
69. *Ibid.*, definitions of forms of genital mutilation derived from Dr. J. A. Verzin, "Sequelae of Female Circumcision," *Tropical Doctor*, October 1975; and Dr. Ahmed Abu-el-Futuh Shandall, "Circumcision and Infibulation of Females," *Sudan Medical Journal*, vol. 5, no. 4, 1967.
70. Patai, *The Arab Mind*, p. 124.
71. Esther Ogunmodede, "Why Circumcize Girls?" excerpted in *Women's International Network News*, 3, no. 4 (Autumn 1977), p. 45.
72. Soheir A. Morsy, "Sex Differences and Folk Illnesses in an Egyptian Village," in *Women in the Muslim World*, eds. Lois Beck and Nikki Keddie (Cambridge, Mass.: Harvard University Press, 1978), p. 611.
73. Fran Hosken, "Clitoridectomy: Female Circumcision in Egypt," *Women's International Network News*, 3, no. 2 (Spring 1977), p. 33.
74. *Ibid.*, p. 34.
75. Ogunmodede, "Why Circumcize Girls?" p. 45.
76. Remi Clignet, *Many Wives, Many Powers* (Evanston, Ill.: Northwestern University Press, 1970), p. 17.
77. *Ibid.*
78. Boserup, *Women's Role*, p. 40.
79. Marie Angelique Savané, "Polygamy: Is It a Necessary Evil?" excerpted from *Famille et Développement*, no. 9, January 1977, in *Women's International Network News*, 3, no. 2 (Spring 1977), p. 56.
80. Louise Lamphere, "Strategies, Cooperation and Conflict Among Women in Domestic Groups," *Women, Culture and Society*, eds. Michele Zimbalist Rosaldo and Louise Lamphere (Stanford, Calif.: Stanford University Press, 1974), p. 107.
81. Clignet, *Many Wives*, pp. 30–31.
82. *Ibid.*, p. 31.

83. Remi Clignet, "Social Change and Sexual Differentiation in the Cameroons and the Ivory Coast," *Signs*, 3, no. 1 (Autumn 1977), p. 253.

84. *Women's International Network News*, Spring 1977, p. 56.

85. Clignet, *Many Wives*, p. 33.

86. Barbara Burris, in agreement with Kathy Barry, Terry Moon, Joann DeLor, Joanne Parrent, and Cate Stadelman, "The Fourth World Manifesto," *Notes from the Third Year: Women's Liberation*, eds. Anne Koedt and Shulamith Firestone, New York, 1971, p. 113.

87. *Ibid.*, p. 115.

88. David C. Gordon, *Women of Algeria, An Essay on Change* (Cambridge, Mass.: Harvard Middle Eastern Monograph Series, 1968), p. 56.

89. Frantz Fanon, quoted from *Dying Colonialism* in Burris, "Fourth World Manifesto," p. 115.

90. Gordon, *Women of Algeria*, pp. 57–58.

91. Gordon, *Women of Algeria*, p. 71.

92. *Ibid.*, p. 64.

93. Fadela M'rabet, "Les Algériennes," excerpts in *Middle Eastern Muslim Women Speak*, eds. Fernea and Bezirgan, p. 324.

94. *New York Post*, June 1978.

95. Hilmi Toros, "Islam: A Persuasive Counterpoint to West," Associated Press, *San Francisco Chronicle*, January 21, 1979.

Chapter 9   Pornography: The Ideology of Cultural Sadism

1. Eberhard and Phyllis Kronhausen, *Pornography and the Law* (New York: Ballantine Books, 1964).

2. *Ibid.*, p. 237.

3. *Ibid.*, p. 245.

4. *Ibid.*, p. 269.

5. Shere Hite, *The Hite Report* (New York: Dell, 1977).

6. Abraham Kaplan, "Obscenity as an Esthetic Category," in *The Pornography Controversy*, ed. Ray Rist (New Brunswick, N.J.: Transaction Books, 1974), p. 22.

7. Susan Sontag, "The Pornographic Imagination," in *Perspectives on Pornography*, ed. Douglas Hughes (New York: St. Martin's Press, 1970), p. 151.

8. Nancy Friday, *My Secret Garden* (New York: Pocket Books, 1974), pp. 3–4.

9. C. G. Jung, *Psyche & Symbol*, ed. Violet deLaszlo (New York: Anchor Books, 1958), p. 123.

10. H. Abelson, *et al.*, "National Survey of Public Attitudes Toward Experience with Erotic Materials," United States Commission on Obscenity and Pornography, Vol. VI

312 CHAPTER NOTES

(Washington, D.C.: Government Printing Office, 1971), p. 7.

11. John H. Gagnon and William Simon, "Raging Menace or Paper Tiger?" in Rist, *The Pornography Controversy*, p. 91.
12. *Playboy*, December 1977, p. 79.
13. *San Francisco Chronicle*, June 2, 1976.
14. Joseph Gabel, *False Consciousness: An Essay on Reification*, trans., Margaret Thompson (New York: Harper Torchbooks, 1975), p. 11 for discussion of ideology as a theoretical crystallization; p. 104 for discussion of autism.
15. *Marquis de Sade: Selections from His Writings and a Study by Simone de Beauvoir*, ed. and trans. Paul Dinnage (New York: Grove Press, 1953), p. 213.
16. Gilbert Lely, *The Marquis de Sade*, trans. Alec Brown (New York: Grove Press, 1961), p .92.
17. Geoffrey Gorer, *The Life and Ideas of the Marquis de Sade* (New York: W. W. Norton, 1962), pp. 29–30.
18. *Ibid.*, p. 30.
19. Marquis de Sade, from "La Philosophie Dans Le Boudoir," in *Marquis de Sade: Selections*, ed. Paul Dinnage, pp.132–33.
20. *Ibid.*, pp. 134–35.
21. *Ibid.*, p. 135.
22. Dr. Richard von Krafft-Ebing, *Psychopathia Sexualis*, trans. F.J. Rebman (New York: Special Books, 1965), p. 131.
23. Havelock Ellis, *Studies in the Psychology of Sex*, Vol. I, Part Two: *Love and Pain* (New York: Random House, 1942), p. 67.
24. *Ibid.*, p. 104.
25. *Ibid.*, p. 166.
26. Sigmund Freud, *Three Contributions to the Theory of Sex* (New York: E. P. Dutton, 1962), p. 2.
27. Sigmund Freud, *Sexuality and The Psychology of Love* (New York: Collier, 1974; copyright Macmillan, 1963), p. 62.
28. *Ibid.*
29. *Ibid.*, p. 64.
30. *Ibid.*, p. 62.
31. Freud, *Three Contributions*, p. 22.
32. Sigmund Freud, *General Psychological Theory* (New York: Collier Books, 1963), p. 92.
33. Peter Berger and Thomas Luchmann, *The Social Construction of Reality* (New York: Anchor Books, 1967), p. 178.
34. Robert J. Stoller, "Sexual Excitement," *Archives of General Psychiatry*, 33 (August 1976), Copyright 1976, American Medical Association, p. 903.

35. *Ibid.*, p. 900.
36. *Ibid.*, p. 903.
37. *Ibid.*
38. *Ibid.*, p. 904.
39. *Ibid.*, p. 903.
40. Edward O. Wilson, *Sociobiology, the New Synthesis* (Cambridge, Mass.: Belknap Press of Harvard University Press, 1975), p. 3.
41. *Ibid.*, p. 4.
42. Edward O. Wilson, *On Human Nature* (Cambridge, Mass.: Harvard University Press, 1978), p. 126.
43. David Barash, "Sociobiology of Rape in Mallards (*Anas platyrhynchos*): Responses of the Mated Male," *Science*, August 19, 1977, 197:4305, p. 789.
44. *Ibid.*
45. *The Report of the Commission on Obscenity and Pornography* (New York: Bantam Books, 1970), p. 1.
46. *Ibid.*, p. 32.
47. *Ibid.*, pp. 57, 58.
48. *Ibid.*, pp. 446–47.
49. Victor B. Cline, "Another View: Pornography Effects, the State of the Art," in *Where Do You Draw the Line*, ed. Victor Cline (Provo, Utah: Brigham Young University Press, 1974), p. 204.
50. Richard Ben-Veniste, "Pornography and Sex Crime: The Danish Experience," United States Commission on Obscenity and Pornography, Technical Report, VII, p. 245.
51. M. J. Goldstein *et al.*, "Exposure to Pornography and Sexual Behavior in Deviant and Normal Groups," U.S. Commission, Technical Report, VII, p. 10.
52. *Report of the Commission on Obscenity and Pornography*, p. 277.
53. Abelson, "National Survey of Public Attitudes," p. 15.
54. Goldstein, "Exposure to Pornography," pp. 27–28.
55. Goldstein, "Exposure to Pornography," p. 27.
56. *Ibid.*, p. 56.
57. *Report of the Commission on Obscenity and Pornography*, p. 281.
58. James Howard, Clifford Reifler and Myron Liptzin, "Effects of Exposure to Pornography," U.S. Commission, Technical Report, VIII, p. 97.
59. *Ibid.*, p. 125.
60. Ben-Veniste, "Pornography and Sex Crime," p. 247.
61. *Ibid.*
62. B. Kutchinsky, "Towards an Explanation of the Decrease in Registered Sex Crimes in Copenhagen," U.S. Commission, Technical Report, VIII, p. 294.

63. *Ibid.*, p. 296.
64. *Report of the Commission on Obscenity and Pornography*, p. 274.
65. Gene Abel *et al.*, "The Components of Rapists' Sexual Arousal," *Archives of General Psychiatry*, 34 (August 1977), Copyright 1977, American Medical Association, p. 898.
66. *Ibid.*
67. *Ibid.*, p. 901.
68. *Ibid.*, p. 897.
69. Simone de Beauvoir, "Must We Burn Sade," trans. Annette Michelson, in *Marquis de Sade: Selections*, ed. Paul Dinnage, p. 44.
70. *Ibid.*
71. Pauline Réage, *Story of O* (New York: Ballantine Books, 1973), p. 16.
72. *Ibid.*, p. 23.
73. De Beauvoir, "Must We Burn Sade," p. 67.
74. *Ibid.*, p. 58.
75. Peter Michelson, "An Apology for Pornography," in Hughes, *Perspective on Pornography*, p. 69.
76. *Ibid.*, p. 68.
77. *Ibid.*
78. Sontag, "Pornographic Imagination," p. 155.
79. *Ibid.*

Chapter 10   From Violence to Values . . . And Beyond

1. Hans Toch, *Violent Men* (Middlesex, England: Penguin Books, 1972), p. 176.
2. *Ibid.*
3. Havelock Ellis, "Analysis of the Sexual Impulse," in *Studies in the Psychology of Sex*, I, Part Two (New York: Random House, 1942), p. 63.
4. Theodor Reik, *Psychology of Sex Relations* (New York: Rinehart, 1945), p. 9.
5. Ellis, "Analysis of Sexual Impulse," p. 65.
6. Sigmund Freud, *Sexuality and the Psychology of Love* (New York: Collier Books, 1974), p. 30.
7. Alfred Kinsey *et al.*, *Sexual Behavior in the Human Female* (Philadelphia: W. B. Saunders, 1953), pp. 624–25.
8. Kinsey, *Sexuality*, p. 624.
9. John Stoltenberg, "Refusing to Be a Man," *WIN*, X:25, July 11, 1974, p. 14.
10. Anthony Pietropinto and Jacqueline Simenauer, *Beyond the Male Myth* (New York: Signet, 1978), p. 170.
11. *Ibid.*, p. 176.

12. *Ibid.*, p. 196.
13. Uniform Crime Reports, 1977 (Washington, D.C.: U.S. Government Printing Office, 1977), p. 171.
14. *Ibid.*, p. 9; statistics derived from table: Victim/Offender Relationship by Sex and Race.
15. *Ibid.*, p. 14.
16. R. D. Rosen, *Psychobabble* (New York: Atheneum, 1978), p. 13.
17. Audre Lorde, "Uses of the Erotic: The Erotic as Power," Private Edition, 1978.
18. Jeanne Cordelier, *The Life: Memoirs of a French Hooker* (New York: Viking Press, 1978), pp. 69–70.
19. Gertrude Jaeger and Philip Selznick, "A Normative Theory of Culture," *American Sociological Review*, 29, no. 5 (October 1964), p. 658.
20. Jaeger and Selznick, "Normative Theory," p. 659.
21. Uniform Crime Reports, 1977, derived from Table 27, p. 175.
22. Theresa Lynch and Marilyn Neckes, "The Cost Effectiveness of Enforcing Prostitution Laws," December 1978 (San Francisco: Unitarian Universalist Committee), p. 67. Percentage for female prostitutes derived from original research.
23. *Ibid.*, p. 13.

INDEX

Human Rights Commission, 57–58, 62–63, 64
International Women's Year Conference (1975), 4, 64–65
Sexual slavery, 62–68
Slavery, survey of (Awad, 1965), 62–63, 72
Working Group on Slavery, 63–64
UNESCO, Report to International Women's Year Conference, 4, 64
U.S. Commission on Obscenity and Pornography, 214, 233–42, 243

Valueless individualism, 262–66
Values, sexual, 37, 266–71, 276
Veiling, 184–86, 197–99, 200
Victimism, 43–46, 47, 49, 169
Vienna, Austria, 102–103
Vietnam, 106, 128
Vietnam War, 71–74, 85
Villach, Austria, 103
Village of Night Girls, 74
Violent Home, The (Gelles), 167
Virginity, 180–81, 183

Vorenberg, Elizabeth, 84
Vorenberg, James, 84

Walker, Lenore, 170
Walkowitz, Judith, 20, 29
Wathey, Richard, 168
Weber, Tom, 73
Weed, Steven, 138, 139, 144
Well of Loneliness, The (Hall), 265
Wertmuller, Lina, 214–16
West, Dr., 149–50
White Slave Trade, The (O'Callaghan), 54, 101
White Slavery, 15, 32–38
Whitten, Les, 69
Whorology, 88
Wife battery, 166–78, 271
Wolfe, William, 142
Wolfgang, Marvin, 235
Women's Social and Political Union, 21, 33
Working Group on Slavery (UN), 63–64
World Health Organization, 191

Yayori, Matsui, 76
Yondorf, Barbara, 130
Youthful Offenders Act (United States), 144

Zanzibar, sexual slavery in, 53–58, 165